Open Source and Libraries

Open Source and Libraries

by

Anil Deshpande | Savita Chowdhary

Wordpen Academics

Publishing Science That Matter

ISBN: 9788119283187 (Hardback)

Published by : WORDPEN ACADEMICS
4736/23, Ansari Road, Darya Ganj,
New Delhi – 110 002
Phone: +91-011-35004336
E-mail: info@wordpenacademics.com

Exclusive Distributor: ***Bio-Green Books, New Delhi***

Preface

Open source refers to software that is freely available for use, modification, and distribution. Unlike proprietary software, which restricts access and control, open source projects encourage transparency, collaboration, and community-driven innovation. Developers, hobbyists, and organizations contribute their expertise to build robust, reliable tools that benefit everyone.

Libraries play a crucial role in software development. They provide reusable code, functions, and modules that simplify complex tasks. Whether you're building a web application, analyzing data, or creating a game, libraries offer a treasure trove of pre-built solutions.

Our overarching goal in presenting this book is to bridge the gap between theory and practice, providing both students and professionals with the requisite knowledge and tools.

We extend our sincere gratitude to all the contributors who have generously shared their expertise, experiences, and innovations. It is our hope that this volume will serve as a valuable resource for researchers, educators, policymakers, and practitioners alike, fostering a deeper understanding and appreciation for the pivotal role of open source and library in shaping the future of sustainable library.

Anil Deshpande | Savita Chowdhary

Contents

1

Open Source Library: Overview

In computer science, a library refers to a collection of precompiled, reusable files, functions, scripts, routines, and other resources that can be referenced by computer programmers, often for software development. An open source library is any library with an open source license, which denotes software that is free to reuse, modify, and/or publish without permission.

Open source library software in computer science provides an easier means for programmers to develop dynamic interfaces by storing readily accessible and frequently used routines and resources, such as classes, configuration data, documentation, help data, message templates, pre-written code and subroutines, type specifications, and values.

Open Source Library means object code that is statically or dynamically linked to the Licensed Software and that contains, or is derived from, any computer source code licensed pursuant to a license that is identified as an open source license by the Open Source Initiative (opensource.org) or other similar licensing or distribution models for computer code offered free of charge.

These precompiled modules are stored in object format and organized in such a way that they can be used by multiple, unconnected programs. An open source library uses a General Public License, which guarantees end users the freedom to legally run, study, share and modify the software.

Open source is source code that is made freely available for possible modification and redistribution. Products include permission to use the source code, design documents, or content of the product. The open-source model is a decentralized software development model that encourages open collaboration. A main principle of open-source software development is peer production, with products such as source code, blueprints, and documentation freely available to the public. The open-source movement in software began as a response to the limitations of proprietary code. The model is used for projects such as in open-source appropriate technology, and open-source drug discovery.

Open source promotes universal access via an open-source or free license to a product's design or blueprint, and universal redistribution of that design or blueprint. Before the phrase open source became widely adopted, developers and producers have used a variety of other terms. Open source gained hold with the rise of the Internet. The open-source software movement arose to clarify copyright, licensing, domain, and consumer issues.

Generally, open source refers to a computer program in which the source code is available to the general public for use or modification from its original design. Code is released under the terms of a software license. Depending on the license terms, others may then download, modify, and publish their version (fork) back to the community.

Many large formal institutions have sprung up to support the development of the open-source movement, including the Apache Software Foundation, which supports community projects such as the open-source framework Apache Hadoop and the open-source HTTP server Apache HTTP.

History of Open Source

The sharing of technological information predates the internet and the personal computer considerably. For instance, in the early years of automobile development a group of capital monopolists owned the rights to a 2-cycle gasoline engine patent originally filed by George B. Selden.

By controlling this patent, they were able to monopolize the industry and force car manufacturers to adhere to their demands, or risk a lawsuit. In 1911, independent automaker Henry Ford won a challenge to the Selden patent. The result was that the Selden patent became virtually worthless and a new association (which would eventually become the Motor Vehicle Manufacturers Association) was formed. The new association instituted a cross-licensing agreement among all US auto manufacturers: although each company would develop technology and file patents, these patents were shared openly and without the exchange of money between all the manufacturers. By the time the US entered World War II, 92 Ford patents and 515 patents from other companies were being shared between these manufacturers, without any exchange of money (or lawsuits).

Very similar to open standards, researchers with access to Advanced Research Projects Agency Network (ARPANET) used a process called Request for Comments to develop telecommunication network protocols. This collaborative process of the 1960s led to the birth of the Internet in 1969.

Early instances of the free sharing of source code include IBM's source releases of its operating systems and other programs in the 1950s and 1960s, and the SHARE user group that formed to facilitate the exchange of software.

In a foreshadowing of the Internet, software with source code included became available on BBS networks in the 1980s. This was sometimes a necessity; distributing software written in BASIC and other interpreted languages can only be distributed as source code as there is no separate portable executable binary to distribute.

Example of BBS systems and networks that gathered source code, and setup up boards specifically to discuss its modification includes WWIV, developed initially in BASIC by Wayne Bell. A culture of "modding" his software and distributing the mods, grew up so extensively that when the software was ported to first Pascal, then C++, its source code continued to be distributed to registered users, who would share mods and compile their own versions of the software. This may have contributed to its being a dominant system and network, despite being outside the Fidonet umbrella that was shared by so many other BBS makers.

The sharing of source code on the Internet began when the Internet was relatively primitive, with software distributed via UUCP, Usenet, and irc, and gopher. BSD, for example, was first widely distributed by posts to comp.os.linux on the Usenet, which is also where its development was discussed. Linux followed in this model.

The label "open source" was adopted by a group of people in the free software movement at a strategy session held at Palo Alto, California, in reaction to Netscape's January 1998 announcement of a source code release for Navigator. The group of individuals at the session included Christine Peterson who suggested "open source", Todd Anderson, Larry Augustin, Jon Hall, Sam Ockman, Michael Tiemann and Eric S. Raymond. Over the next week, Raymond and others worked on spreading the word. Linus Torvalds gave an all-important sanction the following day. Phil Hughes offered a pulpit in Linux Journal. Richard Stallman, pioneer of the free software movement, initially seemed to adopt the term, but later changed his mind. Those people who adopted the term used the opportunity before the release of Navigator's source code to free themselves from the ideology of the term "free software". Netscape released its source code under the Netscape Public License and later under the Mozilla Public License.

In February 1998, Raymond made the first public call to the free software community to adopt the new term. The Open Source Initiative was formed shortly thereafter by Eric Raymond and Bruce Perens.

The term was given a big boost at an event organized in April 1998 by technology publisher Tim O'Reilly. Originally titled the "Freeware Summit" and later known as the "Open Source Summit", The event brought together the leaders of many of the most important free and open-source projects, including Linus Torvalds, Larry Wall, Brian Behlendorf, Eric Allman, Guido van Rossum, Michael Tiemann, Paul Vixie, Jamie Zawinski of Netscape, and Eric Raymond. At that meeting, the confusion caused by the name free software was brought up. Tiemann argued for "sourceware" as a new term, while Raymond argued for "open source." The assembled developers took a vote, and the winner was announced at a press conference that evening.

Starting in the beginning of the 2000s, a number of companies began to publish a small parts of their source code to claim they were open source, while keeping key parts closed. This led to the development of the now widely used terms free open-source software and commercial open-source software to distinguish between truly open and hybrid forms of open source.

Economics

Most economists agree that open-source candidates have an information good (also termed "knowledge good") aspect. In general, this suggests that the original work involves a great deal of time, money, and effort. However, the cost of reproducing the work is very low, so that additional users may be added at zero or near zero cost - this is referred to as the marginal cost of a product. Copyright creates a monopoly so the price charged to consumers can be significantly higher than the marginal cost of production. This allows the author to recoup the cost of making the original work, without needing to find a single customer that can bear the entire cost. Conventional copyright thus creates access costs for consumers who value the work more than the marginal cost but less than the initial production cost. Access costs also pose problems for authors who wish to create a derivative work - such as a copy of a software program modified to fix a bug or add a feature, or a remix of a song - but are unable or unwilling to pay the copyright holder for the right to do so.

Being organized effectively as a consumers' cooperative, the idea of open source is to eliminate the access costs of the consumer and the creators of derivative works by reducing the restrictions of copyright.

Basic economic theory predicts that lower costs would lead to higher consumption and also more frequent creation of derivative works. Additionally some proponents argue that open source also relieves society of the administration and enforcement costs of copyright. Organizations such as Creative Commons have websites where individuals can file for alternative "licenses", or levels of restriction, for their works. These self-made protections free the general society of the costs of policing copyright infringement. Thus, on several fronts, there is an efficiency argument to be made on behalf of open-sourced goods.

However, others argue that because consumers do not pay for the copies, creators are unable to recoup the initial cost of production, and thus have no economic incentive to create in the first place. By this argument, consumers would lose out because some of the goods they would otherwise purchase would not be available at all. In practice, content producers can choose whether to adopt a proprietary license and charge for copies, or an open license. Some goods which require large amounts of professional research and development, such as the pharmaceutical industry (which depends largely on patents, not copyright for intellectual property protection) are almost exclusively proprietary.

Alternatives

Alternative arrangements have also been shown to result in good creation outside of the proprietary model. Examples include:

- Creation for its own sake - for example, Wikipedia editors add content for recreation. Artists have a drive to create. Both communities benefit from free starting material.
- Voluntary after-the-fact donations - used by shareware, street performers, and public broadcasting in the United States.
- Patron - For example, open access publishing relies on institutional and government funding of research faculty, who also have a professional incentive to publish for reputation and career advancement. Works of the U.S. federal government are automatically released into the public domain.
- Freemium - Give away a limited version for free and charge for a premium version (perhaps using a dual license)
- Give away the product and charge for something related - charge for support of open-source enterprise software, give away music but charge for concert admission
- Give away work in order to gain market share - used by artists, in corporate software to spoil a dominant competitor (for example in the browser wars and the Android operating system)

- For own use - Businesses or individual software developers often create software to solve a problem, bearing the full cost of initial creation. They will then open source the solution, and benefit from the improvements others make for their own needs. Communalizing the maintenance burden distributes the cost across more users; free riders can also benefit without undermining the creation process.

Applications

Social and political views have been affected by the growth of the concept of open source. Advocates in one field often support the expansion of open source in other fields. But Eric Raymond and other founders of the open-source movement have sometimes publicly argued against speculation about applications outside software, saying that strong arguments for software openness should not be weakened by overreaching into areas where the story may be less compelling.

The broader impact of the open-source movement, and the extent of its role in the development of new information sharing procedures, remain to be seen.

The open-source movement has inspired increased transparency and liberty in biotechnology research, for example by CAMBIA. Even the research methodologies themselves can benefit from the application of open-source principles.

It has also given rise to the rapidly expanding open-source hardware movement.

In the book Democratizing Innovation it is argued that a trend toward democratized innovation in physical products (e.g. open-source hardware) is occurring like the free and open-source software movement, and that the difference between crowdsourcing and open source is that open-source production is a cooperative activity initiated and voluntarily undertaken by members of the public.

One of the primary geographically diverse communities that is utilizing this developmental method is the scientific community, for example using open-source hardware to reduce the cost of scientific equipment.

Open collaboration

The open-source model is a decentralized software development model that encourages open collaboration, meaning "any system of innovation or production that relies on goal-oriented yet loosely coordinated participants who interact to create a product (or service) of economic value, which they make available to contributors and noncontributors alike." A main principle of open-source software development is peer production, with products such as source code, blueprints, and documentation freely available to the public.

The open-source movement in software began as a response to the limitations of proprietary code. The model is used for projects such as in open-source appropriate technology, and open-source drug discovery.

The open-source model for software development inspired the use of the term to refer to other forms of open collaboration, such as in Internet forums, mailing lists and online communities. Open collaboration is also thought to be the operating principle underlining a gamut of diverse ventures, including TEDx and Wikipedia.

Open collaboration is the principle underlying peer production, mass collaboration, and wikinomics. It was observed initially in open source software, but can also be found in many other instances, such as in Internet forums, mailing lists, Internet communities, and many instances of open content, such as Creative Commons. It also explains some instances of crowdsourcing, collaborative consumption, and open innovation.

Riehle et al. define open collaboration as collaboration based on three principles of egalitarianism, meritocracy, and self-organization. Levine and Prietula define open collaboration as "any system of innovation or production that relies on goal-oriented yet loosely coordinated participants who interact to create a product (or service) of economic value, which they make available to contributors and noncontributors alike."

This definition captures multiple instances, all joined by similar principles. For example, all of the elements — goods of economic value, open access to contribute and consume, interaction and exchange, purposeful yet loosely coordinated work — are present in an open source software project, in Wikipedia, or in a user forum or community.

They can also be present in a commercial website that is based on user-generated content. In all of these instances of open collaboration, anyone can contribute and anyone can freely partake in the fruits of sharing, which are produced by interacting participants who are loosely coordinated.

An annual conference dedicated to the research and practice of open collaboration is the International Symposium on Wikis and Open Collaboration (OpenSym, formerly WikiSym). As per its website, the group defines open collaboration as "collaboration that is egalitarian (everyone can join, no principled or artificial barriers to participation exist), meritocratic (decisions and status are merit-based rather than imposed) and self-organizing (processes adapt to people rather than people adapt to pre-defined processes)."

Open-source license

Open source promotes universal access via an open-source or free license to a product's design or blueprint, and universal redistribution of that design or blueprint. Before the phrase open source became widely adopted, developers and producers used a variety of other terms. Open source gained hold in part due to the rise of the Internet. The open-source software movement arose to clarify copyright, licensing, domain, and consumer issues.

An open-source license is a type of license for computer software and other products that allows the source code, blueprint or design to be used, modified or shared (with or without modification) under defined terms and conditions. This allows end users and commercial companies to review and modify the source code, blueprint or design for their own customization, curiosity or troubleshooting needs.

Open-source licensed software is mostly available free of charge, though this does not necessarily have to be the case. Licenses which only permit non-commercial redistribution or modification of the source code for personal use only are generally not considered as open-source licenses. However, open-source licenses may have some restrictions, particularly regarding the expression of respect to the origin of software, such as a requirement to preserve the name of the authors and a copyright statement within the code, or a requirement to redistribute the licensed software only under the same license (as in a copyleft license). One popular set of open-source software licenses are those approved by the Open Source Initiative (OSI) based on their Open Source Definition (OSD).

Computer software

Open-source software is software whose source code is published and made available to the public, enabling anyone to copy, modify and redistribute the source code without paying royalties or fees. Open-source code can evolve through community cooperation. These communities are composed of individual programmers as well as large companies. Some of the individual programmers who start an open-source project may end up establishing companies offering products or services incorporating open-source programs. Examples of open-source software products are:

Electronics

Open-source hardware is hardware whose initial specification, usually in a software format, are published and made available to the public, enabling anyone to copy, modify and redistribute the hardware and source code without paying royalties or fees. Open-source hardware evolves through community cooperation. These communities are composed of individual hardware/software developers, hobbyists, as well as very large companies. Examples of open-source hardware initiatives are:

- Openmoko: a family of open-source mobile phones, including the hardware specification and the operating system.
- OpenRISC: an open-source microprocessor family, with architecture specification licensed under GNU GPL and implementation under LGPL.
- Sun Microsystems's OpenSPARC T1 Multicore processor. Sun has released it under GPL.
- Arduino, a microcontroller platform for hobbyists, artists and designers.
- GizmoSphere, an open source development platform for the embedded design community; the site includes code downloads and hardware schematics along with free user guides, spec sheets and other documentation.
- Simputer, an open hardware handheld computer, designed in India for use in environments where computing devices such as personal computers are deemed inappropriate.
- LEON: A family of open-source microprocessors distributed in a library with peripheral IP cores, open SPARC V8 specification, implementation available under GNU GPL.
- Tinkerforge: A system of open source stackable microcontroller building blocks. Allows to control motors and read out sensors with the programming languages C, C++, C#, Object Pascal, Java, PHP, Python and Ruby over a USB or Wifi connection on Windows, Linux and Mac OS X. All of the hardware is licensed under CERN OHL (CERN Open Hardware License).
- Open Compute Project: designs for computer data center including power supply, Intel motherboard, AMD motherboard, chassis, racks, battery cabinet, and aspects of electrical and mechanical design.
- Lasersaur, an open source laser cutter.

Beverages

- Open source colas - cola soft drinks, similar to Coca-Cola and Pepsi, whose recipe is open source and developed by volunteers. The taste is said to be comparable to that of the standard beverages. Most corporations producing beverages hold their formulas as closely guarded secrets.
- Vores Øl beer (Open Source Beer) - a beer created by students at the IT-University in Copenhagen together with Superflex, a Copenhagen-

based artist collective, to illustrate how open-source concepts might be applied outside the digital world.

- In 2002, the beer company Brewtopia in Australia started an open-source brewery and invited the general population to be involved in the development and ownership of the brewery, and to vote on the development of every aspect of its beer, Blowfly, and its road to market. In return for their feedback and input, individuals received shares in the company, which is now publicly traded on a stock exchange in Australia. The company has always adhered to its open-source roots and is the only beer company in the world that allows the public to design, customise and develop its own beers online.

Digital content

- Open-content projects organized by the Wikimedia Foundation - Sites such as Wikipedia and Wiktionary have embraced the open-content GFDL and Creative Commons content licenses. These licenses were designed to adhere to principles similar to various open-source software development licenses. Many of these licenses ensure that content remains free for re-use, that source documents are made readily available to interested parties, and that changes to content are accepted easily back into the system. Important sites embracing open-source-like ideals are Project Gutenberg and Wikisource, both of which post many books on which the copyright has expired and are thus in the public domain, ensuring that anyone has free, unlimited access to that content.
- Open ICEcat is an open catalog for the IT, CE and Lighting sectors with product data-sheets based on Open Content License Agreement. The digital content are distributed in XML and URL formats.

Medicine

- Pharmaceuticals - There have been several proposals for open-source pharmaceutical development, which led to the establishment of the Tropical Disease Initiative and the Open Source Drug Discovery for Malaria Consortium.
- Genomics - The term "open-source genomics" refers to the combination of rapid release of sequence data (especially raw reads) and crowdsourced analyses from bioinformaticians around the world that characterised the analysis of the 2011 E. coli O104:H4 outbreak.
- OpenEMR - OpenEMR is an ONC-ATB Ambulatory EHR 2011-2012 certified electronic health records and medical practice management application. It features fully integrated electronic health, records, practice management, scheduling, electronic billing, and is the base for many EHR programs. http://www.open-emr.org/ OpenEMR

Science & engineering

- Research - The Science Commons was created as an alternative to the expensive legal costs of sharing and reusing scientific works in journals etc.
- Research - The Open Source Science Project was created to increase the ability for students to participate in the research process by providing them access to microfunding - which, in turn, offers non-researchers the opportunity to directly invest, and follow, cutting-edge scientific research. All data and methodology is subsequently published in an openly accessible manner under a Creative Commons fair use license.
- Research - The Open Solar Outdoors Test Field (OSOTF) is a grid-connected photovoltaic test system, which continuously monitors the output of a number of photovoltaic modules and correlates their performance to a long list of highly accurate meteorological readings. The OSOTF is organized under open-source principles - All data and analysis is be made freely available to the entire photovoltaic community and the general public.
- Engineering - Hyperloop, a form of high-speed transport proposed by entrepreneur Elon Musk, which he describes as "an elevated, reduced-pressure tube that contains pressurized capsules driven within the tube by a number of linear electric motors."

Society and culture

Open-source culture is the creative practice of appropriation and free sharing of found and created content. Examples include collage, found footage film, music, and appropriation art. Open-source culture is one in which fixations, works entitled to copyright protection, are made generally available. Participants in the culture can modify those products and redistribute them back into the community or other organizations.

The rise of open-source culture in the 20th century resulted from a growing tension between creative practices that involve appropriation, and therefore require access to content that is often copyrighted, and increasingly restrictive intellectual property laws and policies governing access to copyrighted content. The two main ways in which intellectual property laws became more restrictive in the 20th century were extensions to the term of copyright (particularly in the United States) and penalties, such as those articulated in the Digital Millennium Copyright Act (DMCA), placed on attempts to circumvent anti-piracy technologies.

Although artistic appropriation is often permitted under fair-use doctrines, the complexity and ambiguity of these doctrines creates an atmosphere of uncertainty among cultural practitioners. Also, the protective actions of copyright owners create what some call a "chilling effect" among cultural practitioners.

In the late 20th century, cultural practitioners began to adopt the intellectual property licensing techniques of free software and open-source software to make their work more freely available to others, including the Creative Commons.

The idea of an "open-source" culture runs parallel to "Free Culture," but is substantively different. Free culture is a term derived from the free software movement, and in contrast to that vision of culture, proponents of open-source culture (OSC) maintain that some intellectual property law needs to exist to protect cultural producers. Yet they propose a more nuanced position than corporations have traditionally sought. Instead of seeing intellectual property law as an expression of instrumental rules intended to uphold either natural rights or desirable outcomes, an argument for OSC takes into account diverse goods (as in "the Good life") and ends.

One way of achieving the goal of making the fixations of cultural work generally available is to maximally utilize technology and digital media.

In keeping with Moore's law's prediction about processors, the cost of digital media and storage plummeted in the late 20th Century. Consequently, the marginal cost of digitally duplicating anything capable of being transmitted via digital media dropped to near zero. Combined with an explosive growth in personal computer and technology ownership, the result is an increase in general population's access to digital media. This phenomenon facilitated growth in open-source culture because it allowed for rapid and inexpensive duplication and distribution of culture.

Where the access to the majority of culture produced prior to the advent of digital media was limited by other constraints of proprietary and potentially "open" mediums, digital media is the latest technology with the potential to increase access to cultural products. Artists and users who choose to distribute their work digitally face none of the physical limitations that traditional cultural producers have been typically faced with. Accordingly, the audience of an open-source culture faces little physical cost in acquiring digital media.

Open-source culture precedes Richard Stallman's codification of free software with the creation of the Free Software movement. As the public began to communicate through Bulletin Board Systems (BBS) like FidoNet, places like Sourcery Systems BBS were dedicated to providing source code to Public Domain, Shareware and Freeware programs.

Essentially born out of a desire for increased general access to digital media, the Internet is open-source culture's most valuable asset. It is questionable whether the goals of an open-source culture could be achieved without the Internet.

The global network not only fosters an environment where culture can be generally accessible, but also allows for easy and inexpensive redistribution of culture back into various communities. Some reasons for this are as follows. First, the Internet allows even greater access to inexpensive digital media and storage. Instead of users being limited to their own facilities and resources, they are granted access to a vast network of facilities and resources, some free.

Sites such as ccMixter offer up free web space for anyone willing to license their work under a Creative Commons license. The resulting cultural product is then available to download free (generally accessible) to anyone with an Internet connection. Second, users are granted unprecedented access to each other.

Older analog technologies such as the telephone or television have limitations on the kind of interaction users can have. In the case of television there is little, if any interaction between users participating on the network. And in the case of the telephone, users rarely interact with any more than a couple of their known peers.

On the Internet, however, users have the potential to access and meet millions of their peers. This aspect of the Internet facilitates the modification of culture as users are able to collaborate and communicate with each other across international and cultural boundaries. The speed in which digital media travels on the Internet in turn facilitates the redistribution of culture.

Through various technologies such as peer-to-peer networks and blogs, cultural producers can take advantage of vast social networks to distribute their products. As opposed to traditional media distribution, redistributing digital media on the Internet can be virtually costless. Technologies such as BitTorrent and Gnutella take advantage of various characteristics of the Internet protocol (TCP/IP) in an attempt to totally decentralize file distribution.

Government

- Open politics (sometimes known as Open-source politics) is a political process that uses Internet technologies such as blogs, email and polling to provide for a rapid feedback mechanism between political organizations and their supporters. There is also an alternative conception of the term Open-source politics which relates to the development of public policy under a set of rules and processes similar to the open-source software movement.
- Open-source governance is similar to open-source politics, but it applies more to the democratic process and promotes the freedom of information.

Ethics

Open-source ethics is split into two strands:

- Open-source ethics as an ethical school - Charles Ess and David Berry are researching whether ethics can learn anything from an open-source approach. Ess famously even defined the AoIR Research Guidelines as an example of open-source ethics.
- Open-source ethics as a professional body of rules - This is based principally on the computer ethics school, studying the questions of ethics and professionalism in the computer industry in general and software development in particular.

Media

Open-source journalism formerly referred to the standard journalistic techniques of news gathering and fact checking, reflecting open-source intelligence a similar term used in military intelligence circles. Now, open-source journalism commonly refers to forms of innovative publishing of online journalism, rather than the sourcing of news stories by a professional journalist. In the December 25, 2006 issue of TIME magazine this is referred to as user created content and listed alongside more traditional open-source projects such as OpenSolaris and Linux.

Weblogs, or blogs, are another significant platform for open-source culture. Blogs consist of periodic, reverse chronologically ordered posts, using a technology that makes webpages easily updatable with no understanding of design, code, or file transfer required. While corporations, political campaigns and other formal institutions have begun using these tools to distribute information, many blogs are used by individuals for personal expression, political organizing, and socializing.

Some, such as LiveJournal or WordPress, utilize open-source software that is open to the public and can be modified by users to fit their own tastes. Whether the code is open or not, this format represents a nimble tool for people to borrow and re-present culture; whereas traditional websites made the illegal reproduction of culture difficult to regulate, the mutability of blogs makes "open sourcing" even more uncontrollable since it allows a larger portion of the population to replicate material more quickly in the public sphere.

Messageboards are another platform for open-source culture. Messageboards (also known as discussion boards or forums), are places online where people with similar interests can congregate and post messages for the community to read and respond to. Messageboards sometimes have moderators who enforce community standards of etiquette such as banning users who are spammers. Other common board features are private messages (where users can send messages to one another) as well as chat (a way to have a real time conversation online) and image uploading.

Some messageboards use phpBB, which is a free open-source package. Where blogs are more about individual expression and tend to revolve around their authors, messageboards are about creating a conversation amongst its users where information can be shared freely and quickly.

Messageboards are a way to remove intermediaries from everyday life - for instance, instead of relying on commercials and other forms of advertising, one can ask other users for frank reviews of a product, movie or CD. By removing the cultural middlemen, messageboards help speed the flow of information and exchange of ideas.

OpenDocument is an open document file format for saving and exchanging editable office documents such as text documents (including memos, reports, and books), spreadsheets, charts, and presentations.

Organizations and individuals that store their data in an open format such as OpenDocument avoid being locked into a single software vendor, leaving them free to switch software if their current vendor goes out of business, raises their prices, changes their software, or changes their licensing terms to something less favorable.

Open-source movie production is either an open call system in which a changing crew and cast collaborate in movie production, a system in which the end result is made available for re-use by others or in which exclusively open-source products are used in the production. The 2006 movie Elephants Dream is said to be the "world's first open movie", created entirely using open-source technology.

An open-source documentary film has a production process allowing the open contributions of archival material, footage, and other filmic elements, both in unedited and edited form. By doing so, on-line contributors become part of the process of creating the film, helping to influence the editorial and visual material to be used in the documentary, as well as its thematic development. The first open-source documentary film is the non-profit "The American Revolution," which went into production in 2005, and will examine the role media played in the cultural, social and political changes from 1968 to 1974 through the story of radio station WBCN-FM in Boston.

The film is being produced by Lichtenstein Creative Media and the non-profit Filmmakers Collaborative. Open Source Cinema is a website to create Basement Tapes, a feature documentary about copyright in the digital age, co-produced by the National Film Board of Canada.

Open-source film-making refers to a form of film-making that takes a method of idea formation from open-source software, but in this case the 'source' for a filmmaker is raw unedited footage rather than programming code.

It can also refer to a method of film-making where the process of creation is 'open' i.e. a disparate group of contributors, at different times contribute to the final piece.

Open-IPTV is IPTV that is not limited to one recording studio, production studio, or cast. Open-IPTV uses the Internet or other means to pool efforts and resources together to create an online community that all contributes to a show.

Education

Within the academic community, there is discussion about expanding what could be called the "intellectual commons" (analogous to the Creative Commons). Proponents of this view have hailed the Connexions Project at Rice University, OpenCourseWare project at MIT, Eugene Thacker's article on "open-source DNA", the "Open Source Cultural Database", Salman Khan's Khan Academy and Wikipedia as examples of applying open source outside the realm of computer software.

Open-source curricula are instructional resources whose digital source can be freely used, distributed and modified.

Another strand to the academic community is in the area of research. Many funded research projects produce software as part of their work. There is an increasing interest in making the outputs of such projects available under an open-source license. In the UK the Joint Information Systems Committee (JISC) has developed a policy on open-source software. JISC also funds a development service called OSS Watch which acts as an advisory service for higher and further education institutions wishing to use, contribute to and develop open-source software.

Innovation communities

The principle of sharing pre-dates the open-source movement; for example, the free sharing of information has been institutionalized in the scientific enterprise since at least the 19th century. Open-source principles have always been part of the scientific community.

The sociologist Robert K. Merton described the four basic elements of the community - universalism (an international perspective), communalism (sharing information), disinterestedness (removing one's personal views from the scientific inquiry) and organized skepticism (requirements of proof and review) that accurately describe the scientific community today.

These principles are, in part, complemented by US law's focus on protecting expression and method but not the ideas themselves. There is also a tradition of publishing research results to the scientific community instead of keeping all such knowledge proprietary.

One of the recent initiatives in scientific publishing has been open access - the idea that research should be published in such a way that it is free and available to the public. There are currently many open access journals where the information is available free online, however most journals do charge a fee (either to users or libraries for access).

The Budapest Open Access Initiative is an international effort with the goal of making all research articles available free on the Internet.

The National Institutes of Health has recently proposed a policy on "Enhanced Public Access to NIH Research Information." This policy would provide a free, searchable resource of NIH-funded results to the public and with other international repositories six months after its initial publication. The NIH's move is an important one because there is significant amount of public funding in scientific research. Many of the questions have yet to be answered - the balancing of profit vs. public access, and ensuring that desirable standards and incentives do not diminish with a shift to open access.

Farmavita.Net is a community of pharmaceuticals executives that has recently proposed a new business model of open-source pharmaceuticals. The project is targeted to development and sharing of know-how for manufacture of essential and life-saving medicines. It is mainly dedicated to the countries with less developed economies where local pharmaceutical research and development resources are insufficient for national needs. It will be limited to generic (off-patent) medicines with established use. By the definition, medicinal product have a "well-established use" if is used for at least 15 years, with recognized efficacy and an acceptable level of safety. In that event, the expensive clinical test and trial results could be replaced by appropriate scientific literature.

Benjamin Franklin was an early contributor eventually donating all his inventions including the Franklin stove, bifocals, and the lightning rod to the public domain.

New NGO communities are starting to use the open-source technology as a tool. One example is the Open Source Youth Network started in 2007 in Lisboa by ISCA members.

Open innovation is also a new emerging concept which advocate putting R&D in a common pool. The Eclipse platform is openly presenting itself as an Open innovation network.

Arts and recreation

Copyright protection is used in the performing arts and even in athletic activities. Some groups have attempted to remove copyright from such practices.

In 2012, Russian music composer, scientist and Russian Pirate Party member Victor Argonov presented detailed raw files of his electronic opera "2032" under free license CC-BY-NC 3.0. This opera was originally composed and published in 2007 by Russian label MC Entertainment as a commercial product, but then the author changed its status to free. In his blog he said that he decided to open raw files (including wav, midi and other used formats) to the public in order to support worldwide pirate actions against SOPA and PIPA. Several Internet resources, called "2032" the first open source musical opera in history.

Benefits of Open Source Libraries

Libraries are very useful for computer programmers as they provide access to reusable, pre-written, frequently used codes, which drastically reduces the workload as programmers can reference this code instead of writing everything from scratch every time.

The benefits of open source software include

Community: Open source solutions are driven by a large, diverse, and talented community with a common goal of working together to quickly develop improvements and troubleshoot issues.

Cost: Open source libraries and other open source solutions decrease the overall cost of deploying a solution by eliminating any licensing fees.

Reliability: With a diverse and large group of humans reviewing open source libraries and software, open source output is thoroughly tested and tends to be highly robust and reliable.

Security: Having a large number of participants involved in the development of open source solutions increases the chances of discovering and resolving security vulnerabilities.

Transparency: Full visibility into the code base provides transparency, enabling users to develop an expectation as to what they will be working with.

"Open" versus "free" versus "free and open"

Free and open-source software (FOSS) or free/libre and open-source software (FLOSS) is openly shared source code that is licensed without any restrictions on usage, modification, or distribution. Confusion persists about this definition because the "free", also known as "libre", refers to the freedom of the product, not the price, expense, cost, or charge. For example, "being free to speak" is not the same as "free beer".

Conversely, Richard Stallman argues the "obvious meaning" of term "open source" is that the source code is public/accessible for inspection, without necessarily any other rights granted, although the proponents of the term say the conditions in the Open Source Definition must be fulfilled.

"Free and open" should not be confused with public ownership (state ownership), deprivatization (nationalization), anti-privatization (anti-corporate activism), or transparent behavior.

GNU

GNU Manifesto

Richard Stallman

Gratis versus libre (no cost vs no restriction)

Examples of *Open Source Library* in a sentence

- Manuscripts submitted to the California Digital ***Open Source Library*** shall be exempt from the requirements in subdivision (b) of Section 66408 of the Education Code.
- All open educational resources used as learning materials for a degree developed pursuant to this section shall be added to the California Digital ***Open Source Library*** established in Section 66408.
- · This initiative shall use, in addition to any other appropriate resources, those identified, housed, produced, and otherwise found appropriate pursuant to the California Open Education Resources Council established in Section 66409 and the California Digital ***Open Source Library***, also known as the California Open Online Library for Education, established in Section 66408.
- · For global equities we prefer to utilise both hedged and unhedged versions of global equity managed funds or ETFs to pursue the same factors noted in the Australian equities description.
- · All Intellectual Property Rights that are part of the AppwiseCore ***Open Source Library*** (hereinafter the "AppwiseCore Library") will always remain with Appwise.

- Definitions of Proprietary and ***Open Source Library*** Automation Software's: According to Techopedia Proprietary Software: Proprietary software is primarily commercial software that can be bought, leased or licensed from its vendor/developer.
- Among the key ROA issues addressed by the Committee in 2016- 17 were:
- Childcare Regional Skills Investment Plan Funding Allocation QualityThe three Glasgow Colleges also collaborated to procure an ***Open Source Library*** Management System.
- The museum first considered using an ***Open Source Library*** Management System (LMS) OPAC module such as Koha, OPALS or Evergreen.
- The bidder must have supplied, installed, implemented, integrated and commissioned Koha (***Open Source Library*** Management Software) on Linux platform as Library Management System in atleast 3 libraries of repute in India.
- Collection of Historical Tweets Using ***Open Source Library*** While this was a long process, we managed to collect the tweets for all the Dow Jones stocks.

Related to Open Source Library

- Open Source License means any license meeting the Open Source Definition (as promulgated by the Open Source Initiative) or the Free Software Definition (as promulgated by the Free Software Foundation), or any substantially similar license, including any license approved by the Open Source Initiative or any Creative Commons License. "Open Source Licenses" shall include Copyleft Licenses.
- Open Source Code means any software code that is distributed as "free software" or "open source software" or is otherwise distributed publicly in source code form under terms that permit modification and redistribution of such software. Open Source Code includes software code that is licensed under the GNU General Public License, GNU Lesser General Public License, Mozilla License, Common Public License, Apache License, BSD License, Artistic License, or Sun Community Source License.
- Open Source Materials means software or other material that is distributed as "free software," "open source software" or under similar licensing or distribution terms (including the GNU General Public License (GPL), GNU Lesser General Public License (LGPL), Mozilla Public License (MPL), BSD licenses, the Artistic License, the Netscape Public License, the Sun Community Source License (SCSL) the Sun Industry Standards License (SISL) and the Apache License).

- Open Source Software means any Software that is licensed pursuant to: (a) any license that is a license now or in the future approved by the open source initiative and listed at http://www.opensource.org/licenses, which licenses include all versions of the GNU General Public License (GPL), the GNU Lesser General Public License (LGPL), the GNU Affero GPL, the MIT license, the Eclipse Public License, the Common Public License, the CDDL, the Mozilla Public License (MPL), the Artistic License, the Netscape Public License, the Sun Community Source License (SCSL), and the Sun Industry Standards License (SISL); or (b) any license to Software that is considered "free" or "open source software" by the open source foundation or the free software foundation.
- Open-Source Components means any software component that is subject to any open-source copyright license agreement, including any GNU General Public License or GNU Library or Lesser Public License, or other obligation, restriction or license agreement that substantially conforms to the Open Source Definition as prescribed by the Open Source Initiative or otherwise may require disclosure or licensing to any third party of any source code with which such software component is used or compiled.
- Open Source means any software having license terms that require, as a condition of use, modification, or distribution of the software that such software or other software combined or distributed with such software be (i) disclosed or distributed in source code form, (ii) licensed for the purpose of making derivative works, or (iii) redistributable at no charge.
- Company Software means the Company Licensed Software and the Company Proprietary Software.
- Software License means any agreement (including any agreement constituting a Copyright License, Patent License and/or Trademark License) now or hereafter in existence granting to any Credit Party any right, whether exclusive or non-exclusive, to use another Person's Software, or pursuant to which any Credit Party has granted to any other Person, any right, whether exclusive or non-exclusive, to use any Software, whether or not subject to any registration.
- Software Product means any COTS which you propose to provide pursuant to the contract.
- Company Product means any project-based business management and/or sales management software and/or other product that, as of the date the Optionee's employment Terminates, the Company or any of its Affiliates is developing, implementing, marketing and/or selling.

- Application Software means Software formulated to perform specific business or technical functions and interface with the business or technical users of the System and is identified as such in Appendix 4 of the Contract Agreement and such other Software as the parties may agree in writing to be Application Software.
- Third Party Software means software which is proprietary to any third party (other than an Affiliate of the Contractor) which is or will be used by the Contractor for the purposes of providing the Services.
- Company Products means all products or services produced, marketed, licensed, sold, distributed or performed by or on behalf of the Company or any Subsidiary and all products or services currently under development by the Company or any Subsidiary.
- Diagnostic source assembly means the tube housing assembly with a beam-limiting device attached.
- Company Source Code means, collectively, any software source code or database specifications or designs, or any material proprietary information or algorithm contained in or relating to any software source code or database specifications or designs, of any Company-Owned Intellectual Property or Company Products.
- Source Materials means uranium containing the mixture of isotopes occurring in nature; uranium whose content in uranium 235 is less than the normal; thorium; any of the foregoing in the form of metal, alloy, chemical compound or concentrate; any other substance containing one or more of the foregoing in such a concentration as shall be specified by the Council, acting by a qualified majority on a proposal from the Commission.
- Commercial Software means Software developed or regularly used that: (i) has been sold, leased, or licensed to the general public; (ii) has been offered for sale, lease, or license to the general public; (iii) has not been offered, sold, leased, or licensed to the public but will be available for commercial sale, lease, or license in time to satisfy the delivery requirements of this Contract; or (iv) satisfies a criterion expressed in (i), (ii), or (iii) above and would require only minor modifications to meet the requirements of this Contract.
- Software Products means any computer software products, other than Off-the-Shelf-Software, and all computer operating, security or programming software, that is owned by or licensed to any Company Group Member or used, in whole or in part, directly or indirectly, or has been developed or designed for or is in the process of being developed or designed for use, in whole or in part, directly or indirectly, in the conduct of the Business of any nature whatsoever,

including all systems software, all applications software, whether for general business usage (e.g., accounting, finance, word processing, graphics, spreadsheet analysis, etc.) or specific, unique-to-the-Business usage (e.g., telephone call processing, etc.), and any and all documentation and object and source codes related thereto.

- Public Software means any Software that contains, or is derived in any manner (in whole or in part) from, any software that is distributed as free software, open source software (e.g., Linux) or similar licensing or distribution models, including, without limitation, software licensed or distributed under any of the following licenses or distribution models, or licenses or distribution models similar to any of the following: (A) GNU's General Public License (GPL) or Lesser/Library GPL (LGPL), (B) the Artistic License (e.g., PERL), (C) the Mozilla Public License, (D) the Netscape Public License, (E) the Sun Community Source License (SCSL), (F) the Sun Industry Standards License (SISL), (G) the BSD License, and (H) the Apache License.
- Supplier Software means software which is proprietary to the Supplier or its Affiliates which is used or supplied by the Supplier in the provision of the Services; Supplier Staff means all persons employed or engaged by the Supplier together with the Supplier's servants, agents, suppliers, consultants and Sub-Contractors (and all persons employed by any Sub-Contractor together with the Sub-Contractor's servants, consultants, agents, suppliers and Sub-Contractors) used in the performance of its obligations under this Contract; Time and Materials means the pricing mechanism for the Services as may be agreed by the Parties and set out at paragraph Error: Reference source not found in the SOW; TUPE means the Transfer of Undertakings (Protection of Employment) Regulations 2006 (SI 2006/246) as amended or replaced or any other regulations or UK legislation implementing the Acquired Rights Directive; Velocity means the Metric which measures the total number of Story Points for Stories that have been accepted in a Sprint, indicating the rate of progress towards Acceptance of all Stories from the Product Backlog;
- Source material means: (1) uranium or thorium, or any combination thereof, in any physical or chemical form or (2) ores which contain by weight one-twentieth of one percent (0.05 percent) or more of (i) uranium, (ii) thorium or (iii) any combination thereof. Source material does not include special nuclear material.
- SAP Software means: (i) any and all software products and Cloud Services licensed to Customer under the License Agreement as specified in software order forms or Cloud Service Order Forms (or other order forms, schedules or appendices as applicable) thereto;

(ii) any new releases, updates or versions thereof made available through unrestricted shipment pursuant to the respective support agreement or warranty obligation and (iii) any complete or partial copies of any of the foregoing.

- Licensed Software includes error corrections, upgrades, enhancements or new releases, and any deliverables due under a maintenance or service contract (e.g., patches, fixes, PTFs, programs, code or data conversion, or custom programming).
- Source Code for a work means the preferred form of the work for making modifications to it. "Object code" means any non-source form of a work.
- Hosted Software means Samsara's web-based software platform, including the interface accessed online at cloud.samsara.com.
- Seller Software means any software (including firmware and other software embedded in hardware devices) owned, developed (or currently being developed), used, marketed, distributed, licensed or sold by the Seller at any time (other than non-customized third-party software licensed to the Seller for internal use on a non-exclusive basis).

Open-source movement

The open source movement is a broad-reaching movement of individuals who support the use of open source licences for some or all software.. Open source software is made available for anybody to use or modify, as its source code is made available. Some open-source software is based on a share-alike principle, whereby users are free to pass on the software subject to the stipulation that any enhancements or changes are just as freely available to the public, while other open-source projects may be freely incorporated into any derivative work, open-source or proprietary. Open source software promotes learning and understanding through the dissemination of understanding.

The main difference between open-source and traditional proprietary software is in user and property rights, the conditions of use imposed on the user by the software license, as opposed to differences in the programming code. With open source software, such as OpenOffice.org, users are granted the right to both the program's functionality and methodology. With proprietary software programs, such as Microsoft Office, users only have the rights to functionality. Examples of popular open source software products include Mozilla Firefox, Google Chromium, Android and OpenOffice.org.

Programmers who support the open source movement philosophy contribute to the open source community by voluntarily writing and exchanging programming code for software development. The term "open source" requires that no one can discriminate against a group in not sharing the edited code or hinder others from editing their already edited work. This approach to software development allows anyone to obtain and modify open source code. These modifications are distributed back to the developers within the open source community of people who are working with the software. In this way, the identities of all individuals participating in code modification are disclosed and the transformation of the code is documented over time. This method makes it difficult to establish ownership of a particular bit of code but is in keeping with the open source movement philosophy. These goals promote the production of "high quality programs" as well as "working cooperatively with other similarly minded people" to improve open source technologies.

Brief History

In the late 1970s and early 1980s, two different groups were establishing the roots of the current open source software movement. On the east coast, Richard Stallman, formerly of the MIT AI lab, created the GNU project and the Free Software Foundation. The GNU project was aimed to create a free operating system, and used the GNU General Public License (GPL) as the software license to prohibit proprietization of the software, but allow redistribution and modification.

On the US West coast, the Computer Science Research Group (CSRG) of the University of California at Berkeley was adding improvements to the original Unix operating system from AT&T, and developed many applications, which became known as "BSD Unix". These efforts were funded mainly by DARPA contracts, and a dense network of Unix hackers around the world helped to debug, maintain and improve the system. During 1991-1992, two significant events took place:

- In California, Bill Jolitz completed the Net/2 distribution, until it was ready to run on i386-class machines. Net/2 was the result of the effort of the CSRG to make a version of BSD Unix free of AT&T-copyrighted code. He called his work 386BSD, and it quickly became appreciated within the BSD and Unix communities. It included not only a kernel, but also many utilities, making a complete operating system.
- In Finland, Linus Torvalds, a computer science student, unhappy with Tanenbaum's Minix, implemented the first versions of the Linux kernel. Soon, many people were collaborating to make that kernel more and more usable, and added many utilities to make GNU/Linux a real operating system.

In 1993, both GNU/Linux and 386BSD were reasonably stable platforms. Since then, 386BSD has evolved into a family of BSD-based operating systems (NetBSD, FreeBSD, and OpenBSD), while the Linux kernel is used in many GNU/Linux distributions such as Slackware, Debian, Red Hat, SUSE, Mandrake, and many more.

The label "open source" was created and adopted by a group of people in the free software movement at a strategy session held at Palo Alto, California, in reaction to Netscape's January 1998 announcement of a source code release for Navigator.

One of the reasoning behind using the term was that "the [advantage] of using the term open source [is] that the business world usually tries to keep free technologies from being installed." Those people who adopted the term used the opportunity before the release of Navigator's source code to free themselves of the ideological and confrontational connotations of the term "free software".

Later in February 1998, Bruce Perens and Eric S. Raymond founded an organization called Open Source Initiative (OSI) "as an educational, advocacy, and stewardship organization at a cusp moment in the history of that culture."

Evolution

Any technological advance needs a reason to be introduced into society. In the beginning, a difference between hardware and software did not exist. The user and programmer of a computer were one and the same. When the first commercial electronic computer was introduced by IBM in 1952, the machine was hard to maintain and expensive.

Putting the price of the machine aside it was the software that caused the problem when owning one of these computers. Then in 1952, a collaboration of all the owners of the computer got together and created a set of tools. The collaboration of people were in a group called PACT (The Project for the Advancement of Coding techniques).

After passing this hurdle, in 1956, the Eisenhower administration decided to put restrictions on the types of sales AT&T could make. This did not stop the inventors from developing new ideas of how to bring the computer to the mass population. The next step was making the computer more affordable which slowly developed through different companies. Then they had to develop a software which would host multiple users. MIT computation center developed one of the first systems, CTSS (Compatible Time-Sharing System).

This lay the foundation for many more systems to come and what we now call the Open Source Movement.

The Open Source Movement is branched from the free software movement which began in the late 80s with the launching of the GNU/ Linux project by Richard Stallman. Stallman is regarded within the open source community as sharing a key role in the conceptualization of freely shared source code for software development. The term "free software" in the free software movement is meant to imply freedom of software exchange and modification. The term does not refer to any monetary freedom. Both the free software movement and the open source movement share this view of free exchange of programming code, and this is often why both of the movements are sometimes referenced in literature as part of the FOSS or "Free and Open Software" or FLOSS "Free/Libre Open Source" communities.

These movements share fundamental differences in the view on open software. The main, factionalizing difference between the groups is the relationship between open source and proprietary software. Often makers of proprietary software, such as Microsoft, may make efforts to support open source software to remain competitive. Members of the open source community are willing to coexist with the makers of proprietary software and feel that the issue of whether software is open source is a matter of practicality.

In contrast, members of the free software community maintain the vision that all software is a part of freedom of speech and that proprietary software is unethical and unjust. The free software movement openly champions this belief through talks that denounce proprietary software. As a whole the community refuses to support proprietary software. It also is suggested there are external motivations exist for these developers. One motivation is when a programmer fixes a bug or makes a program it benefits others in an open source environment. Another motivation is that a programmer can work on multiple projects at the same time doing something they enjoy. Also, programming in the open source world can lead to commercial job offers or entrance into the venture capital community. These are just a few reasons why open source programmers continue to create and advance software.

While cognizant of the fact that both it and the open source movement share similarities in practical recommendations regarding open source, the free software movement fervently continues to distinguish themselves from the open source movement entirely. The free software movement maintains that it has fundamentally different attitudes towards the relationship between open source and proprietary software. The free software community does not view the open source community as their target grievance, however. Their target grievance is proprietary software itself.

Legal issues

The Open Source Movement has faced a number of legal challenges. Companies that manage open source products have some difficulty securing their trademarks. For example, the scope of "implied license" conjecture remains unclear and can compromise an enterprise's ability to patent productions made with open source software. Another example is the case of companies offering add-ons for purchase; licensees who make additions to the open-source code that are similar to those for purchase may have immunity from patent suits.

In the court case "Jacobsen v Katzer", the plaintiff sued the defendant for failing to put the required attribution notices in his modified version of the software, thereby violating license. The defendant claimed Artistic License in not adhering to the conditions of the software's use, but the wording of the attribution notice decided that this was not the case. "Jacobsen v Katzer" established open source software's equality to proprietary software in the eyes of the law.

In a court case accusing Microsoft of being a monopoly, Linux and open source software was introduced in court to prove that Microsoft had valid competitors and was grouped in with Apple.

There are resources available for those involved open source projects in need of legal advice. The Software Freedom Legal Center features a primer on open source legal issues. International Free and Open Source Software Law Review offers peer-reviewed information for lawyers on free software issues.

Formalization

Richard Stallman, a supporter of the free software movement, was one of the free software and open source movement advocates who proposed an alternative to the private models prevalent in the industry. After developing a nonproprietary operating system called GNU, Stallman founded the Free Software Foundation in 1983. For most of the 1970s and 1980s, organizations such as AT&T, with their Unix operating system initiative, have promoted a policy of shared source code.

Linus Torvalds then built upon Stallman's development in the late 1980s and created the Linux operating system that he released under

Stallman's GNU General Public License. This enabled open source programmers to improve, modify, and develop his system.

The Open Source Initiative (OSI) was also instrumental in the formalization of the Open Source Movement. The OSI was founded by Eric Raymond and Bruce Perens in February 1998 with the purpose of providing general education and advocacy of the open source label through the creation of the Open Source Definition that was based on the Debian Free Software Guidelines. The OSI has become one of the main supporters and advocators of the open source movement.

In February 1998 the open source movement was adopted, formalized, and spearheaded by the Open Source Initiative (OSI), an organization formed to market software "as something more amenable to commercial business use" The OSI owns the trademark "Open Source" The main tool they adopted for this was the Open Source Definition

The "open source" label was conceived at a strategy session that was held on February 3, 1998 in Palo Alto, California and on April 8 of the same year, the attendees of Tim O'Reilly's Free Software Summit voted to promote the use of the term "open source".

Overall, the software developments that have come out of the open source movement have not been unique to the computer science field, but they have been successful in developing alternatives to propriety software. Members of the open source community improve upon code and write programs that can rival much of the propriety software that is already available.

The rhetorical discourse used in open source movements is now being broadened to include a larger group of non-expert users as well as advocacy organizations. Several organized groups such as the Creative Commons and global development agencies have also adopted the open source concepts according to their own aims and for their own purposes.

The factors affecting the Open Source Movement's legal formalization are primarily based on recent political discussion over copyright, appropriation, and intellectual property.

Examples of software that have come out of the open source movement

- Linux - a Unix-Based operating system used predominantly in servers Linux was created by a student in 1991 along with other developers around the world.
- Apache - a leading server software and scripting language on the web

- MySQL - a database management system
- PHP - a widely used open source general-purpose scripting language
- Blender - a 3D graphics and animation software
- OpenOffice.org - an office suite software with word processor, spreadsheet, and presentation capabilities, now forked to LibreOffice after lock-in claims from companies which supported OpenOffice.
- Mozilla - a web browser and e-mail client
- Perl - a programming/scripting language
- Wikipedia - Online encyclopedia open for anyone to update and revise content.

Strengths

- The collaborative nature of the open source community creates software that can offer customizability and, as a result, promotes the adoption of its products.
- The open source community promotes the creation of software that is not proprietary, resulting in lower costs.
- Individuals who have intrinsic interest in code writing and software creation motivate the development of open source software within the community. This differs from proprietary software, which is often motivated through potential monetary gains.
- An open source tool puts the system administrator in control of the level of risk assumed in deploying the tool.
- Open source provides flexibility not available in closed products. The hope is that individuals make improvements to an open tool and will offer those improvements to the original developer and community at large. The give-and-take of the gift economy benefits the entire community.
- Open source licenses and software can be combined with proprietary software. While open source was initially seen as a threat to corporations, some companies found ways to strengthen their proprietary code with open source code, re-releasing it as an improvement.
- In the event of market failure, programmers and innovators work together to make sure that the software still works
- Globalization of Market

The Open Source Movement has allowed smaller businesses to participate in the global economy. Before smaller businesses did not have access to the software needed to participate or compete in the global market. It was the larger corporations, the producers of the networks and software who had the power. "That is, individuals who have access to the software needed to create, organize, or distribute content can plug into and participate in the global community". The creation of the Open Source Movement has created "a degree of global computing access that might have been unthinkable in a world where proprietary was the only option." Individuals or organizations with access to an open source had the means needed to develop technical material for a variety of consumers. The Open Source Movement created equal opportunities for people all over the world to participate in the global economy.

Members of the Open Source Movement stress the importance of differentiating between "open source" software and "free software". Although the two issues are related, they are quite different. The open source movement and the free software movement are different but they work together. Both movements strive for freedom of the internet and dislike the idea of ownership over a website.

For both open source and free software, one can find the source code and executable component easily and for free online. The largest difference is that free software requires any changes to be submitted to the original maker for redistribution, and any derivative software must also be distributed as free software. This is mainly to keep companies from making minor changes to free software and redistributing it as their own, for a price.

A major advantage to open source code is the ability for a variety of different people to edit and fix problems and errors that have occurred. Naturally because there are more people who can edit the material there are more people who can help make the information more credible and reliable. The open source mission statement promises better quality, higher reliability, more flexibility, lower cost, and an end to predatory vendor lock-in. They stress the importance of maintaining the Open Source Definition. This trademark creates a trusted group that connects all users and developers together. To fully understand the Open Source Definition, one must understand certain terms: Free redistribution means that there is no restriction on any party to sell or give away the software to third parties. Source Code means that the program must efficiently publicize the means of obtaining the source code.

Derived works means that the program must allow certain works to be distributed under the same terms. There must be a promise of no discriminating against any certain persons or groups. All of these factors allow for the open source movement to become available to all and easy to access, which is their overall mission. The latest updates from the Open Source Institution took place on January 19, 2011: The OSI collaborated with the Free Software Foundation and together they updated a version of the request that they have sent to the US Department of Justice.

Motivations of Programmers

With the growth and attention on the open source movement, the reasons and motivations of programmers for creating code for free has been under investigation. In a paper from the 15th Annual Congress of the European Economic Association on the open source movement, the incentives of programmers on an individual level as well as on a company or network level were analyzed. What is essentially the intellectual gift giving of talented programmers challenges the "self-interested-economic-agent paradigm," and has made both the public and economists search for an understanding of what the benefits are for programmers.

- Altruism: The argument for altruism is limited as an explanation because though some exists, the programmers do not focus their kindness on more charitable causes. If the generosity of working for free was a viable motivation for such a prevalent movement, it is curious why such a trend has not been seen in industries such as biotechnology that would have a much bigger impact on the public good.
- Community Sharing and Improvement: The online community is an environment that promotes continual improvements, modifications, and contributions to each other's work. A programmer can easily benefit from open source software because by making it public, other testers and subprograms can remove bugs, tailor code to other purposes, and find problems. This kind of peer editing feature of open source software promotes better programs and a higher standard of code.
- Recognition: Though a project may not be associated with a specific individual, the contributors are often recognized and marked on a project's server. This allows for programmers to receive public recognition for their skills, promoting career opportunities and exposure. In fact, the founders of Sun and Netscape began as open source programmers.
- Ego: "If they are somehow assigned to a trivial problem and that is their only possible task, they may spend six months coming up with a bewildering architecture...merely to show their friends and colleagues what a tough nut they are trying to crack." Ego-gratification has been cited as a relevant motivation of programmers because of their competitive community. An OSS (open source software) community has no clear distinction between developers and users, because all users are potential developers. There is a large community of programmers trying to essentially outshine or impress their colleagues. They enjoy having other programmers admire their works and accomplishments, contributing to why OSS projects have a recruiting advantage for unknown talent than a closed-source company.

- Creative Expression: Personal satisfaction also comes from the act of writing software as an equivalent to creative self-expression - it is almost equivalent to creating a work of art. The rediscovery of creativity, which has been lost through the mass production of commercial software products can be a relevant motivation.

Drawbacks

- The structure of the open source community requires that individuals have programming expertise in order to engage in open code modification and exchange. Individuals interested in supporting the open source movement may lack this skill set, but there are many other ways of contributing.
- Programmers and developers comprise a large percentage of the open source community and sought-out technical support and/or documentation may not be useful or clear to open source software lay-users.
- The structure of the open source community is one that involves contributions of multiple developers and programmers; software produced in this fashion may lack standardization and compatibility with various computer applications and capabilities.
- Production can be very limited. Programmers that create open source software often can turn their attention elsewhere very quickly. This opens the door for many bug filled programs and applications out there. Because no one is paid to create it, many projects are never completed.
- In the open source industry, the user decides the quality of the software. A user must learn the skills of software creation independently and then make the appropriate determinations for quality and capabilities.
- Librarians may not be equipped to take on this new responsibility of technologies.
- There is no guarantee that development will happen. It is unknown if an open source project will become usable, especially when a project is started without significant support from one or more organizations. Even if the project does reach a usable stage, it is possible the project can die if there is not enough funding or interest toward it.
- It is sometimes difficult to know that a project exists, and its current status. Especially for open source projects without significant support, there is not much advertising involved in open source software.
- Not much support exists for open source software. Qualified support essentially does not exist. The available support for open source software is predominantly self-motivated discussions found on the

Internet, and since the software is constantly being changed, no manuals or instructions are made.

- There is no guarantee of updates. Although open source software is available to anyone for free, regular updates are not assured since users do not pay for its use.
- Beyond the obvious detriments towards the theoretical success of open source software, there are several factors that contribute to the lack of long-term success in open source projects. One of the most obvious drawback is that without pay or royalty licensing, there is little financial incentive for a programmer to become involved with a project in the first place, or to continue development and support once the initial product is released. This leads to innumerable examples of well-anticipated software being forever condemned to beta versions and unsupported early model products. With donations as the only source of income for a truly open source (and GPL licensed) project, there is almost no certainty in the future of the project simply because of developer abandonment, making it a poor choice for any sort of application in which future versions, support and a long-term plan would be essential, as is the case for most business software.
- Organization's with Enterprise Agreements still pay licensing agreements even if they choose to run alternative open source software. Therefore many organizations are unlikely to consider using alternative products. As a cost saving method of using Microsoft products, many large corporations use enterprise agreements and therefore pay a single company wide IT Licensing fee, at lower cost per product."Organizations with EAs that are interested in alternative products can benefit from the gap-filler scenario, but only after they drop Microsoft Office from their EA at the next renewal and final true-up."

Evidence of open source adoption

Libraries are using open source software to develop information as well as library services. The purpose of open source is to provide a software that is cheaper, reliable and has better quality. The one feature that makes this software so sought after is that it is free. Libraries in particular benefit from this movement because of the resources it provides. They also promote the same ideas of learning and understanding new information through the resources of other people. Open source allows a sense of community. It is an invitation for anyone to provide information about various topics. The open source tools even allow libraries to create web-based catalogs. According to the IT source there are various library programs that benefit from this.

The following are events and applications that have been developed via the open source community as and echo the ideologies of the open source movement.

OpenCourseWare Consortium - an organization composed of various colleges that support open source and share some of their material online. This organization, headed by Massachusetts Institute of Technology, was established to aid in the exchange of open source educational materials.

Wikipedia - user-generated online encyclopedia with sister projects in academic areas, such as Wikiversity - a community dedicated to the creation and exchange of learning materials

Project Gutenberg - prior to the existence of Google Scholar Beta, this was the first supplier of electronic books and the very first free library project

Google - this search engine has led the way in transformation of Web-based applications, such as books, scholarly journals, that are based primarily on open source software. Google continues to make applications based on open software. Recently, in November 2009, Google announced that it would be "enabling people everywhere to find, and read full text legal opinions from U.S. federal and state districts, appellate and supreme courts using Google Scholar"

Microsoft - Before summer of 2008, Microsoft has generally been known as an enemy of the open source community. The company's anti-open source sentiment was enforced by former CEO Steve Ballmer, who referred to Linux, a widely used open source software, as a "malignant cancer". Microsoft also threatened Linux that they would charge royalties for violating 235 of their patents. In 2004, Microsoft lost a European Union court case, and lost the appeal in 2007, and their further appeal in 2012: being convicted of abusing its dominant position. Specifically they had withheld inter-operability information with the open-source Samba (software) project, which can be run on many platforms and aims to "removing barriers to interoperability".

In 2008, however, Sam Ramji, the then head of open source software strategy in Microsoft, began working closely with Bill Gates to develop a pro-open source attitude within the software industry as well as Microsoft itself. Ramji, before leaving the company in 2009, built Microsoft's familiarity and involvement with open source, which is evident in Microsoft's contributions of open source code to Windows Azure, "its new-age web service for building and hosting applications on the net", among other projects. These contributions would have been previously unimaginable by Microsoft. Microsoft's change in attitude about open source and efforts to build a stronger open source community is evidence of the growing adoption and adaption of open source.

Government agencies and infrastructure software - Government Agencies are utilizing open source infrastructure software, like the Linux operating system and the Apache Web-server into software, to manage information. In 2005, a new government lobby was launched under the name National Center for Open Source Policy and Research (NCOSPR) "a non-profit organization promoting the use of open source software solutions within government IT enterprises."

Synthetic Biology- Synthetic Biology is considered the feasibility of the open source movement. This new technology is important and exciting because it promises to enable cheap, lifesaving new drugs as well as helping to yield biofuels that may help to solve our energy problem. Although synthetic biology has not yet come out of its "lab" stage, it has great potential to become industrialized in the near future. In order to industrialize open source science, there are some scientists who are trying to build their own brand of it.

Open Source Movement in the Military- Open source movement has potential to help in the military. The open source software allows anyone to make changes that will improve it. This is a form of invitation for people to put their minds together to grow a software in a cost efficient manner. The reason the military is so interested is because it is possible that this software can increase speed and flexibility.

Although there are security setbacks to this idea due to the fact that anyone has access to change the software, the advantages can outweigh the disadvantages. The fact that the open- source programs can be modified quickly is crucial. A support group was formed to test these theories. The Military Open Source Software Working Group was organized in 2009 and held over 120 military members. Their purpose was to bring together software developers and contractors from the military to discover new ideas for reuse and collaboration.

Overall, open-source software in the military is an intriguing idea that has potential drawbacks but they are not enough to offset the advantages.

Open Source in Education- Colleges and organizations use software predominantly online to educate their students. Open source technology is being adopted by many institutions because it can save these institutions from paying companies to provide them with these administrative software systems. One of the first major colleges to adopt an open source system was Colorado State University in 2009 with many others following after that. Colorado State Universities system was produced by the Kuali Foundation who has become a major player in open source administrative systems. The Kuali Foundation defines itself as a group of organizations that aims to "build and sustain open source software for higher education, by higher education." There are many other examples of open source instruments being used in education other than the Kuali Foundation as well.

"For educators, The Open Source Movement allowed access to software that could be used in teaching students how to apply the theories they were learning". With open networks and software, teachers are able to share lessons, lectures, and other course materials within a community. OpenTechComm is a program that is dedicated to "open access, open use, and open edits- text book or pedagogical resource that teachers of technical and professional communication courses at every level can rely on to craft free offerings to their students." As stated earlier, access to programs like this would be much more cost efficient for educational departments.

Open Source in Healthcare- Created in June 2009 by the nonprofit eHealthNigeria, the open source software OpenMRS is used to document health care in Nigeria. The use of this software began in Kaduna, Nigeria to serve the purpose of public health.

OpenMRS manages features such as alerting health care workers when patients show warning signs for conditions and records births and deaths daily, among other features. The success of this software is caused by its ease of use for those first being introduced to the technology, compared to more complex proprietary healthcare software available in first world countries. This software is community-developed and can be used freely by anyone, characteristic of open source applications. So far, OpenMRS is being used in Rwanda, Mozambique, Haiti, India, China, and the Philippines.

The impact of open source in healthcare is also observed by Apelon Inc, the "leading provider of terminology and data interoperability solutions". Recently, its Distributed Terminology System (Open DTS) began supporting the open source MySQL database system.

This essentially allows for open source software to be used in healthcare, lessening the dependence on expensive proprietary healthcare software. Due to open source software, the healthcare industry has available a free open source solution to implement healthcare standards. Not only does open source benefit healthcare economically, but the lesser dependence on proprietary software allows for easier integration of various systems, regardless of the developer.

Software

Generally, open source refers to a computer program in which the source code is available to the general public for use for any (including commercial) purpose, or modification from its original design. Open-source code is meant to be a collaborative effort, where programmers improve upon the source code and share the changes within the community. Code is released under the terms of a software license. Depending on the license terms, others may then download, modify, and publish their version (fork) back to the community.

List of free and open-source software packages

Open-source license, a copyright license that makes the source code available with a product. The Open Source Definition, as used by the Open Source Initiative for open source software.

Open-source model, a decentralized software development model that encourages open collaboration.

Open-source software, software which permits the use and Imodification of its source code History of free and open-source software.

- Open-source software advocacy.
- Open-source software development.
- Open-source-software movement.
- Open-source video games
- List of open-source video games
- Business models for open-source software
- Comparison of open-source and closed-source software
- Diversity in open-source software

MapGuide Open Source, a web-based map-making platform to develop and deploy web mapping applications and geospatial web services (not to be confused with OpenStreetMap (OSM), a collaborative project to create a free editable map of the world).

Ideologically related movements

The open access movement is a movement that is similar in ideology to the open source movement. Members of this movement maintain that academic material should be readily available to provide help with "future research, assist in teaching and aid in academic purposes." The Open access movement aims to eliminate subscription fees and licensing restrictions of academic materials

The free culture movement is a movement that seeks to achieve a culture that engages in collective freedom via freedom of expression, free public access to knowledge and information, full demonstration of creativity and innovation in various arenas and promotion of citizen liberties.

Creative Commons is an organization that "develops, supports, and stewards legal and technical infrastructure that maximizes digital creativity, sharing, and innovation."

It encourages the use of protected properties online for research, education, and creative purposes in pursuit of a universal access. Creative Commons provides an infrastructure through a set of copyright licenses and tools that creates a better balance within the realm of "all rights reserved" properties.

The Creative Commons license offers a slightly more lenient alternative to "all rights reserved" copyrights for those who do not wish to exclude the use of their material.

Society

The rise of open-source culture in the 20th century resulted from a growing tension between creative practices that involve require access to content that is often copyrighted, and restrictive intellectual property laws and policies governing access to copyrighted content.

The two main ways in which intellectual property laws became more restrictive in the 20th century were extensions to the term of copyright (particularly in the United States) and penalties, such as those articulated in the Digital Millennium Copyright Act (DMCA), placed on attempts to circumvent anti-piracy technologies.

Although artistic appropriation is often permitted under fair-use doctrines, the complexity and ambiguity of these doctrines creates an atmosphere of uncertainty among cultural practitioners. Also, the protective actions of copyright owners create what some call a "chilling effect" among cultural practitioners.

The idea of an "open-source" culture runs parallel to "Free Culture," but is substantively different. Free culture is a term derived from the free software movement, and in contrast to that vision of culture, proponents of open-source culture (OSC) maintain that some intellectual property law needs to exist to protect cultural producers. Yet they propose a more nuanced position than corporations have traditionally sought.

Instead of seeing intellectual property law as an expression of instrumental rules intended to uphold either natural rights or desirable outcomes, an argument for OSC takes into account diverse goods (as in "the Good life") and ends.

Sites such as ccMixter offer up free web space for anyone willing to license their work under a Creative Commons license. The resulting cultural product is then available to download free (generally accessible) to anyone with an Internet connection. Older, analog technologies such as the telephone or television have limitations on the kind of interaction users can have.

Through various technologies such as peer-to-peer networks and blogs, cultural producers can take advantage of vast social networks to distribute their products. As opposed to traditional media distribution, redistributing digital media on the Internet can be virtually costless. Technologies such as BitTorrent and Gnutella take advantage of various characteristics of the Internet protocol (TCP/IP) in an attempt to totally decentralize file distribution.

Government

Open politics (sometimes known as Open-source politics) is a political process that uses Internet technologies such as blogs, email and polling to provide for a rapid feedback mechanism between political organizations and their supporters.

There is also an alternative conception of the term Open-source politics which relates to the development of public policy under a set of rules and processes similar to the open-source software movement.

Open-source governance is similar to open-source politics, but it applies more to the democratic process and promotes the freedom of information.

Open-source political campaigns refer specifically to political campaigns.

The South Korean government wants to increase its use of free and open-source software, in order to decrease its dependence on proprietary software solutions. It plans to make open standards a requirement, to allow the government to choose between multiple operating systems and web browsers. Korea's Ministry of Science, ICT & Future Planning is also preparing ten pilots on using open-source software distributions.

Ethics

Open-source ethics is split into two strands:

Open-source ethics as an ethical school – Charles Ess and David Berry are researching whether ethics can learn anything from an open-source approach. Ess famously even defined the AoIR Research Guidelines as an example of open-source ethics.

Open-source ethics as a professional body of rules – This is based principally on the computer ethics school, studying the questions of ethics and professionalism in the computer industry in general and software development in particular.

Religion

Irish philosopher Richard Kearney has used the term "open-source Hinduism" to refer to the way historical figures such as Mohandas Gandhi and Swami Vivekananda worked upon this ancient tradition.

Media

Open-source journalism formerly referred to the standard journalistic techniques of news gathering and fact checking, reflecting open-source intelligence, a similar term used in military intelligence circles. Now, open-source journalism commonly refers to forms of innovative publishing of online journalism, rather than the sourcing of news stories by a professional journalist. In the 25 December 2006 issue of TIME magazine this is referred to as user created content and listed alongside more traditional open-source projects such as OpenSolaris and Linux.

Weblogs, or blogs, are another significant platform for open-source culture. Blogs consist of periodic, reverse chronologically ordered posts, using a technology that makes webpages easily updatable with no understanding of design, code, or file transfer required. While corporations, political campaigns and other formal institutions have begun using these tools to distribute information, many blogs are used by individuals for personal expression, political organizing, and socializing. Some, such as LiveJournal or WordPress, utilize open-source software that is open to the public and can be modified by users to fit their own tastes. Whether the code is open or not, this format represents a nimble tool for people to borrow and re-present culture; whereas traditional websites made the illegal reproduction of culture difficult to regulate, the mutability of blogs makes "open sourcing" even more uncontrollable since it allows a larger portion of the population to replicate material more quickly in the public sphere.

Messageboards are another platform for open-source culture. Messageboards (also known as discussion boards or forums), are places online where people with similar interests can congregate and post messages for the community to read and respond to. Messageboards sometimes have moderators who enforce community standards of etiquette such as banning spammers. Other common board features are private messages (where users can send messages to one another) as well as chat (a way to have a real time conversation online) and image uploading. Some messageboards use phpBB, which is a free open-source package. Where blogs are more about individual expression and tend to revolve around their authors, messageboards are about creating a conversation amongst its users where information can be shared freely and quickly.

Messageboards are a way to remove intermediaries from everyday life—for instance, instead of relying on commercials and other forms of advertising, one can ask other users for frank reviews of a product, movie or CD. By removing the cultural middlemen, messageboards help speed the flow of information and exchange of ideas.

OpenDocument is an open document file format for saving and exchanging editable office documents such as text documents (including memos, reports, and books), spreadsheets, charts, and presentations. Organizations and individuals that store their data in an open format such as OpenDocument avoid being locked into a single software vendor, leaving them free to switch software if their current vendor goes out of business, raises their prices, changes their software, or changes their licensing terms to something less favorable.

Open-source movie production is either an open call system in which a changing crew and cast collaborate in movie production, a system in which the result is made available for re-use by others or in which exclusively open-source products are used in the production. The 2006 movie Elephants Dream is said to be the "world's first open movie", created entirely using open-source technology.

An open-source documentary film has a production process allowing the open contributions of archival material footage, and other filmic elements, both in unedited and edited form, similar to crowdsourcing. By doing so, on-line contributors become part of the process of creating the film, helping to influence the editorial and visual material to be used in the documentary, as well as its thematic development. The first open-source documentary film is the non-profit WBCN and the American Revolution, which went into development in 2006, and will examine the role media played in the cultural, social and political changes from 1968 to 1974 through the story of radio station WBCN-FM in Boston. The film is being produced by Lichtenstein Creative Media and the non-profit Center for Independent Documentary.

Open Source Cinema is a website to create Basement Tapes, a feature documentary about copyright in the digital age, co-produced by the National Film Board of Canada. Open-source film-making refers to a form of film-making that takes a method of idea formation from open-source software, but in this case the 'source' for a filmmaker is raw unedited footage rather than programming code. It can also refer to a method of film-making where the process of creation is 'open' i.e. a disparate group of contributors, at different times contribute to the final piece.

Open-IPTV is IPTV that is not limited to one recording studio, production studio, or cast. Open-IPTV uses the Internet or other means to pool efforts and resources together to create an online community that all contributes to a show.

Education

Within the academic community, there is discussion about expanding what could be called the "intellectual commons" (analogous to the Creative Commons). Proponents of this view have hailed the Connexions Project at Rice University, OpenCourseWare project at MIT, Eugene Thacker's article on "open-source DNA", the "Open Source Cultural Database", Salman Khan's Khan Academy and Wikipedia as examples of applying open source outside the realm of computer software.

Open-source curricula are instructional resources whose digital source can be freely used, distributed and modified.

Another strand to the academic community is in the area of research. Many funded research projects produce software as part of their work. Due to the benefits of sharing software openly in scientific endeavours, there is an increasing interest in making the outputs of research projects available under an open-source license. In the UK the Joint Information Systems Committee (JISC) has developed a policy on open-source software. JISC also funds a development service called OSS Watch which acts as an advisory service for higher and further education institutions wishing to use, contribute to and develop open-source software.

On 30 March 2010, President Barack Obama signed the Health Care and Education Reconciliation Act, which included $2 billion over four years to fund the TAACCCT program, which is described as "the largest

OER (open education resources) initiative in the world and uniquely focused on creating curricula in partnership with industry for credentials in vocational industry sectors like manufacturing, health, energy, transportation, and IT".

Innovation communities

The principle of sharing pre-dates the open-source movement; for example, the free sharing of information has been institutionalized in the scientific enterprise since at least the 19th century. Open-source principles have always been part of the scientific community. The sociologist Robert K. Merton described the four basic elements of the community—universalism (an international perspective), communalism (sharing information), objectivity (removing one's personal views from the scientific inquiry) and organized skepticism (requirements of proof and review) that describe the (idealised) scientific community.

These principles are, in part, complemented by US law's focus on protecting expression and method but not the ideas themselves. There is also a tradition of publishing research results to the scientific community instead of keeping all such knowledge proprietary. One of the recent initiatives in scientific publishing has been open access—the idea that research should be published in such a way that it is free and available to the public. There are currently many open access journals where the information is available free online, however most journals do charge a fee (either to users or libraries for access). The Budapest Open Access Initiative is an international effort with the goal of making all research articles available free on the Internet.

The National Institutes of Health has recently proposed a policy on "Enhanced Public Access to NIH Research Information". This policy would provide a free, searchable resource of NIH-funded results to the public and with other international repositories six months after its initial publication. The NIH's move is an important one because there is significant amount of public funding in scientific research. Many of the questions have yet to be answered—the balancing of profit vs. public access, and ensuring that desirable standards and incentives do not diminish with a shift to open access.

Benjamin Franklin was an early contributor eventually donating all his inventions including the Franklin stove, bifocals, and the lightning rod to the public domain.

New NGO communities are starting to use the open-source technology as a tool. One example is the Open Source Youth Network started in 2007 in Lisboa by ISCA members.

Open innovation is also a new emerging concept which advocate putting R&D in a common pool. The Eclipse platform is openly presenting itself as an Open innovation network.

Arts and recreation

Copyright protection is used in the performing arts and even in athletic activities. Some groups have attempted to remove copyright from such practices.

In 2012, Russian music composer, scientist and Russian Pirate Party member Victor Argonov presented detailed raw files of his electronic opera "2032" under free license CC-BY-NC 3.0 (later relicensed under CC-BY-SA 4.0). This opera was originally composed and published in 2007 by Russian label MC Entertainment as a commercial product, but then the author changed its status to free. In his blog he said that he decided to open raw files (including wav, midi and other used formats) to the public in order to support worldwide pirate actions against SOPA and PIPA. Several Internet resources called "2032" the first open-source musical opera in history.

Other related movements

This article or section may need to be cleaned up or summarized because it has been split from/to Open-source software movement.

The following are events and applications that have been developed via the open source community, and echo the ideologies of the open source movement.

Open Education Consortium — an organization composed of various colleges that support open source and share some of their material online. This organization, headed by Massachusetts Institute of Technology, was established to aid in the exchange of open source educational materials.

Wikipedia — user-generated online encyclopedia with sister projects in academic areas, such as Wikiversity — a community dedicated to the creation and exchange of learning materials [failed verification]

Project Gutenberg — prior to the existence of Google Scholar Beta, this was the first supplier of electronic books and the very first free library project.

Synthetic Biology- This new technology is potentially important because it promises to enable cheap, lifesaving new drugs as well as helping to yield biofuels that may help to solve our energy problem. Although synthetic biology has not yet come out of its "lab" stage, it has potential to become industrialized in the near future. In order to industrialize open source science, there are some scientists who are trying to build their own brand of it.

Ideologically-related movements

The open-access movement is a movement that is similar in ideology to the open source movement. Members of this movement maintain that academic material should be readily available to provide help with "future research, assist in teaching and aid in academic purposes." The Open access movement aims to eliminate subscription fees and licensing restrictions of academic materials

The free-culture movement is a movement that seeks to achieve a culture that engages in collective freedom via freedom of expression, free public access to knowledge and information, full demonstration of creativity and innovation in various arenas and promotion of citizen liberties.

Creative Commons is an organization that "develops, supports, and stewards legal and technical infrastructure that maximizes digital creativity, sharing, and innovation."

It encourages the use of protected properties online for research, education, and creative purposes in pursuit of a universal access. Creative Commons provides an infrastructure through a set of copyright licenses and tools that creates a better balance within the realm of "all rights reserved" properties. The Creative Commons license offers a slightly more lenient alternative to "all rights reserved" copyrights for those who do not wish to exclude the use of their material.

The Zeitgeist Movement is an international social movement that advocates a transition into a sustainable "resource-based economy" based on collaboration in which monetary incentives are replaced by commons-based ones with everyone having access to everything (from code to products) as in "open source everything".

While its activism and events are typically focused on media and education, TZM is a major supporter of open source projects worldwide since they allow for uninhibited advancement of science and technology, independent of constraints posed by institutions of patenting and capitalist investment.

P2P Foundation is an "international organization focused on studying, researching, documenting and promoting peer to peer practices in a very broad sense". Its objectives incorporate those of the open source movement, whose principles are integrated in a larger socio-economic model.

2

Open Source Technologies that Changed the World

Open source technology is a growing trend in GIS, but what is it? Open source software is software in which the source code used to create the program is freely available for the public to view, edit, and redistribute. Any type of software program can be open source, including operating systems (e.g., Linux), databases (e.g., PostgreSQL), applications (e.g., OpenOffice.org), games, and even programming languages (e.g., Python).

Open source software is identified by the type of license it is released under. These licenses include the Apache 2.0 license, the Microsoft Public License, and the GNU General Public License. While there are some variations, most open source licenses require that the source code be freely available and users are free to modify the source code and redistribute the software and derived works.

Non-open source software is called closed source or proprietary software.

The open source license encourages a shared community approach to the development, extension, and patching of open source software. Most open source projects have a dedicated group that moderates and directs the core software development and ensures that needed new features are being developed, bugs are being fixed, and the supporting documentation remains current. Sometimes an open source project will "fork," meaning a group of developers will lead the development of the software that is independent of the original project. Improvements in the "fork" project could either become incorporated into the core project or evolve into a completely new project.

Isn't Open Source Free?

A common misconception is that open source software is free, meaning without cost. While often true, that is not always the case. Open source only requires that a program's source code be freely available; the program itself may still be sold commercially. So what's the difference between a program's source code and the program itself?

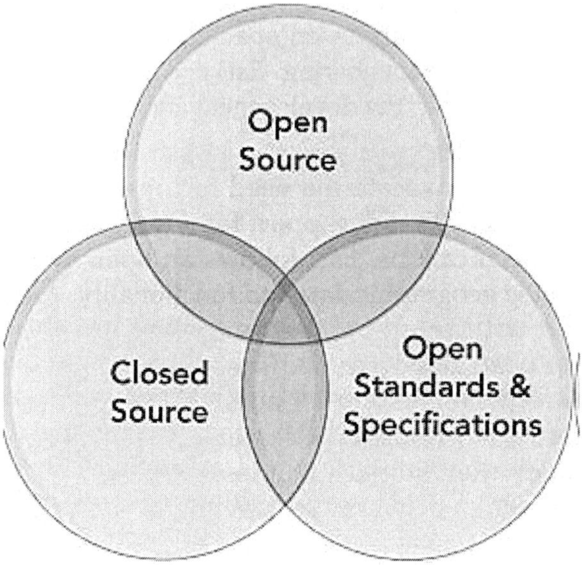

Developers create a software program by writing its source code using a computer programming language, such as C++ or Java. The source code is a series of commands, processes, and interfaces that tell the computer program how to behave. A computer cannot look at source code and know how to run the program.

The source code needs to be translated from the developer's programming language to a machine binary language (0s and 1s) that the computer can read.

The developer does this translation by running the source code through another program called a compiler. The compiler translates the source code into the binary language that the computer can read and execute. Compilers not only make it possible for computers to run the program but also make the programs more efficient by optimizing the file sizes and checking for errors. Since it is often difficult to reverse the translation, compiling helps protect the integrity of the source code.

Open Source vs. Open Specifications

Another common misconception about open source technology is that it is completely open and can freely read and write any data format. However, that is not the case. Formats, specifications, reference models, and procedures that help establish interoperability between programs and devices are called open specifications. PNG, RSS, HTML, and Esri's shapefile are all examples of openly published specifications.

The Open Geospatial Consortium, Inc. (OGC), is an international organization for developing open specifications for geospatial data, services, processes, and data sharing. Esri is a principal member of OGC and actively participates in the development and implementation of many of these standards.

Esri continues to advocate the need for open access to geographic data and functionality through support for widely adopted and practical standards and specifications. Esri follows an open system strategy for accessing and using geographic data and functionality. ArcGIS is designed and engineered with interoperability and extensibility in mind and conforms to the open standards and specifications that are necessary to implement enterprise systems. Users can incorporate GIS in any application on a variety of desktop, server, and mobile platforms and use geographic information stored in almost any format, accessed from a variety of databases, or delivered as a web service.

Open Source or ArcGIS?

Deciding between open source and ArcGIS is not an either/or question. Esri encourages users to choose a hybrid model, a combination of open source and closed source technology, based on their needs.

Esri recommends the use of open source technology to enhance users' Esri experience. Esri supports the Red Hat Enterprise Linux and SUSE Linux operating systems. Geodatabases can be created on the open source RDBMS PostgreSQL. ArcGIS Server can use open source web servers, such as Apache Tomcat, to distribute GIS services.

Esri also integrates the best open source components in ArcGIS. Since ArcGIS 9, the software has integrated Python, the open source programming language, and at ArcGIS 10 introduced ArcPy, a Python site package, to simplify and automate Python scripting. The new Python window in ArcMap allows users to simplify and automate their geoprocessing workflows. The ArcGIS Desktop web help includes a list of all open source tools, languages, and libraries used in ArcGIS. In fact, there are over 80 open source components, including GDAL libraries.

Esri has released numerous APIs and Software Developer Kits (SDKs) to improve GIS interoperability. Many of these APIs and SDKs work with open source development environments, such as Eclipse or Sun's Java Studio Creator. Esri's most recent API, the File Geodatabase API, while not yet open source, opens up the file geodatabase for developers to create applications that access file geodatabases from a variety of outside environments without using ArcObjects.

Esri's Open Source Solutions

ArcGIS Editor for OpenStreetMap is an open source add-on for ArcGIS Desktop that allows users to become active members of the growing OpenStreetMap (OSM) community. OpenStreetMap is an open and freely available database of geographic data.

ArcGIS Editor for OpenStreetMap allows users to download data from the OSM server to a local geodatabase and use the familiar ArcGIS editing environment to create, modify, or delete the OSM data. The editor includes the OSM geodatabase schema and symbology template to simplify editing. Users can then upload their changes back to the OSM servers to share with the entire OSM community.

ArcGIS Editor for OpenStreetMap, its documentation, and its source code are available on CodePlex (esriurl.com/OSMEditor), Microsoft's open source repository, and released under the Microsoft Public License.

Esri Geoportal Server is a free open source product that helps organizations manage and publish metadata describing their geospatial resources so that others can discover and use those resources. Geoportal Server can act as the nexus for an international framework of spatial data resources for enhanced collaboration and data sharing among various government and private agencies. Geoportal Server does not require an ArcGIS license.

Geoportal Server supports standards-based clearinghouse and metadata discovery applications. It was released under the Apache 2.0 open source license, which allows developers to freely customize and redistribute the software. Esri uses SourceForge (esriurl.com/geoportalserver) to host and distribute the Geoportal Server software, documentation, and source code. SourceForge is a familiar platform for open source development, which makes it easy for open source developers to incorporate their changes and improvements to products.

Esri is excited to be part of the evolving open source community, including sponsoring and participating in open source geospatial conferences, such as FOSS4G and State of the Map. These events are opportunities to learn more about the needs of open source geospatial developers and users to enhance and improve Esri's open source offerings and interoperability and, most importantly, build a larger and stronger community of all geospatial developers and users.

A DEFINITION OF OPEN SOURCE

Open source technology is defined as the production and development philosophy of allowing end users and developers to not only see the source code of software, but modify it as well. The Linux operating system is a one of the best-known examples of open source software technology.

The Linux operating system's open source paradigm is in direct contrast to Microsoft's approach to development and production of its popular Windows operating system. Unlike Linux, Windows is built on a closed source paradigm that does not allow the end user the ability to see or edit the code that makes up the operating system. In fact, certain aspects of the end-user license for the Windows operating system specifically forbids the end user from attempting to view or modify the code that makes up the software. Such attempts are often known as reverse engineering or reverse compiling.

How Open Source Worksa

Although software is not the only product governed by a open source licenses, it is the most popular, lending itself well to manipulation of its code and add-ons. Open source provides a transparent platform upon which anyone with the skills to do so can add to the development and production of the software either for release as a new incarnation of the software for others to use or for strictly in-house development only.

" One issue that has come up repeatedly in open source has to do with the copyrights assigned to the original software and any modifications made to it. As outlined in most open source license agreements, ownership of the software can never transfer to anyone who modifies the software. This usually makes it impossible for a developer to take open source software, modify it, and then sell it.

Most money made from open source software comes in the form of support for the software technology and its many additions, add-ons, and modifications that often ensue. Although most open source software is available to download free, license remains with the original creator of the software and does not transfer to anyone regardless of any modifications, improvements, or add-ons made to the open source software. Although free to download, the software is not free in the sense that the end user can do whatever he/she wants to it including selling it.

Open source technology has spawned an open source culture among programmers and developers who embrace the open source philosophy. Many open source initiatives begin to spite the large corporations who dominate the markets with expensive, complicated, and over-commercialized software. In fact, many Linux developers are committed to producing software that rivals or even surpasses the flexibility and compatibility of such software giants as Microsoft, Apple, and IBM.

Open-source-appropriate technology

Open-source-appropriate technology (OSAT) refers to "appropriate technology" (technology that is designed with special consideration to the environmental, ethical, cultural, social, political, and economical aspects of the community it is intended for) that are designed in the same fashion as free and open-source software; that is, developed in the open and licensed in such a way as to allow their designs to be used, modified and distributed freely.

Benefits

Open source is a development method for appropriate technology that harnesses the power of distributed peer review and transparency of process. Appropedia is an example of open-source appropriate technology. There anyone can both learn how to make and use AT free of concerns about patents. At the same time anyone can also add to the collective open-source knowledge base by contributing ideas, observations, experimental data, deployment logs, etc. It has been claimed that the potential for open-source-appropriate technology to drive applied sustainability is enormous. The built in continuous peer-review can result in better quality, higher reliability, and more flexibility than conventional design/patenting of technologies. The free nature of the knowledge also obviously provides lower costs, particularly for those technologies that do not benefit to a large degree from scale of manufacture. Finally, OSAT also enables the end to predatory intellectual property lock-in. This is particularly important in the context of technology focused on relieving suffering and saving lives in the developing world.

The "open-source" model can act as a driver of sustainable development. There are (at least) three good reasons:

1. It enables production as well as consumption;

2. It enables localization for communities that do not have the resources to tempt commercial developers to provide local versions of their products;

3. It can be free as in "gratis" as well as free as in "libre", an important consideration for developing communities.

Ethical considerations

Although developing world problems are portioned remarkably low support for solutions, many researchers, companies, and academics do work on products meant to assist sustainable development. Vinay Gupta has suggested that those developers agree to three principles:

1. I will not permit any human being to be deprived of life-giving technology by the profit motive.

2. Any works that I patent I will make available to others who are engaged in humanitarian activity for free, except where this would breach other contractual responsibilities.

3. I will not use patent law to slow the pace of innovation or service delivery to the needy under any circumstances.

Support in the literature

- It has been investigated how open sharing of designs, specifications, and technical information can enhance effectiveness, widespread use, and innovation of appropriate technology.
- OSAT has been proposed as a new model of enabling innovation for sustainable development.
- OSAT has been claimed to assist in development of medical technology particularly for the developing world.
- It has been claimed that the sharing of design processes, appropriate tools, and technical information enables more effective and rapid development of appropriate technologies for both industrialized and non-industrialized regions. In addition, it is claimed that this sharing will require the appropriate-technology community to adopt open standards/licenses, document knowledge, and build on previous work.

OSAT in education

- At the university level, the use of open-source-appropriate technology classroom projects has been shown to be successful in forging the connection between physics and social benefit: This approach has the potential to use university students' access to resources and testing equipment in furthering the development of appropriate technology. Similarly OSAT has been used as a tool for improving service learning. MIT has completed a study looking at the usefulness of using appropriate technology education and its relation to OSAT.
- It has been proposed that the evolution of the open-source 3D printers can enable a new method of development for OSAT

Criticism

It has been claimed that the decline of the appropriate technology movement is said to be part of the 'remasculinization' of US after the

Vietnam War through the Reagan regime. According to Pursell, it was said have failed because of the inability to counter advocates of agribusiness, large private utilities, and multinational construction companies. These groups maintained the elitist, narrow and traditional definition of the word 'technology' to forward their interests, and not those of the developing world. Recently, several barriers to OSAT deployment have been identified:

- AT seen as inferior or "poor person's" technology
- Technical transferability and robustness of AT
- Insufficient funding
- Weak institutional support
- The challenges of distance and time in tackling rural poverty.

Operating system

An operating system (OS) is a collection of software that manages computer hardware resources and provides common services for computer programs. The operating system is an essential component of the system software in a computer system. Application programs usually require an operating system to function.

Time-sharing operating systems schedule tasks for efficient use of the system and may also include accounting software for cost allocation of processor time, mass storage, printing, and other resources.

For hardware functions such as input and output and memory allocation, the operating system acts as an intermediary between programs and the computer hardware, although the application code is usually executed directly by the hardware and will frequently make a system call to an OS function or be interrupted by it. Operating systems can be found on almost any device that contains a computer-from cellular phones and video game consoles to supercomputers and web servers.

Examples of popular modern operating systems include Android, BSD, iOS, Linux, OS X, QNX, Microsoft Windows, Windows Phone, and IBM z/OS. All these, except Windows, Windows Phone and z/OS, share roots in UNIX.

TYPES OF OPERATING SYSTEMS

Real-time

A real-time operating system is a multitasking operating system that aims at executing real-time applications. Real-time operating systems often use specialized scheduling algorithms so that they can achieve a deterministic nature of behavior. The main objective of real-time operating systems is their quick and predictable response to events. They have an event-driven or time-sharing design and often aspects of both. An event-driven system switches between tasks based on their priorities or external events while time-sharing operating systems switch tasks based on clock interrupts.

Multi-user

A multi-user operating system allows multiple users to access a computer system at the same time. Time-sharing systems and Internet servers can be classified as multi-user systems as they enable multiple-user access to a computer through the sharing of time. Single-user operating systems have only one user but may allow multiple programs to run at the same time.

Multi-tasking vs. single-tasking

A multi-tasking operating system allows more than one program to be running at the same time, from the point of view of human time scales. A single-tasking system has only one running program. Multi-tasking can be of two types: pre-emptive and co-operative. In pre-emptive multitasking, the operating system slices the CPU time and dedicates one slot to each of the programs. Unix-like operating systems such as Solaris and Linux support pre-emptive multitasking, as does AmigaOS. Cooperative multitasking is achieved by relying on each process to give time to the other processes in a defined manner. 16-bit versions of Microsoft Windows used cooperative multi-tasking. 32-bit versions of both Windows NT and Win9x, used pre-emptive multi-tasking. Mac OS prior to OS X used to support cooperative multitasking.

Distributed

A distributed operating system manages a group of independent computers and makes them appear to be a single computer. The development of networked computers that could be linked and communicate with each other gave rise to distributed computing. Distributed computations are carried out on more than one machine. When computers in a group work in cooperation, they make a distributed system.

Embedded

Embedded operating systems are designed to be used in embedded computer systems. They are designed to operate on small machines like

PDAs with less autonomy. They are able to operate with a limited number of resources. They are very compact and extremely efficient by design. Windows CE and Minix 3 are some examples of embedded operating systems.

HISTORY

Early computers were built to perform a series of single tasks, like a calculator. Basic operating system features were developed in the 1950s, such as resident monitor functions that could automatically run different programs in succession to speed up processing.

Operating systems did not exist in their modern and more complex forms until the early 1960s. Hardware features were added, that enabled use of runtime libraries, interrupts, and parallel processing. When personal computers became popular in the 1980s, operating systems were made for them similar in concept to those used on larger computers.

In the 1940s, the earliest electronic digital systems had no operating systems. Electronic systems of this time were programmed on rows of mechanical switches or by jumper wires on plug boards.

These were special-purpose systems that, for example, generated ballistics tables for the military or controlled the printing of payroll checks from data on punched paper cards. After programmable general purpose computers were invented, machine languages (consisting of strings of the binary digits 0 and 1 on punched paper tape) were introduced that sped up the programming process (Stern, 1981).

In the early 1950s, a computer could execute only one program at a time. Each user had sole use of the computer for a limited period of time and would arrive at a scheduled time with program and data on punched paper cards and/or punched tape. The program would be loaded into the machine, and the machine would be set to work until the program completed or crashed. Programs could generally be debugged via a front panel using toggle switches and panel lights.

It is said that Alan Turing was a master of this on the early Manchester Mark 1 machine, and he was already deriving the primitive conception of an operating system from the principles of the Universal Turing machine.

Later machines came with libraries of programs, which would be linked to a user's program to assist in operations such as input and output and generating computer code from human-readable symbolic code. This was the genesis of the modern-day operating system. However, machines still ran a single job at a time. At Cambridge University in England the job queue was at one time a washing line from which tapes were hung with different colored clothes-pegs to indicate job-priority.

Mainframes

Through the 1950s, many major features were pioneered in the field of operating systems, including batch processing, input/output interrupt, buffering, multitasking, spooling, runtime libraries, link-loading, and programs for sorting records in files. These features were included or not included in application software at the option of application programmers, rather than in a separate operating system used by all applications.

In 1959 the SHARE Operating System was released as an integrated utility for the IBM 704, and later in the 709 and 7090 mainframes, although it was quickly supplanted by IBSYS/IBJOB on the 709, 7090 and 7094.

During the 1960s, IBM's OS/360 introduced the concept of a single OS spanning an entire product line, which was crucial for the success of the System/360 machines. IBM's current mainframe operating systems are distant descendants of this original system and applications written for OS/360 can still be run on modern machines.

OS/360 also pioneered the concept that the operating system keeps track of all of the system resources that are used, including program and data space allocation in main memory and file space in secondary storage, and file locking during update. When the process is terminated for any reason, all of these resources are re-claimed by the operating system.

The alternative CP-67 system for the S/360-67 started a whole line of IBM operating systems focused on the concept of virtual machines. Other operating systems used on IBM S/360 series mainframes included systems developed by IBM: COS/360 (Compatibility Operating System), DOS/360 (Disk Operating System), TSS/360 (Time Sharing System), TOS/360 (Tape Operating System), BOS/360 (Basic Operating System), and ACP (Airline Control Program), as well as a few non-IBM systems: MTS (Michigan Terminal System), MUSIC (Multi-User System for Interactive Computing), and ORVYL (Stanford Timesharing System).

Control Data Corporation developed the SCOPE operating system in the 1960s, for batch processing.

In cooperation with the University of Minnesota, the Kronos and later the NOS operating systems were developed during the 1970s, which supported simultaneous batch and timesharing use. Like many commercial timesharing systems, its interface was an extension of the Dartmouth BASIC operating systems, one of the pioneering efforts in timesharing and programming languages. In the late 1970s, Control Data and the University of Illinois developed the PLATO operating system, which used plasma panel displays and long-distance time sharing networks. Plato was remarkably innovative for its time, featuring real-time chat, and multi-user graphical games.

In 1961, Burroughs Corporation introduced the B5000 with the MCP, (Master Control Program) operating system. The B5000 was a stack machine designed to exclusively support high-level languages with no machine language or assembler, and indeed the MCP was the first OS to be written exclusively in a high-level language - ESPOL, a dialect of ALGOL. MCP also introduced many other ground-breaking innovations, such as being the first commercial implementation of virtual memory. During development of the AS400, IBM made an approach to Burroughs to licence MCP to run on the AS400 hardware.

This proposal was declined by Burroughs management to protect its existing hardware production. MCP is still in use today in the Unisys ClearPath/MCP line of computers.

UNIVAC, the first commercial computer manufacturer, produced a series of EXEC operating systems. Like all early main-frame systems, this batch-oriented system managed magnetic drums, disks, card readers and line printers. In the 1970s, UNIVAC produced the Real-Time Basic (RTB) system to support large-scale time sharing, also patterned after the Dartmouth BC system.

General Electric and MIT developed General Electric Comprehensive Operating Supervisor (GECOS), which introduced the concept of ringed security privilege levels. After acquisition by Honeywell it was renamed General Comprehensive Operating System (GCOS).

Digital Equipment Corporation developed many operating systems for its various computer lines, including TOPS-10 and TOPS-20 time sharing systems for the 36-bit PDP-10 class systems. Prior to the widespread use of UNIX, TOPS-10 was a particularly popular system in universities, and in the early ARPANET community.

From the late 1960s through the late 1970s, several hardware capabilities evolved that allowed similar or ported software to run on more than one system. Early systems had utilized microprogramming to implement features on their systems in order to permit different underlying computer architectures to appear to be the same as others in a series. In fact, most 360s after the 360/40 (except the 360/165 and 360/168) were microprogrammed implementations.

The enormous investment in software for these systems made since the 1960s caused most of the original computer manufacturers to continue to develop compatible operating systems along with the hardware. Notable supported mainframe operating systems include:

- Burroughs MCP - B5000, 1961 to Unisys Clearpath/MCP, present.
- IBM OS/360 - IBM System/360, 1966 to IBM z/OS, present.
- IBM CP-67 - IBM System/360, 1967 to IBM z/VM, present.
- UNIVAC EXEC 8 - UNIVAC 1108, 1967, to OS 2200 Unisys Clearpath Dorado, present.

Microcomputers

The first microcomputers did not have the capacity or need for the elaborate operating systems that had been developed for mainframes and minis; minimalistic operating systems were developed, often loaded from ROM and known as monitors.

One notable early disk operating system was CP/M, which was supported on many early microcomputers and was closely imitated by Microsoft's MS-DOS, which became wildly popular as the operating system chosen for the IBM PC (IBM's version of it was called IBM DOS or PC DOS). In the '80s, Apple Computer Inc. (now Apple Inc.) abandoned its popular Apple II series of microcomputers to introduce the Apple Macintosh computer with an innovative Graphical User Interface (GUI) to the Mac OS.

The introduction of the Intel 80386 CPU chip with 32-bit architecture and paging capabilities, provided personal computers with the ability to run multitasking operating systems like those of earlier minicomputers and mainframes. Microsoft responded to this progress by hiring Dave Cutler, who had developed the VMS operating system for Digital Equipment Corporation.

He would lead the development of the Windows NT operating system, which continues to serve as the basis for Microsoft's operating systems line. Steve Jobs, a co-founder of Apple Inc., started NeXT Computer Inc., which developed the NEXTSTEP operating system. NEXTSTEP would later be acquired by Apple Inc. and used, along with code from FreeBSD as the core of Mac OS X.

The GNU Project was started by activist and programmer Richard Stallman with the goal of creating a complete free software replacement to the proprietary UNIX operating system.

While the project was highly successful in duplicating the functionality of various parts of UNIX, development of the GNU Hurd kernel proved to be unproductive. In 1991, Finnish computer science student Linus Torvalds, with cooperation from volunteers collaborating over the Internet, released the first version of the Linux kernel. It was soon merged with the GNU user space components and system software to form a complete operating system.

Since then, the combination of the two major components has usually been referred to as simply "Linux" by the software industry, a naming convention that Stallman and the Free Software Foundation remain opposed to, preferring the name GNU/Linux. The Berkeley Software Distribution, known as BSD, is the UNIX derivative distributed by the University of California, Berkeley, starting in the 1970s. Freely distributed and ported to many minicomputers, it eventually also gained a following for use on PCs, mainly as FreeBSD, NetBSD and OpenBSD.

Examples of operating systems

UNIX and UNIX-like operating systems

Unix was originally written in assembly language. Ken Thompson wrote B, mainly based on BCPL, based on his experience in the MULTICS project. B was replaced by C, and Unix, rewritten in C, developed into a large, complex family of inter-related operating systems which have been influential in every modern operating system (see History).

The UNIX-like family is a diverse group of operating systems, with several major sub-categories including System V, BSD, and Linux. The name "UNIX" is a trademark of The Open Group which licenses it for use with any operating system that has been shown to conform to their definitions. "UNIX-like" is commonly used to refer to the large set of operating systems which resemble the original UNIX.

Unix-like systems run on a wide variety of computer architectures. They are used heavily for servers in business, as well as workstations in academic and engineering environments. Free UNIX variants, such as Linux and BSD, are popular in these areas.

Four operating systems are certified by The Open Group (holder of the Unix trademark) as Unix. HP's HP-UX and IBM's AIX are both descendants of the original System V Unix and are designed to run only on their respective vendor's hardware. In contrast, Sun Microsystems's Solaris Operating System can run on multiple types of hardware, including x86 and Sparc servers, and PCs. Apple's OS X, a replacement for Apple's earlier (non-Unix) Mac OS, is a hybrid kernel-based BSD variant derived from NeXTSTEP, Mach, and FreeBSD.

Unix interoperability was sought by establishing the POSIX standard. The POSIX standard can be applied to any operating system, although it was originally created for various Unix variants.

BSD and its descendants

A subgroup of the Unix family is the Berkeley Software Distribution family, which includes FreeBSD, NetBSD, and OpenBSD. These operating systems are most commonly found on webservers, although they can also function as a personal computer OS. The Internet owes much of its existence to BSD, as many of the protocols now commonly used by computers to connect, send and receive data over a network were widely implemented and refined in BSD. The World Wide Web was also first demonstrated on a number of computers running an OS based on BSD called NextStep.

BSD has its roots in Unix. In 1974, University of California, Berkeley installed its first Unix system. Over time, students and staff in the computer science department there began adding new programs to make things easier, such as text editors. When Berkeley received new VAX computers in 1978 with Unix installed, the school's undergraduates modified Unix even more in order to take advantage of the computer's hardware possibilities. The Defense Advanced Research Projects Agency of the US Department of Defense took interest, and decided to fund the project. Many schools, corporations, and government organizations took notice and started to use Berkeley's version of Unix instead of the official one distributed by AT&T.

Steve Jobs, upon leaving Apple Inc. in 1985, formed NeXT Inc., a company that manufactured high-end computers running on a variation of BSD called NeXTSTEP. One of these computers was used by Tim Berners-Lee as the first webserver to create the World Wide Web.

Developers like Keith Bostic encouraged the project to replace any non-free code that originated with Bell Labs. Once this was done, however, AT&T sued. Eventually, after two years of legal disputes, the BSD project came out ahead and spawned a number of free derivatives, such as FreeBSD and NetBSD.

OS X

OS X (formerly "Mac OS X") is a line of open core graphical operating systems developed, marketed, and sold by Apple Inc., the latest of which is pre-loaded on all currently shipping Macintosh computers. OS X is the successor to the original Mac OS, which had been Apple's primary operating system since 1984. Unlike its predecessor, OS X is a UNIX operating system built on technology that had been developed at NeXT through the second half of the 1980s and up until Apple purchased the company in early 1997.

The operating system was first released in 1999 as Mac OS X Server 1.0, with a desktop-oriented version (Mac OS X v10.0 "Cheetah") following in March 2001. Since then, six more distinct "client" and "server" editions of OS X have been released, until the two were merged in OS X 10.7 "Lion". The most recent version is OS X 10.9 "Mavericks", which was announced on June 10, 2013, and released on October 22, 2013. Releases of OS X v10.0 through v10.8 are named after big cats. Starting with v10.9, "Mavericks", OS X versions are named after inspirational places in California.

Prior to its merging with OS X, the server edition - OS X Server - was architecturally identical to its desktop counterpart and usually ran on Apple's line of Macintosh server hardware. OS X Server included work group management and administration software tools that provide simplified access to key network services, including a mail transfer agent, a Samba server, an LDAP server, a domain name server, and others. With Mac OS X v10.7 Lion, all server aspects of Mac OS X Server have been integrated into the client version and the product re-branded as "OS X" (dropping "Mac" from the name). The server tools are now offered as an application.

Linux and GNU

Linux (or GNU/Linux) is a Unix-like operating system that was developed without any actual Unix code, unlike BSD and its variants. Linux can be used on a wide range of devices from supercomputers to wristwatches. The Linux kernel is released under an open source license, so anyone can read and modify its code. It has been modified to run on a large variety of electronics. Although estimates suggest that Linux is used on 1.82% of all personal computers, it has been widely adopted for use in servers and embedded systems (such as cell phones). Linux has superseded Unix in most places, and is used on the 10 most powerful supercomputers in the world. The Linux kernel is used in some popular distributions, such as Red Hat, Debian, Ubuntu, Linux Mint and Google's Android.

The GNU project is a mass collaboration of programmers who seek to create a completely free and open operating system that was similar to Unix but with completely original code. It was started in 1983 by Richard Stallman, and is responsible for many of the parts of most Linux variants.

Thousands of pieces of software for virtually every operating system are licensed under the GNU General Public License. Meanwhile, the Linux kernel began as a side project of Linus Torvalds, a university student from Finland. In 1991, Torvalds began work on it, and posted information about his project on a newsgroup for computer students and programmers. He received a wave of support and volunteers who ended up creating a full-fledged kernel. Programmers from GNU took notice, and members of both projects worked to integrate the finished GNU parts with the Linux kernel in order to create a full-fledged operating system.

Google Chromium OS

Chromium is an operating system based on the Linux kernel and designed by Google. Since Chromium OS targets computer users who spend most of their time on the Internet, it is mainly a web browser with limited ability to run local applications, though it has a built-in file manager and media player. Instead, it relies on Internet applications (or Web apps) used in the web browser to accomplish tasks such as word processing.

Microsoft Windows

Microsoft Windows is a family of proprietary operating systems designed by Microsoft Corporation and primarily targeted to Intel architecture based computers, with an estimated 88.9 percent total usage share on Web connected computers. The newest version is Windows 8 for workstations and Windows Server 2012 for servers. Windows 7 recently overtook Windows XP as most used OS.

Microsoft Windows originated in 1985 as an operating environment running on top of MS-DOS, which was the standard operating system shipped on most Intel architecture personal computers at the time. In 1995, Windows 95 was released which only used MS-DOS as a bootstrap. For backwards compatibility, Win9x could run real-mode MS-DOS and 16 bits Windows 3.x drivers. Windows ME, released in 2000, was the last version in the Win9x family. Later versions have all been based on the Windows NT kernel. Current versions of Windows run on IA-32 and x86-64 microprocessors, although Windows 8 will support ARM architecture. In the past, Windows NT supported non-Intel architectures.

Server editions of Windows are widely used. In recent years, Microsoft has expended significant capital in an effort to promote the use of Windows as a server operating system. However, Windows' usage on servers is not as widespread as on personal computers, as Windows competes against Linux and BSD for server market share.

Other

There have been many operating systems that were significant in their day but are no longer so, such as AmigaOS; OS/2 from IBM and Microsoft; Mac OS, the non-Unix precursor to Apple's Mac OS X; BeOS; XTS-300; RISC OS; MorphOS and FreeMint. Some are still used in niche markets and continue to be developed as minority platforms for enthusiast communities and specialist applications. OpenVMS formerly from DEC, is still under active development by Hewlett-Packard. Yet other operating systems are used almost exclusively in academia, for operating systems education or to do research on operating system concepts. A typical example of a system that fulfills both roles is MINIX, while for example Singularity is used purely for research.

Other operating systems have failed to win significant market share, but have introduced innovations that have influenced mainstream operating systems, not least Bell Labs' Plan 9.

Components

The components of an operating system all exist in order to make the different parts of a computer work together. All user software needs to go through the operating system in order to use any of the hardware, whether it be as simple as a mouse or keyboard or as complex as an Internet component.

Kernel

With the aid of the firmware and device drivers, the kernel provides the most basic level of control over all of the computer's hardware devices. It manages memory access for programs in the RAM, it determines which programs get access to which hardware resources, it sets up or resets the CPU's operating states for optimal operation at all times, and it organizes the data for long-term non-volatile storage with file systems on such media as disks, tapes, flash memory, etc.

Program execution

The operating system provides an interface between an application program and the computer hardware, so that an application program can interact with the hardware only by obeying rules and procedures programmed into the operating system. The operating system is also a set of services which simplify development and execution of application programs. Executing an application program involves the creation of a process by the operating system kernel which assigns memory space and other resources, establishes a priority for the process in multi-tasking systems, loads program binary code into memory, and initiates execution of the application program which then interacts with the user and with hardware devices.

Interrupts

Interrupts are central to operating systems, as they provide an efficient way for the operating system to interact with and react to its environment. The alternative - having the operating system "watch" the various sources of input for events (polling) that require action - can be found in older systems with very small stacks (50 or 60 bytes) but are unusual in modern systems with large stacks. Interrupt-based programming is directly supported by most modern CPUs.

Interrupts provide a computer with a way of automatically saving local register contexts, and running specific code in response to events. Even very basic computers support hardware interrupts, and allow the programmer to specify code which may be run when that event takes place.

When an interrupt is received, the computer's hardware automatically suspends whatever program is currently running, saves its status, and runs computer code previously associated with the interrupt; this is analogous to placing a bookmark in a book in response to a phone call. In modern operating systems, interrupts are handled by the operating system's kernel. Interrupts may come from either the computer's hardware or from the running program.

When a hardware device triggers an interrupt, the operating system's kernel decides how to deal with this event, generally by running some processing code. The amount of code being run depends on the priority of the interrupt (for example: a person usually responds to a smoke detector alarm before answering the phone). The processing of hardware interrupts is a task that is usually delegated to software called device driver, which may be either part of the operating system's kernel, part of another program, or both. Device drivers may then relay information to a running program by various means.

A program may also trigger an interrupt to the operating system. If a program wishes to access hardware for example, it may interrupt the operating system's kernel, which causes control to be passed back to the kernel. The kernel will then process the request. If a program wishes additional resources (or wishes to shed resources) such as memory, it will trigger an interrupt to get the kernel's attention.

Modes

Modern CPUs support multiple modes of operation. CPUs with this capability use at least two modes: protected mode and supervisor mode. The supervisor mode is used by the operating system's kernel for low level tasks that need unrestricted access to hardware, such as controlling how memory is written and erased, and communication with devices like graphics cards.

Protected mode, in contrast, is used for almost everything else. Applications operate within protected mode, and can only use hardware by communicating with the kernel, which controls everything in supervisor mode. CPUs might have other modes similar to protected mode as well, such as the virtual modes in order to emulate older processor types, such as 16-bit processors on a 32-bit one, or 32-bit processors on a 64-bit one.

When a computer first starts up, it is automatically running in supervisor mode. The first few programs to run on the computer, being the BIOS or EFI, bootloader, and the operating system have unlimited access to hardware - and this is required because, by definition, initializing a protected environment can only be done outside of one. However, when the operating system passes control to another program, it can place the CPU into protected mode.

In protected mode, programs may have access to a more limited set of the CPU's instructions. A user program may leave protected mode only by triggering an interrupt, causing control to be passed back to the kernel. In this way the operating system can maintain exclusive control over things like access to hardware and memory.

The term "protected mode resource" generally refers to one or more CPU registers, which contain information that the running program isn't allowed to alter. Attempts to alter these resources generally causes a switch to supervisor mode, where the operating system can deal with the illegal operation the program was attempting (for example, by killing the program).

Memory management

Among other things, a multiprogramming operating system kernel must be responsible for managing all system memory which is currently in use by programs. This ensures that a program does not interfere with memory already in use by another program. Since programs time share, each program must have independent access to memory.

Cooperative memory management, used by many early operating systems, assumes that all programs make voluntary use of the kernel's memory manager, and do not exceed their allocated memory. This system of memory management is almost never seen any more, since programs often contain bugs which can cause them to exceed their allocated memory. If a program fails, it may cause memory used by one or more other programs to be affected or overwritten.

Malicious programs or viruses may purposefully alter another program's memory, or may affect the operation of the operating system itself. With cooperative memory management, it takes only one misbehaved program to crash the system.

Memory protection enables the kernel to limit a process' access to the computer's memory. Various methods of memory protection exist, including memory segmentation and paging. All methods require some level of hardware support (such as the 80286 MMU), which doesn't exist in all computers.

In both segmentation and paging, certain protected mode registers specify to the CPU what memory address it should allow a running program to access. Attempts to access other addresses will trigger an interrupt which will cause the CPU to re-enter supervisor mode, placing the kernel in charge.

This is called a segmentation violation or Seg-V for short, and since it is both difficult to assign a meaningful result to such an operation, and because it is usually a sign of a misbehaving program, the kernel will generally resort to terminating the offending program, and will report the error.

Windows 3.1-Me had some level of memory protection, but programs could easily circumvent the need to use it. A general protection fault would be produced, indicating a segmentation violation had occurred; however, the system would often crash anyway.

Virtual memory

The use of virtual memory addressing (such as paging or segmentation) means that the kernel can choose what memory each program may use at any given time, allowing the operating system to use the same memory locations for multiple tasks.

If a program tries to access memory that isn't in its current range of accessible memory, but nonetheless has been allocated to it, the kernel will be interrupted in the same way as it would if the program were to exceed its allocated memory. (See section on memory management.) Under UNIX this kind of interrupt is referred to as a page fault.

When the kernel detects a page fault it will generally adjust the virtual memory range of the program which triggered it, granting it access to the memory requested. This gives the kernel discretionary power over where a particular application's memory is stored, or even whether or not it has actually been allocated yet.

In modern operating systems, memory which is accessed less frequently can be temporarily stored on disk or other media to make that space available for use by other programs. This is called swapping, as an area of memory can be used by multiple programs, and what that memory area contains can be swapped or exchanged on demand.

"Virtual memory" provides the programmer or the user with the perception that there is a much larger amount of RAM in the computer than is really there.

Multitasking

Multitasking refers to the running of multiple independent computer programs on the same computer; giving the appearance that it is performing the tasks at the same time. Since most computers can do at most one or two things at one time, this is generally done via time-sharing, which means that each program uses a share of the computer's time to execute.

An operating system kernel contains a piece of software called a scheduler which determines how much time each program will spend executing, and in which order execution control should be passed to programs. Control is passed to a process by the kernel, which allows the program access to the CPU and memory.

Later, control is returned to the kernel through some mechanism, so that another program may be allowed to use the CPU. This so-called passing of control between the kernel and applications is called a context switch.

An early model which governed the allocation of time to programs was called cooperative multitasking. In this model, when control is passed to a program by the kernel, it may execute for as long as it wants before explicitly returning control to the kernel. This means that a malicious or malfunctioning program may not only prevent any other programs from using the CPU, but it can hang the entire system if it enters an infinite loop.

Modern operating systems extend the concepts of application preemption to device drivers and kernel code, so that the operating system has preemptive control over internal run-times as well.

The philosophy governing preemptive multitasking is that of ensuring that all programs are given regular time on the CPU. This implies that all programs must be limited in how much time they are allowed to spend on the CPU without being interrupted. To accomplish this, modern operating system kernels make use of a timed interrupt. A protected mode timer is set by the kernel which triggers a return to supervisor mode after the specified time has elapsed. (See above sections on Interrupts and Dual Mode Operation.)

On many single user operating systems cooperative multitasking is perfectly adequate, as home computers generally run a small number of well tested programs. The AmigaOS is an exception, having pre-emptive multitasking from its very first version. Windows NT was the first version of Microsoft Windows which enforced preemptive multitasking, but it didn't reach the home user market until Windows XP (since Windows NT was targeted at professionals).

Disk access and file systems

Access to data stored on disks is a central feature of all operating systems. Computers store data on disks using files, which are structured in specific ways in order to allow for faster access, higher reliability, and to make better use out of the drive's available space.

The specific way in which files are stored on a disk is called a file system, and enables files to have names and attributes. It also allows them to be stored in a hierarchy of directories or folders arranged in a directory tree.

Early operating systems generally supported a single type of disk drive and only one kind of file system. Early file systems were limited in their capacity, speed, and in the kinds of file names and directory structures they could use.

These limitations often reflected limitations in the operating systems they were designed for, making it very difficult for an operating system to support more than one file system.

While many simpler operating systems support a limited range of options for accessing storage systems, operating systems like UNIX and Linux support a technology known as a virtual file system or VFS.

An operating system such as UNIX supports a wide array of storage devices, regardless of their design or file systems, allowing them to be accessed through a common application programming interface (API). This makes it unnecessary for programs to have any knowledge about the device they are accessing. A VFS allows the operating system to provide programs with access to an unlimited number of devices with an infinite variety of file systems installed on them, through the use of specific device drivers and file system drivers.

A connected storage device, such as a hard drive, is accessed through a device driver. The device driver understands the specific language of the drive and is able to translate that language into a standard language used by the operating system to access all disk drives. On UNIX, this is the language of block devices.

When the kernel has an appropriate device driver in place, it can then access the contents of the disk drive in raw format, which may contain one or more file systems. A file system driver is used to translate the commands used to access each specific file system into a standard set of commands that the operating system can use to talk to all file systems. Programs can then deal with these file systems on the basis of filenames, and directories/folders, contained within a hierarchical structure.

They can create, delete, open, and close files, as well as gather various information about them, including access permissions, size, free space, and creation and modification dates.

Various differences between file systems make supporting all file systems difficult. Allowed characters in file names, case sensitivity, and the presence of various kinds of file attributes makes the implementation of a single interface for every file system a daunting task.

Operating systems tend to recommend using (and so support natively) file systems specifically designed for them; for example, NTFS in Windows and ext3 and ReiserFS in Linux.

However, in practice, third party drives are usually available to give support for the most widely used file systems in most general-purpose operating systems (for example, NTFS is available in Linux through NTFS-3g, and ext2/3 and ReiserFS are available in Windows through third-party software).

Support for file systems is highly varied among modern operating systems, although there are several common file systems which almost all operating systems include support and drivers for. Operating systems vary on file system support and on the disk formats they may be installed on. Under Windows, each file system is usually limited in application to certain media; for example, CDs must use ISO 9660 or UDF, and as of Windows Vista, NTFS is the only file system which the operating system can be installed on. It is possible to install Linux onto many types of file systems. Unlike other operating systems, Linux and UNIX allow any file system to be used regardless of the media it is stored in, whether it is a hard drive, a disc (CD, DVD...), a USB flash drive, or even contained within a file located on another file system.

Device drivers

A device driver is a specific type of computer software developed to allow interaction with hardware devices. Typically this constitutes an interface for communicating with the device, through the specific computer bus or communications subsystem that the hardware is connected to, providing commands to and/or receiving data from the device, and on the other end, the requisite interfaces to the operating system and software applications.

It is a specialized hardware-dependent computer program which is also operating system specific that enables another program, typically an operating system or applications software package or computer program running under the operating system kernel, to interact transparently with a hardware device, and usually provides the requisite interrupt handling necessary for any necessary asynchronous time-dependent hardware interfacing needs.

The key design goal of device drivers is abstraction. Every model of hardware (even within the same class of device) is different. Newer models also are released by manufacturers that provide more reliable or better performance and these newer models are often controlled differently. Computers and their operating systems cannot be expected to know how to control every device, both now and in the future.

To solve this problem, operating systems essentially dictate how every type of device should be controlled. The function of the device driver is then to translate these operating system mandated function calls into device specific calls. In theory a new device, which is controlled in a new manner, should function correctly if a suitable driver is available. This new driver will ensure that the device appears to operate as usual from the operating system's point of view.

Under versions of Windows before Vista and versions of Linux before 2.6, all driver execution was co-operative, meaning that if a driver entered an infinite loop it would freeze the system. More recent revisions of these operating systems incorporate kernel preemption, where the kernel interrupts the driver to give it tasks, and then separates itself from the process until it receives a response from the device driver, or gives it more tasks to do.

Networking

Currently most operating systems support a variety of networking protocols, hardware, and applications for using them. This means that computers running dissimilar operating systems can participate in a common network for sharing resources such as computing, files, printers, and scanners using either wired or wireless connections. Networks can essentially allow a computer's operating system to access the resources of a remote computer to support the same functions as it could if those resources were connected directly to the local computer.

This includes everything from simple communication, to using networked file systems or even sharing another computer's graphics or sound hardware. Some network services allow the resources of a computer to be accessed transparently, such as SSH which allows networked users direct access to a computer's command line interface.

Client/server networking allows a program on a computer, called a client, to connect via a network to another computer, called a server. Servers offer (or host) various services to other network computers and users. These services are usually provided through ports or numbered access points beyond the server's network address. Each port number is usually associated with a maximum of one running program, which is responsible for handling requests to that port. A daemon, being a user program, can in turn access the local hardware resources of that computer by passing requests to the operating system kernel.

Many operating systems support one or more vendor-specific or open networking protocols as well, for example, SNA on IBM systems, DECnet on systems from Digital Equipment Corporation, and Microsoft-specific protocols (SMB) on Windows. Specific protocols for specific tasks may also be supported such as NFS for file access. Protocols like ESound, or esd can be easily extended over the network to provide sound from local applications, on a remote system's sound hardware.

Security

A computer being secure depends on a number of technologies working properly. A modern operating system provides access to a number of resources, which are available to software running on the system, and to external devices like networks via the kernel.

The operating system must be capable of distinguishing between requests which should be allowed to be processed, and others which should not be processed. While some systems may simply distinguish between "privileged" and "non-privileged", systems commonly have a form of requester identity, such as a user name. To establish identity there may be a process of authentication. Often a username must be quoted, and each username may have a password. Other methods of authentication, such as magnetic cards or biometric data, might be used instead. In some cases, especially connections from the network, resources may be accessed with no authentication at all (such as reading files over a network share). Also covered by the concept of requester identity is authorization; the particular services and resources accessible by the requester once logged into a system are tied to either the requester's user account or to the variously configured groups of users to which the requester belongs.

In addition to the allow/disallow model of security, a system with a high level of security will also offer auditing options. These would allow tracking of requests for access to resources (such as, "who has been reading this file?"). Internal security, or security from an already running program is only possible if all possibly harmful requests must be carried out through interrupts to the operating system kernel. If programs can directly access hardware and resources, they cannot be secured.

External security involves a request from outside the computer, such as a login at a connected console or some kind of network connection. External requests are often passed through device drivers to the operating system's kernel, where they can be passed onto applications, or carried out directly. Security of operating systems has long been a concern because of highly sensitive data held on computers, both of a commercial and military nature. The United States Government Department of Defense (DoD) created the Trusted Computer System Evaluation Criteria (TCSEC) which is a standard that sets basic requirements for assessing the effectiveness of security.

This became of vital importance to operating system makers, because the TCSEC was used to evaluate, classify and select trusted operating systems being considered for the processing, storage and retrieval of sensitive or classified information.

Network services include offerings such as file sharing, print services, email, web sites, and file transfer protocols (FTP), most of which can have compromised security. At the front line of security are hardware devices known as firewalls or intrusion detection/prevention systems. At the operating system level, there are a number of software firewalls available, as well as intrusion detection/prevention systems. Most modern operating systems include a software firewall, which is enabled by default. A software firewall can be configured to allow or deny network traffic to or from a service or application running on the operating system. Therefore, one can install and be running an insecure service, such as Telnet or FTP, and not have to be threatened by a security breach because the firewall would deny all traffic trying to connect to the service on that port.

An alternative strategy, and the only sandbox strategy available in systems that do not meet the Popek and Goldberg virtualization requirements, is the operating system not running user programs as native code, but instead either emulates a processor or provides a host for a p-code based system such as Java.

Internal security is especially relevant for multi-user systems; it allows each user of the system to have private files that the other users cannot tamper with or read.

Internal security is also vital if auditing is to be of any use, since a program can potentially bypass the operating system, inclusive of bypassing auditing.

User interface

Every computer that is to be operated by an individual requires a user interface. The user interface is usually referred to as a shell and is essential if human interaction is to be supported. The user interface views the directory structure and requests services from the operating system that will acquire data from input hardware devices, such as a keyboard, mouse or credit card reader, and requests operating system services to display prompts, status messages and such on output hardware devices, such as a video monitor or printer. The two most common forms of a user interface have historically been the command-line interface, where computer commands are typed out line-by-line, and the graphical user interface, where a visual environment (most commonly a WIMP) is present.

Graphical user interfaces

Most of the modern computer systems support graphical user interfaces (GUI), and often include them. In some computer systems, such as the original implementation of Mac OS, the GUI is integrated into the kernel.

While technically a graphical user interface is not an operating system service, incorporating support for one into the operating system kernel can allow the GUI to be more responsive by reducing the number of context switches required for the GUI to perform its output functions.

Other operating systems are modular, separating the graphics subsystem from the kernel and the Operating System. In the 1980s UNIX, VMS and many others had operating systems that were built this way.

Linux and Mac OS X are also built this way. Modern releases of Microsoft Windows such as Windows Vista implement a graphics subsystem that is mostly in user-space; however the graphics drawing routines of versions between Windows NT 4.0 and Windows Server 2003 exist mostly in kernel space. Windows 9x had very little distinction between the interface and the kernel.

Many computer operating systems allow the user to install or create any user interface they desire. The X Window System in conjunction with GNOME or KDE Plasma Desktop is a commonly found setup on most Unix and Unix-like (BSD, Linux, Solaris) systems.

A number of Windows shell replacements have been released for Microsoft Windows, which offer alternatives to the included Windows shell, but the shell itself cannot be separated from Windows.

Numerous Unix-based GUIs have existed over time, most derived from X11. Competition among the various vendors of Unix (HP, IBM, Sun) led to much fragmentation, though an effort to standardize in the 1990s to COSE and CDE failed for various reasons, and were eventually eclipsed by the widespread adoption of GNOME and K Desktop Environment.

Prior to free software-based toolkits and desktop environments, Motif was the prevalent toolkit/desktop combination (and was the basis upon which CDE was developed).

Graphical user interfaces evolve over time. For example, Windows has modified its user interface almost every time a new major version of Windows is released, and the Mac OS GUI changed dramatically with the introduction of Mac OS X in 1999.

Real-time operating systems

A real-time operating system (RTOS) is an operating system intended for applications with fixed deadlines (real-time computing). Such applications include some small embedded systems, automobile engine controllers, industrial robots, spacecraft, industrial control, and some large-scale computing systems.

An early example of a large-scale real-time operating system was Transaction Processing Facility developed by American Airlines and IBM for the Sabre Airline Reservations System.

Embedded systems that have fixed deadlines use a real-time operating system such as VxWorks, PikeOS, eCos, QNX, MontaVista Linux and RTLinux. Windows CE is a real-time operating system that shares similar APIs to desktop Windows but shares none of desktop Windows' codebase.

Symbian OS also has an RTOS kernel (EKA2) starting with version 8.0b. Some embedded systems use operating systems such as Palm OS, BSD, and Linux, although such operating systems do not support real-time computing.

OPERATING SYSTEM DEVELOPMENT AS A HOBBY

Operating system development is one of the most complicated activities in which a computing hobbyist may engage. A hobby operating system may be classified as one whose code has not been directly derived from an existing operating system, and has few users and active developers.

In some cases, hobby development is in support of a "homebrew" computing device, for example, a simple single-board computer powered by a 6502 microprocessor. Or, development may be for an architecture already in widespread use. Operating system development may come from entirely new concepts, or may commence by modeling an existing operating system. In either case, the hobbyist is his/her own developer, or may interact with a small and sometimes unstructured group of individuals who have like interests.

Examples of a hobby operating system include ReactOS and Syllable.

Diversity of operating systems and portability

Application software is generally written for use on a specific operating system, and sometimes even for specific hardware. When porting the application to run on another OS, the functionality required by that application may be implemented differently by that OS (the names of functions, meaning of arguments, etc.) requiring the application to be adapted, changed, or otherwise maintained.

This cost in supporting operating systems diversity can be avoided by instead writing applications against software platforms like Java or Qt. These abstractions have already borne the cost of adaptation to specific operating systems and their system libraries.

Another approach is for operating system vendors to adopt standards. For example, POSIX and OS abstraction layers provide commonalities that reduce porting costs.

Open-Source Software for Libraries

All the new software available is truly amazing. It's still far from comprehensive but it can provide a good start if you're looking for stuff to try. FOSS4LIB is a much larger directory of library-specific open-source projects you might also look at.

Digital Repositories

DSpace is a turnkey institutional repository application

Greenstone is a suite of software for building and distributing digital library collections. It provides a new way of organizing information and publishing it on the Internet or on CD-ROM. Greenstone is produced by the New Zealand Digital Library Project at the University of Waikato, and developed and distributed in cooperation with UNESCO and the Human Info NGO. It is open-source, multilingual software, issued under the terms of the GNU General Public License.

Email Ticket Manager

Brimir is built on Ruby on Rails (instead of PHP) and ... allows you to send and receive support emails through a friendly web interface. Received emails are converted to tickets. It's free to set up on your own server or there's a hosted version for $20/month.

ILS

Evergreen, a highly-scalable software for libraries that helps library patrons find library materials, and helps libraries manage, catalog, and circulate those materials, no matter how large or complex the libraries. Evergreen is open source software, freely licensed under the GNU GPL.

Koha, the first free and open source software library automation package (ILS). Development is sponsored by libraries of varying types and sizes, volunteers, and support companies from around the world.

OpenBiblio is an easy to use, open source, automated library system written in PHP containing OPAC, circulation, cataloging, and staff administration functionality.

The purpose of this project is to provide a cost effective library automation solution for private collections, clubs, churches, schools, or public libraries.

NewGenLib (NGL) is an outcome of collaboration between Verus and Kesavan Institute of Information and Knowledge management. NGL is developed and maintained by Verus Solutions and Kesavan Institute has provided the domain expertise.

It provides many basic ILS functions as well as having several social media functions buit in.

SOPAC (Social Online Public Access Catalog) is a module for the Drupal CMS that provides true integration of your library catalog system with the power of the Drupal content management system while allowing users to tag, rate, and review your holdings. User input is then incorporated into the discovery index so that SOPAC becomes a truly community-driven catalog system.

Images

The key goals of The Commons on Flickr are to firstly show you hidden treasures in the world's public photography archives, and secondly to show how your input and knowledge can help make these collections even richer.

Gimp is an open-source photo manipulation program. It's very powerful but has a reputation for not being user-friendly. Fortunately the user-interface has been much improved, making it a very usable option.

Intranet

Brushtail is a open source intranet suitable for public libraries.

Miscellanious

WordPress is web software you can use to create a beautiful website or blog. We like to say that WordPress is both free and priceless at the same time. The core software is built by hundreds of community volunteers, and when you're ready for more there are thousands of plugins and themes available to transform your site into almost anything you can imagine.

Over 25 million people have chosen WordPress to power the place on the web they call "home" - we'd love you to join the family. Drupal is an open source content management platform powering millions of websites and applications. It's built, used, and supported by an active and diverse community of people around the world.

SubjectsPlus sprang from the loins (more or less) of Pirate Source, developed by the Joyner Library at East Carolina University. It became abandonware, and with permission, an expanded version of this original software was open sourced and renamed SubjectsPlus.

Development was undertaken at the Ithaca College Library, and now the University of Miami Libraries. Many people have contributed to SP over the years. It does several things: subject guides, a staff list, database list, FAQs and a suggestion box.

LimeSurvey an open-source survey application, lists a number of features, including csv import/export and basic statistical analysis.

Publishing

Open Journal Systems (OJS) is a journal management and publishing system that has been developed by the Public Knowledge Project through its federally funded efforts to expand and improve access to research. OJS assists with every stage of the refereed publishing process, from submissions through to online publication and indexing.

Scribus is an Open Source program that brings professional page layout to Linux, BSD UNIX, Solaris, OpenIndiana, GNU/Hurd, Mac OS X, OS/2 Warp 4, eComStation, Haiku and Windows desktops with a combination of press-ready output and new approaches to page design.

Underneath a modern and user-friendly interface, Scribus supports professional publishing features, such as color separations, CMYK and spot colors, ICC color management, and versatile PDF creation. It can be used for professional-looking newsletters, posters, anything you need to do with type.

Reserves

ReservesDirect is free, open-source software that manages electronic and physical library materials reserved for university courses. It contains staff interfaces for uploading or creating reserves and managing courses, instructor interfaces for uploading and managing electronic reserve materials directly, and student interfaces for viewing reserve materials from the web and on mobile devices.

While electronic reserves can be used out of the box, use for physical library reserves will require additional integration work with your institution's integrated library system.

WUBS (Web User Booking System) has been developed at Loughborough University Library to allow online booking of resources (rooms, PCs, etc) directly by end users. It has been in production use at Loughborough since October 2004.

Resource Directory

The Collection Workflow Integration System (CWIS, pronounced see-wis) is free, open source software designed to assemble, organize, and share collections of data about resources. CWIS conforms to international and academic standards for metadata. CWIS was created to help build collections of science, technology, engineering, and math (STEM) resources and connect them to NSF's National Science Digital Library and other STEM education channels. However, the software can be (and is being) used for a wide variety of other purposes.

Teaching

Moodle is a Course Management System (CMS), also known as a Learning Management System (LMS) or a Virtual Learning Environment (VLE). It is a Free web application that educators can use to create effective online learning sites.

ATutor is an Open Source Web-based Learning Management System (LMS) used to develop and deliver online courses. Administrators can install or update ATutor in minutes, develop custom themes to give ATutor a new look, and easily extend its functionality with feature modules. Educators can quickly assemble, package, and redistribute Web-based instructional content, easily import prepackaged content, and conduct their courses online.

Digital Library Software

The Greenstone Digital Library Software from the New Zealand Digital Library project provides a new way of organizing information and making it available over the Internet. Collections of information comprise large numbers of documents (typically several thousand to several million), and a uniform interface is provided to them.

Libraries include many collections, individually organized -- though bearing a strong family resemblance. The structure of a collection is determined by a configuration file. Existing collections range from newspaper articles to technical documents, from educational journals to oral history, from visual art to videos, from MIDI pop music collections to ethnic folksongs.

Making information available using Greenstone is far more than just "putting it on the Web." The information becomes searchable, browsable, and maintainable. Each collection, prior to presentation, undergoes a "building" process that, once established, is fully automatic. This creates all the structures used for access at run-time. Searching utilizes various indexes of text and/or metadata, while browsing utilizes metadata such as title and author. When new material appears, it is incorporated into the collection by rebuilding.

To address the broad demands of digital libraries, the system is public and extensible. Issued under the Gnu public license, users are invited to contribute modifications and enhancements. Widely used internationally, Greenstone supports collections in many different languages. Greenstone CD-ROMs have been published by the United Nations and other humanitarian agencies for distribution in developing countries.

Information collections built by Greenstone combine full-text search with browsing indexes based on different metadata types. There are several ways for users to find information, although they differ between collections depending on the metadata available and the collection design.

the Global Help Project's Humanity Development Library (HDL) is being searched for chapters matching the word butterfly . (Also visible on this About page is information about how the collection is organized and the principles governing its use.) The default search interface is a simple one, suitable for casual users.

Advanced searching -- which allows Boolean expressions, phrase searching, and case and stemming control -- can be enabled from a "Preferences" page . This particular collection contains indexes of chapters, section titles, and entire books.

The same collection is browsed by subject; by clicking the bookshelf icons, the user has discovered an item under Animal Husbandry.

Clicking a book icon displays the front cover on the left of Figure 3, and the table of contents is automatically constructed at the start of the document . The current focus, Introduction and Summary, is shown in bold: its text starts further down the page.

Searching is full-text, and -- depending on the collection -- users select indexes built from different parts of the full text or the metadata. Some collections have separate indexes of full documents, sections, paragraphs, titles, and section headings, each of which can be searched for particular words or phrases. When browsing, users examine data structures created from metadata: lists of authors, titles, dates; hierarchical classifications; and so on. Structures for both searching and browsing are specified by instructions in the configuration file, and can be rebuilt entirely automatically. No information is inserted by hand.

Each document may be hierarchically organized into logical sections, each of which comprises paragraphs. Metadata such as author, title, date, keywords, may be associated with documents, or with individual sections. This is the raw material for indexes. It must either be provided explicitly (for example, in an accompanying spreadsheet) or be derived automatically from the source documents. Metadata is stored with the document for internal use.

The software is organized so that "plugins" import documents and transform them into a standard XML form with metadata included. There are plugins for plain text documents; HTML, Word, PostScript and PDF files; email; and common bibliographic formats. New plugins can easily be written -- several have been specially produced for proprietary formats. If the collection contains source documents in different forms, it is just a matter of specifying the necessary plugins. Plugins also perform metadata conversion, whether from internal sources such as HTML's <title> and <meta> tags or Word's "summary" properties, or from externally-specified XML or spreadsheet files. Many collections express metadata in ad hoc ways: these require bespoke plugins. Some plugins also extract metadata from documents using text mining techniques. There are plugins that identify languages and extract acronyms , historical dates, email addresses, keyphrases, etc.

Modules called "classifiers" build browsing structures from metadata -- alphabetic lists, dates, hierarchical classifications, etc.

The Humanity Development Library collection shown in the example above has four metadata indexes.

You can access publications through a subject hierarchy using the subjects button (Figure 2)]; by title, which displays a list of books in alphabetic order (Figure 4) ; by organization (i.e., Dublin Core "publisher"); or by a list of hints defined by the collection's editors (how to) . Dublin Core forms a base that is extended to accommodate idiosyncratic requirements of collection designers.

The Unicode character set is used throughout, so documents -- and interfaces -- can be in any language. Collections have been produced in English, French , Spanish , German, Maori , Chinese , Russian , and Arabic , and Greenstone has interfaces in all these languages and more -- including a text-only version for visually impaired users .

Collections can contain text, pictures, audio and video clips , and music . Most non-textual material is linked to textual documents or accompanied by textual captions to support searching and browsing. Compression technology is used throughout to ensure best use of storage.

The system includes an "administrative" function whereby specified users can examine the composition of all collections, protect documents so that they can only be accessed by registered users on presentation of a password, and so on. User activity logs record all queries made to every Greenstone collection (though this facility can be disabled).

Although primarily designed for web access, collections can be printed on self-installing Windows CD-ROMs with a built-in webserver and the same web interface. These operate standalone on all Windows versions -- a requirement that complicates the software design but is crucial for users in underdeveloped countries seeking access to humanitarian aid collections .

The system operates under Unix, Windows, and Mac OS/X, and works with standard Web servers. A flexible process structure allows different collections to be served by different computers and yet presented to the user as part of the same digital library -- and even, seamlessly, as part of the same collection . Existing collections can be updated and new ones brought on-line at any time, without bringing the system down -- the interface process checks periodically and automatically adds new collections to the list presented to the user.

The Collector

The structure of each collection is determined at set up. This includes specifying the format (or formats) of source documents, deciding how to display the documents on the screen, determining what the source of metadata will be, choosing what full-text searching and browsing facilities should be provided, and outlining how the search and browsing results should be displayed. Once a collection is in place, new documents in the same format can be added automatically.

The Greenstone "Collector" is an interactive subsystem for managing and accessing collections . The Collector can be used to:

- create a new collection with the same structure as an existing one;
- create a new collection with a different structure;
- add new material to an existing collection;
- modify the structure of an existing collection;
- delete a collection;
- write an existing collection to a self-contained, self-installing Windows CD-ROM.

Imagine you are using the Collector to create a new collection from (let us say) a set of html files stored locally. First, an explanatory Web page appears asking you whether you want to work with an existing collection (see the first two options above) or build a new one (see the remaining options).

Either way you must log in before proceeding. Collections are built on a Greenstone server which is, in general, accessed remotely. Because arbitrary users cannot be allowed to build collections, access authorization is required. Thus a central library can, if desired, offer a service to people wishing to build information collections on it. Users who run Greenstone on their own computer may build collections locally, but must still log in to prevent arbitrary users of their library from building collections.

Dialog structure

Upon completion of login, a new page appears that shows the sequence of steps involved in collection building:

1. Collection information
2. Source data
3. Configuring the collection
4. Building the collection
5. Viewing the collection.

The first step specifies the collection's name and associated information -- Figure 5 provides an example of how this interaction might appear. The second step defines where the source data will come from. The third step tailors the configuration options, which requires considerable understanding of what is going on -- this step is really for advanced users. In the fourth step, all the (computer's) work is done -- the system makes all the indexes and gathers together all information required to make the collection operate. Finally, the new collection can be viewed.

These steps appear as a linear sequence of buttons at the bottom of each Collector page so that users can keep track of where they are. Buttons change color to reflect the current stage. The display is modeled after the "wizards" that are widely used to guide users through the installation of new commercial software.

Collection information

The first step, collection information (shown in Figure 5), is to enter some information about the new collection. The title is a short phrase used to identify the collection. The email address is used for diagnostic reports in case any problems arise with the collection. The user also enters the text that appears under About this collection (e.g., Figure 1). An arrow appears at the bottom of the screen to indicate the user's position in the collection-building sequence -- in this case the collection information stage. The user proceeds by clicking the green button, labeled source data.

Source data

Next the user specifies the source text that comprises the collection. The collection is either completely new or a "clone" of an existing one. Creating a new collection with totally novel structure is a major undertaking, and most new collections are clones of existing ones. The user chooses which collection to clone from a pull-down menu. Most Greenstone installations have several different collections. The document file types in the new collection should be amongst those in the one being cloned, the same metadata should be available, and the metadata should be specified in the same way. However, Greenstone is equipped with sensible defaults. If document files with an unexpected format are encountered, they are simply omitted from the collection (with a warning message). If the metadata needed for a particular browser is unavailable for a particular document, that document will be omitted from the browser.

When creating a completely new collection, a bland collection configuration file is provided that accepts most document types and generates a searchable index of the full text and a title browser since this metadata is normally available.

Boxes are provided to indicate where the source documents are located. Any number of input sources can be specified. Specifications can be

- a directory name on the Greenstone server system (beginning with "file://")
- an address beginning with "http://" for files to be downloaded from the Web
- an address beginning with "ftp://" for files to be downloaded using FTP.

In each case of "file://" or "ftp://" the collection will include all files in the specified directory, any directories it contains, any files and directories they contain, and so on. If a filename is specified, that file alone is included. For "http://" the collection will mirror the specified Web site.

Configuring and building the collection

The construction and presentation of all collections is controlled by specifications in a configuration file (see below). Advanced users may use the next page to alter the settings in this file. Most, however, will proceed directly to the final stage where the computer "builds" the new collection.

Up to this point, the responses to the dialog have merely been recorded in a temporary file. The building stage is where the action takes place. First, an internal name is chosen for the collection, based on the title that has been supplied. Then a directory structure is created that includes subdirectories to receive, index and present the source documents. A recursive file system copy command is issued to retrieve source documents already on the file system; for offsite files a web mirroring package is used to copy the specified site along with any related image files.

Next, the documents are converted into a standard XML form. Appropriate plugins to perform this operation must be specified in the collection configuration file. This done, the copied files are deleted: the collection can always be rebuilt from the information stored in the XML files.

Then the full-text searching indexes and browsing structures specified in the collection configuration file are created. Finally, the result of the building process is moved to the area for active collections. This precaution ensures that if a version of this collection already exists, it continues to be served right up until the new one is ready. The software assigns a global, persistent identifier to each document to ensure that the changeover is almost always invisible to users.

The building stage is potentially time-consuming. Small collections take a minute or so but large ones can take a day or more. The Web is not a supportive environment for lengthy activities. A button is provided that allows the user to stop the building process immediately, but users cannot be prevented from leaving the building page. If they do, the Collector continues regardless.

Progress is displayed in a status area at the bottom of the building screen, updated every few seconds. Warnings are issued if any of the following occur:

- non-existent input files or URLs are requested,
- there is no plugin that can process a file, or
- associated files -- such as images embedded in html documents -- are missing.

Users should monitor progress by keeping this window open in their browser. If any errors terminate the process, they appear here.

Viewing the collection

When the collection is built and installed, a View collection button becomes active. Clicking this button takes the user directly to the newly built collection. Also, email is sent to the collection's contact email address and to the digital library administrator whenever a collection is created (or modified). This allows those responsible to monitor what is happening on the system.

Working with existing collections

Four additional facilities are provided when working with existing collections: adding new material, modifying the collection structure, deleting the collection, and printing it on a CD-ROM.

The same dialog structure is used to add new material to an existing collection, but entry is at the "source data" stage. New data is copied as before and converted to XML, joining any existing imported material. Revisions of old documents should perhaps replace existing ones rather than being treated as entirely new. However, this is so difficult to determine that all new documents are added to the collection unless they are textually identical to existing ones. While an imperfect process, in practice the browsing structures are sufficiently clear to make it easy to ignore near-duplicates. The aim of the Collector is to support the most common collection-building tasks in a straightforward manner. If greater control is necessary, it can be achieved by using a suite of command-line scripts instead of the Collector interface.

The structure of existing collections is modified by editing their configuration file. Here, the dialog is entered at the "configuring the collection" stage. To delete a collection, select it from a list and confirm its deletion. Only collections built by the Collector can actually be removed -- others (typically built by advanced users working from the command line) are not shown in the list. It would be nice to be able to selectively delete material from a collection through the Collector, but this functionality does not yet exist. At present this must be done from the command line by inspecting the file system.

Finally, to write an existing collection to a CD-ROM, select the collection and it is automatically massaged into a disk image in a standard directory.

The Collection Configuration File

Figure 6 shows a collection configuration file. Some of the information in it was gathered from the user during the Collector dialog. The indexes line builds a single index comprising the text of all the documents. The classify line builds an alphabetic classifier of the title metadata.

A permissive list of plugins is included. ZIPPlug uncompresses any Zipped files, and makes them available to the other plugins. "GML" is the name of the internal XML document format, and GMLPlug processes previously imported documents. TEXTPlug, HTMLPlug and EMAILPlug process documents of the appropriate types, identified by their file extension. RecPlug (for "recursive") expands subdirectories and pours their contents into the plugin list, thereby traversing arbitrary directory hierarchies.

More indicative of Greenstone's power than the generic structure shown in Figure 6 is the ease with which other facilities can be added. To choose just a few examples:

- A full-text, searchable index of titles could be added by augmenting the indexes line with one extra item.
- If authors' names were encoded in the Web pages using the html metaname construct, a corresponding index of authors could also be added by expanding the indexes line.

- With author metadata, an alphabetic author browser would require an additional classify line.
- Word and/or PDF documents could be included by specifying the appropriate plugins.
- Language metadata could be inferred by specifying an "extract-language" option to each plugin.
- With language metadata present, a separate index could be built for document text in each language.
- Acronyms could be extracted from the text automatically and a list of acronyms added.
- Keyphrases could be extracted from each document and a keyphrase browser added.
- A phrase hierarchy could be extracted from the full text of the documents and made available for browsing.
- The format of any of these browsers, or of the documents themselves when they were displayed, or of the search results list, could all be altered by appropriate "format" statements.

Skilled users could add any of these features to the collection by making a small change to the information presented during the "Configuring the collection" stage. However, we do not anticipate that many casual users will operate at this level. More likely, someone who wants to build new collections of a certain type will arrange for an expert to construct a prototype collection with the desired structure, and proceed to clone that into further collections with the same structure but different material.

Conclusion

Although open source software is often free to download and use, open source licenses rarely transfer any ownership of the software to the end user or developer. Open source is not limited to software. Open source philosophies have been applied to everything from medicine to soft drink formulas. The result is higher commitment and even cult status among the developers and users of open source technologies. For more on open source, read the second article in this series that discusses the advantages and disadvantages of using and developing open source technologies.

Is open source software only important to computer programmers?

No. Open source technology and open source thinking both benefit programmers and non-programmers.

Because early inventors built much of the Internet itself on open source technologies—like the Linux operating system and the Apache Web server application—anyone using the Internet today benefits from open source software.

Every time computer users view web pages, check email, chat with friends, stream music online, or play multiplayer video games, their computers, mobile phones, or gaming consoles connect to a global network of computers using open source software to route and transmit their data to the "local" devices they have in front of them. The computers that do all this important work are typically located in faraway places that users don't actually see or can't physically access—which is why some people call these computers "remote computers."

More and more, people rely on remote computers when performing tasks they might otherwise perform on their local devices. For example, they may use online word processing, email management, and image editing software that they don't install and run on their personal computers. Instead, they simply access these programs on remote computers by using a Web browser or mobile phone application. When they do this, they're engaged in "remote computing."

Some people call remote computing "cloud computing," because it involves activities (like storing files, sharing photos, or watching videos) that incorporate not only local devices but also a global network of remote computers that form an "atmosphere" around them.

Cloud computing is an increasingly important aspect of everyday life with Internet-connected devices. Some cloud computing applications, like Google Apps, are proprietary. Others, like own Cloud and Next cloud, are open source.

Cloud computing applications run "on top" of additional software that helps them operate smoothly and efficiently, so people will often say that software running "underneath" cloud computing applications acts as a "platform" for those applications. Cloud computing platforms can be open source or closed source. OpenStack is an example of an open source cloud computing platform.

Why do people prefer using open source software?

People prefer open source software to proprietary software for a number of reasons, including:

Control. Many people prefer open source software because they have more control over that kind of software. They can examine the code to make sure it's not doing anything they don't want it to do, and they can change parts of it they don't like. Users who aren't programmers also benefit from open source software, because they can use this software for any purpose they wish—not merely the way someone else thinks they should.

Training. Other people like open source software because it helps them become better programmers. Because open source code is publicly accessible, students can easily study it as they learn to make better software. Students can also share their work with others, inviting comment and critique, as they develop their skills. When people discover mistakes in programs' source code, they can share those mistakes with others to help them avoid making those same mistakes themselves.

Security. Some people prefer open source software because they consider it more secure and stable than proprietary software. Because anyone can view and modify open source software, someone might spot and correct errors or omissions that a program's original authors might have missed.

And because so many programmers can work on a piece of open source software without asking for permission from original authors, they can fix, update, and upgrade open source software more quickly than they can proprietary software.

Stability. Many users prefer open source software to proprietary software for important, long-term projects. Because programmers publicly distribute the source code for open source software, users relying on that software for critical tasks can be sure their tools won't disappear or fall into disrepair if their original creators stop working on them.

Additionally, open source software tends to both incorporate and operate according to open standards.

Doesn't "open source" just mean something is free of charge?

No. This is a common misconception about what "open source" implies, and the concept's implications are not only economic.

Open source software programmers can charge money for the open source software they create or to which they contribute. But in some cases, because an open source license might require them to release their source code when they sell software to others, some programmers find that charging users money for software services and support (rather than for the software itself) is more lucrative. This way, their software remains free of charge, and they make money helping others install, use, and troubleshoot it.

While some open source software may be free of charge, skill in programming and troubleshooting open source software can be quite valuable. Many employers specifically seek to hire programmers with experience working on open source software.

3

Participating in Open Source Communities

When a project is open source, that means anybody is free to use, study, modify, and distribute your project for any purpose. These permissions are enforced through an open source license. Open source is powerful because it lowers the barriers to adoption and collaboration, allowing people to spread and improve projects quickly. Also because it gives users a potential to control their own computing, relative to closed source. For example, a business using open source software has the option to hire someone to make custom improvements to the software, rather than relying exclusively on a closed source vendor's product decisions.

One of open source's biggest draws is that it does not cost money. "Free of charge", however, is a byproduct of open source's overall value. Because an open source license requires that anyone can use, modify, and share your project for nearly any purpose, projects themselves tend to be free of charge. If the project cost money to use, anyone could legally make a copy and use the free version instead.

As a result, most open source projects are free, but "free of charge" is not part of the open source definition. There are ways to charge for open source projects indirectly through dual licensing or limited features, while still complying with the official definition of open source.

Open source has become the de facto way to build software — not only in tech, but across diverse industries. As companies use open source code to build their own commercial products and services, they also see the strategic value of contributing back to those projects.

However, diving in without an understanding of those projects, their communities, and how they operate can lead to frustrations for those companies as well as the open source communities. Approaching open source contributions without a strategy can tarnish a company's reputation in the open source community and incur legal risks.

This guide covers what it means to contribute to open source as an organization and how to become a good corporate citizen. Learn how open source projects are structured, how to contribute, why it's important to devote internal developer resources to participation, and why it's important to create a strategy for open source participation and management.

It might be impossible to find an organization today that doesn't benefit in some way from open source software. Some companies, like Intel, IBM, and Samsung, have entire open source programs devoted to contributing to open source communities. Other companies become consumers of open source almost accidentally when the software is brought in by system administrators or developers.

While some of these contributions may come from organizations that just want to give back to the community, there are plenty of strong business reasons to contribute to the open source software projects used within your organization. Here are just a few of the benefits of contributing:

Attract talent. When you rely on open source software, the best place to find people who know the project inside and out is in the community for that project. By working publicly in the community, you can attract people who see that they can get paid to work on their favorite open source project. When your employees are working side by side with these people every day, they can help you identify good fits for your company. (See also: our guide on Recruiting Developers.)

Lower maintenance costs. Companies that start fixing bugs or adding new features and functionality to an open source project without contributing them back into the upstream project quickly learn that upgrading later to add new features or apply security fixes can be a nightmare that drives maintenance costs through the roof.

Contributing your changes back into the upstream project means that they will automatically be included in future updates without incurring additional maintenance costs.

Influence the direction. In an open source project, new features and functionality come from contributions that inevitably influence the project's direction. If you want a project to offer functionality important to your organization, then you need to have active contributors who can any implement potential changes. Through your contributions, you can influence the project's direction (assuming that your changes align with the project's goals).

However, you need to be a bit careful about how you engage these communities to avoid perception problems or other issues with your contributions. Every open source project has slightly different norms, expectations, and processes that need to be thoroughly understood before your organization should begin contributing. This can be achieved by having someone join the community and spend some time observing, or you can hire someone who already has a proven track record of participation in the community.

How open source projects are managed

At first glance, open source projects may look chaotic. People who are completely new to open source software often wonder how a group of random people can throw code together with a resulting stable product used by millions of people. It doesn't take long to realize that this isn't how open source software works. Almost every open source project has some structure, and the best projects will have the structure and project governance clearly described on the project website or in the documentation. (GitHub's guides for contributors have a great overview of project anatomy.)

While the exact governance model varies widely across projects, there are some commonalities:

Leader: At a minimum, there should be someone responsible for making the final decision about features, releases, and other activities. In some cases, this is a single person, for example, Linus Torvalds is the original author and has the final say on anything related to the Linux kernel. In other projects, there may be one or more committees responsible for various aspects of a project, like the Core Technical Committee that governs the Node.js project.

Maintainers: Most leaders delegate some of the decisions to people who are responsible for maintaining specific parts of the project, and in large projects, these maintainers may also delegate to people who are responsible for subcomponents of their portion. For example, Linus Torvalds delegates Linux kernel documentation decisions to Jonathan Corbet.

Committers: Some projects also have groups of people who have contributed to the project and are considered reliable and responsible enough to be allowed to commit directly to all or some parts of the project, rather than having to submit to a maintainer for review. Contributions from committers are still subject to review by maintainers or project leaders and may be reverted if there are any concerns about the contribution.

Contributors: Many people contribute to open source projects with code, documentation and other contributions. These contributions are usually subject to a review from an experienced committer and / or maintainer before the contributions are included.

Users: The most important group of people in an open source project is likely to be the ones who actually use the product, since users give the project a purpose and help it grow. These valuable members of the community can provide feedback about features, bug reports and more.

The community is one of the things that can make or break an open source project, and having a strong, vibrant, and diverse open source community is important to the project's success.

All of the people in the roles listed above are part of this community along with people filling other critical roles in the project for documentation, marketing, user support, and so much more.

How contributions work

The contribution process varies depending on the open source project. For example:

Projects have different guidelines with information about coding style, language, formatting, bug / ticket numbers, release timing, and more.

Some projects require signed contributor agreements, while others have signed-off-by or other processes.

The project may require patches to be posted to the mailing list, but others will ask for pull requests.

These are just a few ways that the contribution style might differ, so it's important to start by reading the documentation about how to contribute. Many projects will include this documentation as a CONTRIBUTING or README file in the home directory of the code repository, but if not, you may need to dig into the documentation or community section of the website to find the documentation.

It's also a good idea to read some of the other documentation, community guidelines, and code of conduct if they are available to make sure that you understand exactly what behavior is expected within a particular project.

If you are a first-time contributor to a project, you might consider finding a mentor or an experienced project member who can review your work and provide you with some feedback as you prepare your first couple of contributions.

After submitting a contribution using the process described in the documentation, you will need to be available to respond to feedback. Common feedback would include questions about how something works or why you chose a particular approach along with suggestions for improvements or requests for changes. This feedback can be tough sometimes, so it helps to assume that the feedback is in the spirit of making your contribution better and avoid getting defensive.

You may need to go through several rounds of resubmission and additional feedback before your code is accepted, and in some cases it may be rejected. There are many valid reasons why something might not be accepted, so don't take it personally if your code is rejected, and if possible, try to learn more about why your contribution was not accepted to help increase the chances of getting your next contribution included.

Keep in mind that if your contribution was accepted, you may be expected to maintain it over the long-term. This is especially true for large contributions, new features, or standalone code, like a driver for a specific piece of hardware. For small contributions and bug fixes, it is unlikely that there will be any long-term maintenance expected.

What it means for an organization to contribute

Over the years, the relationship between some open source projects and the companies or other organizations that use or contribute to those projects has been a bit rocky.

Organizations are often accustomed to forming business relationships in ways that don't usually work for open source projects, so some organizations struggle to understand how to contribute productively.

Another challenge is that an organization can seem self-serving or troublesome if its needs aren't aligned with the needs of the open source project. This can cause an open source community to become suspicious of the motives behind an organization's contributions.

In the past, some organizations have tried to make huge contributions that weren't aligned with the goals of the project, and in certain projects, this history may make it harder for the community to trust organizations.

However, there are also many success stories. One is the Linux kernel, where organizations contribute in meaningful ways.

The most common and easiest way for an organization to contribute to an open source project is to pay employees who have a significant amount of time devoted to participation in open source projects. In order for this to be successful, those employees need to understand the contribution processes and norms within that project to increase the chances that their contributions will be accepted. If your organization is new to a project or new to open source, consider hiring someone who has already contributed and is known within the open source project you want to contribute to; they can provide guidance on contributing successfully. Experienced contributors might be willing to mentor your employees as they pursue an open source career path. (See our guide on Recruiting Open Source Developers.)

Most projects offer other ways for organizations to participate, but these are likely to vary by project. Open source projects and the foundations that support them often need resources that organizations can provide, including infrastructure, funding, marketing, legal services, and much more. Many projects allow companies to sponsor or join a project more formally by contributing funding and/or people in exchange for some advisory role in the project or enhanced visibility.

How to be a good corporate citizen when participating in an open source project

If there is an underlying theme for this guide and for open source in general, it's that every project is different. Every time you join an open source project, you'll need to spend some time orienting yourself to the project and learning how it works.

For organizations participating in an open source project, each employee will need to go through this learning process for each project they participate in. Here are a few things that can help you get started off on the right foot.

Join the community. Each community will have slightly different ways of participating and different channels. Read the documentation to find out about the community and join the key communication channels. These channels may include mailing lists, forums, IRC, Slack, bug trackers, source code repositories, and more.

Lurk first. After you've joined the community, spend a significant amount of time lurking and reading the archives to soak up the culture before you start contributing. You'll want to understand the norms and expectations of this community before you participate. The more time you spend reading and listening, the more likely it is that your first contribution will be well received.

Understand the governance. Read the documentation or website sections about project governance and leadership before contributing. You'll want to understand how decisions are made within the project and who makes the decisions for various types of contributions.

Start small. Tackle a simple bug or documentation fix to start. It will be easier to learn the process and correct mistakes on a small contribution that isn't critical to your organization's needs. Make your mistakes on small and less significant contributions as you work up to the more complex contributions that your organization needs.

Now that your organization has figured out how to make those first small contributions, you'll need to build on those contributions to begin making larger contributions and having a bigger impact in the project.

Build relationships at events. Relationships on a personal and organizational level are an important aspect of participating in an open source community. One of the best ways to build lasting relationships with other project members is by attending events. There is nothing quite like meeting someone in person to help understand them as a human being on the other side of their email address or online handle.

These events have a varied mix of people from project leaders and passionate users of the product to direct participation from many of the organizations through sponsorships, booths, and demos to show how the organization contributes. Most of these events would not be possible without financial support from sponsoring organizations that allow us to get together and learn from each other while helping to achieve the goals of the project.

Include the community early and often. Some organizations make the mistake of developing big chunks of code in house and then dumping them into the open source project, which is almost never seen as a positive way to engage with the community. The reality is that open source projects can be complex, and what seems like an obvious change might have far reaching side effects in other parts of the project. Any significant change is likely to require some community discussion before it moves to implementation to make sure that there are no side effects and that the solution is aligned with the broader goals for the project.

While you discuss it with the community, it can help to focus on the problem, rather than a specific solution, before you invest too much time in the creation of a body of code. (See Jon Corbet's guide on How to Participate in the Linux Kernel Community)

Contribute upstream. This refers to the practice of sending any changes you make to an open source project back to the original maintainers for inclusion into an upcoming release of the software. If your organization is new to open source, you may need to spend some time educating your employees about the importance of upstreaming contributions. In some cases, people may think it will be easier to do a quick and dirty patch to get something working in your infrastructure and not bother with cleaning it up and going through the process of getting it accepted into the upstream project.

However, over the long-term, the quick patch that needs to be tested, updated and reapplied during every upgrade cycle is almost always going to take more time and effort than upstreaming it. This behavior can also be perceived as selfish within the community, since others might also benefit from your fixes, so it could also harm your organization's reputation in open source communities.

Open-source. SOFTWARE

Open-source software (OSS) is computer software with its source code made available and licensed with a license in which the copyright holder provides the rights to study, change and distribute the software to anyone and for any purpose. Open-source software is very often developed in a public, collaborative manner. Open-source software is the most prominent example of open-source development and often compared to (technically defined) user-generated content or (legally defined) open-content movements.

A report by the Standish Group (from 2008) states that adoption of open-source software models has resulted in savings of about $60 billion per year to consumers.

Definitions

The Open Source Initiative's definition is widely recognized as the standard or de facto definition. Eric.S.Raymond and Bruce Perens formed the organization in February 1998. With about 20 years of evidence from case histories of closed and open development already provided by the Internet, OSI{Open Source Initiative} continued to present the "open source" case to commercial businesses. They sought to bring a higher profile to the practical benefits of freely available source code, and wanted to bring major software businesses and other high-tech industries into open source. OSI uses The Open Source Definition to determine whether it considers a software license open source. The definition was based on the Debian Free Software Guidelines, written and adapted primarily by Perens. Perens did not base his writing on the "four freedoms" of Free Software from the FSF, which were only widely available later.

Under Perens' definition, open source describes a broad general type of software license that makes source code available to the general public with relaxed or non-existent copyright restrictions. The principles, as stated, say absolutely nothing about trademark or patent use and require absolutely no cooperation to ensure that any common audit or release regime applies to any derived works. It is an explicit "feature" of open source that it may put no restrictions on the use or distribution by any organization or user. It forbids this, in principle, to guarantee continued access to derived works even by the major original contributors.

However, Richard Stallman of the Free Software Foundation flatly opposes the term "Open Source" being applied to what they refer to as "free software". Although it is clear that legally free software does qualify as open source, Stallman considers that the category is abusive. Critics also oppose the professed pragmatism of the Open Source Initiative, as they fear that the free software ideals of freedom and community are threatened by compromising on the FSF's idealistic standards for software freedom. Increasingly, the consensus term "free and open source software" is used by the communities at large to describe the common ground between free software and open source software.

Proliferation of the term

While the term "open source" applied originally only to the source code of software, it is now being applied to many other areas such as Open source ecology, a movement to decentralize technologies so that any human can use them. However, it is often misapplied to other areas which have different and competing principles, which overlap only partially.

Open software licensing

A license defines the rights and obligations that a licensor grants to a licensee. Open source licenses grant licensees the right to copy, modify and redistribute source code (or content). These licenses may also impose obligations (e.g., modifications to the code that are distributed must be made available in source code form, an author attribution must be placed in a program/ documentation using that open source).

Authors initially derive a right to grant a license to their work based on the legal theory that upon creation of a work the author owns the copyright in that work. What the author/licensor is granting when they grant a license to copy, modify and redistribute their work is the right to use the author's copyrights. The author still retains ownership of those copyrights, the licensee simply is allowed to use those rights, as granted in the license, so long as they maintain the obligations of the license. The author does have the option to sell/assign, versus license, their exclusive right to the copyrights to their work; whereupon the new owner/assignee controls the copyrights. The ownership of the copyright (the "rights") is separate and distinct from the ownership of the work (the "thing") - a person can own a copy of a piece of code (or a copy of a book) without the rights to copy, modify or redistribute copies of it.

When an author contributes code to an open source project (e.g., Apache.org) they do so under an explicit license (e.g., the Apache Contributor License Agreement) or an implicit license (e.g., the open source license under which the project is already licensing code). Some open source projects do not take contributed code under a license, but actually require (joint) assignment of the author's copyright in order to accept code contributions into the project (e.g., OpenOffice.org and its Joint Copyright Assignment agreement). Placing code (or content) in the public domain is a way of waiving an author's (or owner's) copyrights in that work. No license is granted, and none is needed, to copy, modify or redistribute a work in the public domain.

Examples of free software license / open source licenses include Apache License, BSD license, GNU General Public License, GNU Lesser General Public License, MIT License, Eclipse Public License and Mozilla Public License.

The proliferation of open-source licenses is one of the few negative aspects of the open-source movement because it is often difficult to understand the legal implications of the differences between licenses.With more than 180,000 open source projects available and its more than 1400 unique licenses, the complexity of deciding how to manage open-source usage within "closed-source" commercial enterprises have dramatically increased. Some are home-grown while others are modeled after mainstream FOSS licenses such as Berkeley Software Distribution ("BSD"), Apache, MIT-style (Massachusetts Institute of Technology), or GNU General Public License ("GPL").

In view of this, open source practitioners are starting to use classification schemes in which FOSS licenses are grouped (typically based on the existence and obligations imposed by the copyleft provision; the strength of the copyleft provision).

An important legal milestone for the open source / free software movement was passed in 2008, when the US federal appeals court ruled that free software licences definitely do set legally binding conditions on the use of copyrighted work, and they are therefore enforceable under existing copyright law. As a result, if end-users do violate the licensing conditions, their license disappears, meaning they are infringing copyright.

Certifications

Certification can help to build higher user confidence. Certification could be applied to the simplest component that can be used by developers to build the simplest module to a whole software system. There have been numerous institutions involving in this area of the open source software including The International Institute of Software Technology / United Nations University. UNU/IIST is a non-profit research and education institution of The United Nations. It is currently involved in a project known as "The Global Desktop Project". This project aims to build a desktop interface that every end-user is able to understand and interact with, thus crossing the language and cultural barriers. It is drawing huge attention from parties involved in areas ranging from application development to localization. Furthermore, this project will improve developing nations' access to information systems. UNU/IIST aims to achieve this without any compromise in the quality of the software. It believes a global standard can be maintained by introducing certifications and is currently organizing conferences in order to explore frontiers in the field.

Alternatively, assurance models (such as DO178B) have already solved the "certification" approach for software. This approach is tailorable and can be applied to OSS, but only if the requisite planning and execution, design, test and traceability artifacts are generated.

OPEN-SOURCE SOFTWARE DEVELOPMENT

Development model

In his 1997 essay The Cathedral and the Bazaar, open-source evangelist Eric S. Raymond suggests a model for developing OSS known as the bazaar model. Raymond likens the development of software by traditional methodologies to building a cathedral, "carefully crafted by individual wizards or small bands of mages working in splendid isolation". He suggests that all software should be developed using the bazaar style, which he described as "a great babbling bazaar of differing agendas and approaches."

In the traditional model of development, which he called the cathedral model, development takes place in a centralized way. Roles are clearly defined. Roles include people dedicated to designing (the architects), people responsible for managing the project, and people responsible for implementation. Traditional software engineering follows the cathedral model. Fred P. Brooks in his book The Mythical Man-Month advocates this model. He goes further to say that in order to preserve the architectural integrity of a system, the system design should be done by as few architects as possible. The bazaar model, however, is different. In this model, roles are not clearly defined. Gregorio Robles suggests that software developed using the bazaar model should exhibit the following patterns:

Users should be treated as co-developers

The users are treated like co-developers and so they should have access to the source code of the software. Furthermore users are encouraged to submit additions to the software, code fixes for the software, bug reports, documentation etc. Having more co-developers increases the rate at which the software evolves. Linus's law states, "Given enough eyeballs all bugs are shallow." This means that if many users view the source code, they will eventually find all bugs and suggest how to fix them.

Note that some users have advanced programming skills, and furthermore, each user's machine provides an additional testing environment. This new testing environment offers that ability to find and fix a new bug.

Early releases

The first version of the software should be released as early as possible so as to increase one's chances of finding co-developers early.

Frequent integration

Code changes should be integrated (merged into a shared code base) as often as possible so as to avoid the overhead of fixing a large number of bugs at the end of the project life cycle. Some open source projects have nightly builds where integration is done automatically on a daily basis.

Several versions

There should be at least two versions of the software. There should be a buggier version with more features and a more stable version with fewer features. The buggy version (also called the development version) is for users who want the immediate use of the latest features, and are willing to accept the risk of using code that is not yet thoroughly tested. The users can then act as co-developers, reporting bugs and providing bug fixes.

High modularization

The general structure of the software should be modular allowing for parallel development on independent components.

Dynamic decision making structure

There is a need for a decision making structure, whether formal or informal, that makes strategic decisions depending on changing user requirements and other factors. Cf. Extreme programming.

Data suggests, however, that OSS is not quite as democratic as the bazaar model suggests. An analysis of five billion bytes of free/open source code by 31,999 developers shows that 74% of the code was written by the most active 10% of authors. The average number of authors involved in a project was 5.1, with the median at 2.

Considerations for software producsers

Software experts and researchers on open source software have identified several advantages and disadvantages. The main advantage for business is that open source is a good way for business to achieve greater penetration of the market. Companies that offer open source software are able to establish an industry standard and, thus, gain competitive advantage. It has also helped build developer loyalty as developers feel empowered and have a sense of ownership of the end product.

Moreover, lower costs of marketing and logistical services are needed for OSS. OSS also helps companies keep abreast of technology developments. It is a good tool to promote a company's image, including its commercial products. The OSS development approach has helped produce reliable, high quality software quickly and inexpensively.

The term "open source" was originally intended to be trademarkable; however, the term was deemed too descriptive, so no trademark exists. Besides, it offers the potential for a more flexible technology and quicker innovation. It is said to be more reliable since it typically has thousands of independent programmers testing and fixing bugs of the software. It is flexible because modular systems allow programmers to build custom interfaces, or add new abilities to it and it is innovative since open source programs are the product of collaboration among a large number of different programmers. The mix of divergent perspectives, corporate objectives, and personal goals speeds up innovation.

Moreover, free software can be developed in accord with purely technical requirements. It does not require thinking about commercial pressure that often degrades the quality of the software. Commercial pressures make traditional software developers pay more attention to customers' requirements than to security requirements, since such features are somewhat invisible to the customer.

It is sometimes said that the open source development process may not be well defined and the stages in the development process, such as system testing and documentation may be ignored. However this is only true for small (mostly single programmer) projects.

Larger, successful projects do define and enforce at least some rules as they need them to make the teamwork possible. In the most complex projects these rules may be as strict as reviewing even minor change by two independent developers.

Not all OSS initiatives have been successful, for example SourceXchange and Eazel. Software experts and researchers who are not convinced by open source's ability to produce quality systems identify the unclear process, the late defect discovery and the lack of any empirical evidence as the most important problems (collected data concerning productivity and quality). It is also difficult to design a commercially sound business model around the open source paradigm.

Consequently, only technical requirements may be satisfied and not the ones of the market. In terms of security, open source may allow hackers to know about the weaknesses or loopholes of the software more easily than closed-source software.

It depends on control mechanisms in order to create effective performance of autonomous agents who participate in virtual organizations.

Development tools

In OSS development, the participants, who are mostly volunteers, are distributed among different geographic regions, so there is need for tools to aid participants to collaborate in source code development. Often, these tools are also available as OSS.

Revision control systems such as Concurrent Versions System (CVS) and later Subversion (SVN) and Git, and the GNU Compiler Collection are examples of tools that help centrally manage the source code files and the changes to those files for a software project. These tools are themselves OSS.

Utilities that automate testing, compiling, and bug reporting help preserve stability and support of software projects that have numerous developers but no managers, quality controller, or technical support. Building systems that report compilation errors among different platforms include Tinderbox. Commonly used bugtrackers include Bugzilla and GNATS.

Tools such as mailing lists, IRC, and instant messaging provide means of Internet communication between developers. The Web is also a core feature of all of the above systems. Some sites centralize all the features of these tools as a software development management system, including GNU Savannah, SourceForge, and BountySource.

Projects and organizations

Some of the "more prominent organizations" involved in OSS development include the Apache Software Foundation, creators of the Apache web server; the Linux Foundation, a nonprofit which as of 2012 employed Linus Torvalds, the creator of the Linux operating system kernel; the Eclipse Foundation, home of the Eclipse software development platform; the Debian Project, creators of the influential Debian GNU/ Linux distribution; the Mozilla Foundation, home of the Firefox web browser; and OW2, European-born community developing open source middleware. New organizations tend to have a more sophisticated governance model and their membership is often formed by legal entity members.

Several open source programs have become defining entries in their space, including the GIMP image editing system; Sun's Java programming language and environment; the MySQL database system; the FreeBSD Unix operating system; Sun's OpenOffice.org office productivity suite; and the Wireshark network packet sniffer and protocol analyser.

Open Source development is often performed "live and in public", using services provided for free on the Internet, such as the Launchpad and SourceForge web sites.

Open Source Software Institute is a membership-based, non-profit (501 (c)(6)) organization established in 2001 that promotes the development and implementation of open source software solutions within US Federal, state and local government agencies. OSSI's efforts have focused on promoting adoption of open source software programs and policies within Federal Government and Defense and Homeland Security communities.

Open Source for America is a group created to raise awareness in the U.S. Federal Government about the benefits of open source software. Their stated goals are to encourage the government's use of open source software, participation in open source software projects, and incorporation of open source community dynamics to increase government transparency.

Mil-OSS is a group dedicated to the advancement of OSS use and creation in the military.

Funding

Unlike proprietary off-the-shelf software, which comes with restrictive copyright licenses, open source software can be given away for no charge. This means that its creators cannot require each user to pay a license fee to fund development. Instead, a number of alternative models for funding its development have emerged.

Software can be developed as a consulting project for one or more customers. The customers pay to direct the developers' efforts: to have bugs prioritized and fixed or features added. Companies or independent consultants can also charge for training, installation, technical support, or customization of the software.

Another approach to funding is to provide the software freely, but sell licenses to proprietary add-ons such as data libraries. For instance, an open-source CAD program may require parts libraries which are sold on a subscription or flat-fee basis. Open-source software can also promote the sale of specialized hardware that it interoperates with, as in the case of the Asterisk telephony software, developed by a manufacturer of PC telephony hardware (Digium).

Many open source software projects have begun as research projects within universities, as personal projects of students or professors, or as tools to aid scientific research.

The influence of universities and research institutions on open source shows in the number of projects named after their host institutions, such as BSD Unix, CMU Common Lisp, or the NCSA HTTPd which evolved into Apache.

Companies may employ developers to work on open-source projects that are useful to the company's infrastructure: in this case, it is developed not as a product to be sold but as a sort of shared public utility.

A local bug-fix or solution to a software problem, written by a developer either at a company's request or to make his/her own job easier, can be released as an open-source contribution without costing the company anything. A larger project such as the Linux kernel may have contributors from dozens of companies which use and depend upon it, as well as hobbyist and research developers.

Also, there exists stipends to support the development of open source software like Google's Summer of Code founded 2005.

A new funding approach for open source projects is crowdfunding, organized over web platforms like Kickstarter, Indiegogo, or Bountysource.

COMPARISONS WITH OTHER SOFTWARE LICENSING/ DEVELOPMENT MODELS

Closed source / proprietary software

The debate over open source vs. closed source (alternatively called proprietary software) is sometimes heated.

The top four reasons (as provided by Open Source Business Conference survey) individuals or organizations choose open source software are:

1. lower cost,
2. security,
3. no vendor 'lock in', and
4. better quality.

Since innovative companies no longer rely heavily on software sales, proprietary software has become less of a necessity. As such, things like open source content management system-or CMS-deployments are becoming more commonplace.

In 2009, the US White House switched its CMS system from a proprietary system to Drupal open source CMS. Further, companies like Novell (who traditionally sold software the old-fashioned way) continually debate the benefits of switching to open source availability, having already switched part of the product offering to open source code. In this way, open source software provides solutions to unique or specific problems. As such, it is reported that 98% of enterprise-level companies use open source software offerings in some capacity.

With this market shift, more critical systems are beginning to rely on open source offerings, allowing greater funding (such as US Department of Homeland Security grants) to help "hunt for security bugs." According to a pilot study of organisations adopting (or not adopting) OSS; several factors of statistical significance were observed in the manager's beliefs in relation to (a) attitudes toward outcomes, (b) the influences and behav iours of others and (c) their ability to act. Many advocates argue that open source software is inherently safer because any person can view, edit, and change code. A study of the Linux source code has 0.17 bugs per 1000 lines of code while proprietary software generally scores 20-30 bugs per 1000 lines.

Free software

The main difference is that by choosing one term over the other (i.e. either "open source" or "free software") one lets others know about what one's goals are. As Richard Stallman puts it, "Open source is a development methodology; free software is a social movement."

Critics have said that the term "open source" fosters an ambiguity of a different kind such that it confuses the mere availability of the source with the freedom to use, modify, and redistribute it. Developers have used the alternative terms Free/open source Software (FOSS), or Free/Libre/open source Software (FLOSS), consequently, to describe open source software which is also free software.

The term "open source" was originally intended to be trademarkable; however, the term was deemed too descriptive, so no trademark exists. The OSI would prefer that people treat open source as if it were a trademark, and use it only to describe software licensed under an OSI approved license.OSI Certified is a trademark licensed only to people who are distributing software licensed under a license listed on the Open Source Initiative's list.

Open-source software and free software are different terms for software which comes with certain rights, or freedoms, for the user. They describe two approaches and philosophies towards free software. Open source and free software (or software libre) both describe software which is free from onerous licensing restrictions. It may be used, copied, studied, modified and redistributed without restriction. Free software is not the same as freeware, software available at zero price.

The definition of open source software was written to be almost identical to the free software definition. There are very few cases of software that is free software but is not open source software, and vice versa. The difference in the terms is where they place the emphasis. "Free software" is defined in terms of giving the user freedom. This reflects the goal of the free software movement. "Open source" highlights that the source code is viewable to all; proponents of the term usually emphasize the quality of the software and how this is caused by the development models which are possible and popular among free and open source software projects.

The FSF believes that knowledge of the concept of freedom is an essential requirement, insists on the use of the term free, and separates itself from the open source movement.

Open-source vs. source-available

Although the OSI definition of "open source software" is widely accepted, a small number of people and organizations use the term to refer to software where the source is available for viewing, but which may not legally be modified or redistributed. Such software is more often referred to as source-available, or as shared source, a term coined by Microsoft in 2001. While in 2007 two shared source licenses were certified by the OSI, most of the shared source licenses are still source-available only.

In 2007 Michael Tiemann, president of OSI, had criticized companies such as SugarCRM for promoting their software as "open source" when in fact it did not have an OSI-approved license. In SugarCRM's case, it was because the software is so-called "badgeware" since it specified a "badge" that must be displayed in the user interface (SugarCRM has since switched to GPLv3). Another example was Scilab prior to version 5, which called itself "the open source platform for numerical computation" but had a license that forbade commercial redistribution of modified versions.

Because OSI does not have a registered trademark for the term "open source", its legal ability to prevent such usage of the term is limited, but Tiemann advocates using public opinion from OSI, customers, and community members to pressure such organizations to change their license or to use a different term.

The creative commons licenses, designed mainly for media but sometimes used for software, offers license clause elements which allow licensing in the spectrum between Open-source, source-available, and public domain.

History

End of 1990s: Foundation of the Open Source Initative

In 1997, Eric Raymond published The Cathedral and the Bazaar, a reflective analysis of the hacker community and free software principles. The paper received significant attention in early 1998, and was one factor in motivating Netscape Communications Corporation to release their popular Netscape Communicator Internet suite as free software. This code is today better known as Mozilla Firefox and Thunderbird.

Netscape's act prompted Raymond and others to look into how to bring the FSF's free software ideas and perceived benefits to the commercial software industry. They concluded that FSF's social activism was not appealing to companies like Netscape, and looked for a way to rebrand the free software movement to emphasize the business potential of sharing and collaborating on software source code. The new name they chose was "open source", and quickly Bruce Perens, publisher Tim O'Reilly,

Linus Torvalds, and others signed on to the rebranding. The Open Source Initiative was founded in February 1998 to encourage use of the new term and evangelize open-source principles.

While the Open Source Initiative sought to encourage the use of the new term and evangelize the principles it adhered to, commercial software vendors found themselves increasingly threatened by the concept of freely distributed software and universal access to an application's source code. A Microsoft executive publicly stated in 2001 that "open source is an intellectual property destroyer. I can't imagine something that could be worse than this for the software business and the intellectual-property business." This view perfectly summarizes the initial response to FOSS by some software corporations.

However, while FOSS has historically played a role outside of the mainstream of private software development, companies as large as Microsoft have begun to develop official open-source presences on the Internet. IBM, Oracle, Google and State Farm are just a few of the companies with a serious public stake in today's competitive open-source market. There has been a significant shift in the corporate philosophy concerning the development of free and open-source software (FOSS).

The free software movement was launched in 1983. In 1998, a group of individuals advocated that the term free software should be replaced by open-source software (OSS) as an expression which is less ambiguous and more comfortable for the corporate world. Software developers may want to publish their software with an open-source license, so that anybody may also develop the same software or understand its internal functioning. With open-source software, generally anyone is allowed to create modifications of it, port it to new operating systems and processor architectures, share it with others or, in some cases, market it. Scholars Casson and Ryan have pointed out several policy-based reasons for adoption of open source - in particular, the heightened value proposition from open source (when compared to most proprietary formats) in the following categories:

- Security
- Affordability
- Transparency
- Perpetuity
- Interoperability
- Flexibility
- Localization-particularly in the context of local governments (who make software decisions). Casson and Ryan argue that "governments

have an inherent responsibility and fiduciary duty to taxpayers" which includes the careful analysis of these factors when deciding to purchase proprietary software or implement an open-source option.

The Open Source Definition, notably, presents an open-source philosophy, and further defines the terms of usage, modification and redistribution of open-source software. Software licenses grant rights to users which would otherwise be reserved by copyright law to the copyright holder. Several open-source software licenses have qualified within the boundaries of the Open Source Definition.

The most prominent and popular example is the GNU General Public License (GPL), which "allows free distribution under the condition that further developments and applications are put under the same licence", thus also free. While open-source distribution presents a way to make the source code of a product publicly accessible, the open-source licenses allow the authors to fine tune such access.

The open source label came out of a strategy session held on April 7, 1998 in Palo Alto in reaction to Netscape's January 1998 announcement of a source code release for Navigator (as Mozilla). A group of individuals at the session included Tim O'Reilly, Linus Torvalds, Tom Paquin, Jamie Zawinski, Larry Wall, Brian Behlendorf, Sameer Parekh, Eric Allman, Greg Olson, Paul Vixie, John Ousterhout, Guido van Rossum, Philip Zimmermann, John Gilmore and Eric S. Raymond.

They used the opportunity before the release of Navigator's source code to clarify a potential confusion caused by the ambiguity of the word "free" in English.

Many people claimed that the birth of the Internet, since 1969, started the open source movement, while others do not distinguish between open-source and free software movements.

The Free Software Foundation (FSF), started in 1985, intended the word "free" to mean freedom to distribute (or "free as in free speech") and not freedom from cost (or "free as in free beer"). Since a great deal of free software already was (and still is) free of charge, such free software became associated with zero cost, which seemed anti-commercial.

The Open Source Initiative (OSI) was formed in February 1998 by Eric S. Raymond and Bruce Perens. With at least 20 years of evidence from case histories of closed software development versus open development already provided by the Internet developer community, the OSI presented the "open source" case to commercial businesses, like Netscape. The OSI hoped that the usage of the label "open source," a term suggested by Peterson of the Foresight Institute at the strategy session, would eliminate ambiguity, particularly for individuals who perceive "free software" as anti-commercial. They sought to bring a higher profile to the practical benefits of freely available source code, and they wanted to bring major software businesses and other high-tech industries into open source.

Perens attempted to register "open source" as a service mark for the OSI, but that attempt was impractical by trademark standards. Meanwhile, due to the presentation of Raymond's paper to the upper management at Netscape-Raymond only discovered when he read the Press Release, and was called by Netscape CEO Jim Barksdale's PA later in the day-Netscape released its Navigator source code as open source, with favorable results.

Current applications

Widely used open-source software

Open source software projects are built and maintained by a network of volunteer programmers. Prime examples of open-source products are the Apache HTTP Server, the e-commerce platform osCommerce and the internet browser Mozilla Firefox.

One of the most successful open-source products is the GNU/Linux operating system, an open-source Unix-like operating system, and its derivative Android, an operating system for mobile devices. In some fields, open software is the norm, like in voice over IP applications with Asterisk (PBX).

Business applications

There are a number of commonly recognized barriers to the adoption of open-source software by enterprises. These barriers include the perception that open-source licenses are viral, lack of formal support and training, the velocity of change, and a lack of a long-term roadmap. The majority of these barriers are risk-related.

From the other side, not all proprietary projects disclose exact future plans, not all open-source licenses are equally viral and many serious OSS projects (especially operating systems) actually make money from paid support and documentation.

A commonly employed business strategy of commercial open-source software firms is the dual-license strategy, as demonstrated by Ingres, MySQL, Alfresco, Sleepycat and others.

Another business strategy could be adapted from existing Internet micro-payments systems including flattr and paypal.

Non-software use

The principles of open source have been adapted for many forms of user-generated content and technology, including open-source hardware, Wikipedia, and open-access publishing.

Supporters of the open content movement advocate some restrictions of use, requirements to share changes, and attribution to other authors of the work.

This "culture" or ideology takes the view that the principles apply more generally to facilitate concurrent input of different agendas, approaches and priorities, in contrast with more centralized models of development such as those typically used in commercial companies.

SOURCEFORGE.NET

SourceForge is a web-based source code repository. It acts as a centralized location for software developers to control and manage free and open source software development. It was the first to offer this service for free to open source projects. The website runs a version of SourceForge Enterprise Edition, forked from the last open-source version available. As of May 2013, the SourceForge repository hosts more than 300,000 projects and has more than 3 million registered users, although not all are active. The domain sourceforge.net attracted at least 33 million visitors by August 2009 according to a Compete.com survey.

SourceForge offers free access to hosting and tools for developers of free / open source software, competing with other providers such as GitHub, RubyForge, Tigris.org, BountySource, Launchpad, BerliOS, JavaForge, GNU Savannah, and Gitorious.

Concept

SourceForge is web-based source code repository, which acts as a centralized location for free and open source software projects. It was the first to offer this service for free to open source projects. Project developers have access to centralized storage and tools for managing projects, although it is best known for providing revision control systems such as CVS, SVN, Bazaar, Git or Mercurial. Major features (amongst others) include project wikis, metrics and analysis, access to a MySQL database, and unique sub-domain URLs (such as http://project-name.sourceforge.net).

The vast number of users at SourceForge.net (over 3 million as of 2013) exposes prominent projects to a variety of developers, and can create a positive feedback loop. As a project's activity rises, SourceForge.net's internal ranking system makes it more visible to other developers who may join and contribute to it. Given that many open source projects fail due to lack of developer support, exposure to such a large community of developers can continually breathe new life into a project.

Revenue model

Sourceforge's traditional revenue model is through advertising banner sales on their website. In 2006, sourceforge inc reported quarterly takings of USD$6.5 million. In 2009, sourceforge reported a gross quarterly income of $23 million through media and e-commerce streams. In 2011, a revenue of USD $20 million was reported for the combined value of the sourceforge, slashdot and freecode holdings, prior to sourceforge's acquisition. More recently additional revenue generation schemes, such as bundleware models, have been trialled, with the goal of further improving sourceforge's revenue.

History

SourceForge, founded 1999 by VA Software, was the first provider of a centralized location for free and open source software developers to control and manage software development and offering this service for free.

Temporary bans in China Golden Shield Project In September 2002, SourceForge.net was temporarily banned in China.

The website was banned again in China, for about a month, in July 2008. On Aug 6, 2012, SourceForge.net was banned again. Several days later the ban was lifted.

Attacks and outage of SourceForge.net

SourceForge has faced critical attacks on its databases. In 2006, attackers targeted the SourceForge.net database and most of its users were advised to change their passwords in order to remain secure. In December 2007, SourceForge.net was offline for a while due to another attack. Nobody knew exactly what had happened, since there were no reports about the outage.

On January 27, 2011, SourceForge faced another attempt. The attack was mainly against some of the developer infrastructure and resulted in the exploitation of several SourceForge.net servers. SourceForge said, "The attack resulted in an exploit of several SourceForge.net servers, and we have proactively shut down a handful of developer centric services to safeguard data and protect the majority of our services"

According to a SourceForge.net announcement on their blog as a short term response, they have taken down services such as CVS Hosting, ViewVC (web-based code browsing), New Release upload capability, and Interactive Shell services. The company is silent about the type of attack and from where those attempts were made.

Suit by SCPP

Société civile des Producteurs de Phonogrammes en France (SCPP) is an umbrella group for a variety of organizations in France. In November, 2008, SCPP initiated a suit against Sourceforge.net, Vuze, Limewire, and Morpheus for hosting the P2P file-sharing application Shareaza that "facilitates mass copyright infringement". SourceForge was not sued for hosting copyrighted material itself, but for hosting Vuze.

Apache relicense

In June 2012, SourceForge released its underlying software, named Allura, under the Apache license which was then accepted by Apache foundation for incubation.

Attackers compromised a download mirror server

On September 26, 2012 it was announced that attackers compromised a download mirror server for the SourceForge software repository, rigging the installer package for phpMyAdmin, a web based MySQL Server interface, with a backdoor.

Acquisition

In September 2012, Dice Holdings acquired SourceForge from its previous owner Geeknet.

DevShare adware controversy

In July, 2013, SourceForge announced that it will provide project owners an optional feature called DevShare, which places closed-source ad-supported content into the binary installers and gives the project part of the ad revenue. Opinions of this new feature vary, with some complaining about downloaders not being as aware of what they are getting or being able to trust that the downloaded content, whereas others see it as a reasonably harmless option that keeps individual projects and users in control.

In November 2013, GIMP, a popular free image manipulation program, removed its download from SourceForge, citing misleading download buttons that can potentially confuse customers, as well as SourceForge's own Windows installer, which bundles third-party offers. In a statement, GIMP called SourceForge a once "useful and trustworthy place to develop and host FLOSS applications" that now faces "a problem with the ads they allow on their sites..."

Reception

Usage

As of May 2013, the SourceForge repository hosts more than 300,000 projects and has more than 3 million registered users, although not all are active. The domain sourceforge.net attracted at least 33 million visitors by August 2009 according to a Compete.com survey.

Country restrictions

In its terms of use, SourceForge states that its services are not available to users in countries on the sanction list of the U.S. Office of Foreign Assets Control (including Cuba, Iran, North Korea, Sudan and Syria). Since 2008, access to the secure server (used for making contributions to the site) has been blocked for people from those countries. As of January 2010, all access including downloads is blocked for those users. This means that all people whose IP addresses appear to belong to those countries are prevented from using the site.

These restrictions have drawn criticism as being counter to the free software movement, the open source software movement and the principles of making software available to all without discrimination.

APACHE SOFTWARE FOUNDATION

The Apache Software Foundation /??pæt?i?/ (ASF) is an American non-profit corporation (classified as 501(c)(3) in the United States) to support Apache software projects, including the Apache HTTP Server. The ASF was formed from the Apache Group and incorporated in Delaware, U.S., in June 1999.

The Apache Software Foundation is a decentralized community of developers. The software they produce is distributed under the terms of the Apache License and is therefore free and open source software (FOSS). The Apache projects are characterized by a collaborative, consensus-based development process and an open and pragmatic software license. Each project is managed by a self-selected team of technical experts who are active contributors to the project. The ASF is a meritocracy, implying that membership of the foundation is granted only to volunteers who have actively contributed to Apache projects. The ASF is considered a second generation open-source organization, in that commercial support is provided without the risk of platform lock-in.

Among the ASF's objectives are: to provide legal protection to volunteers working on Apache projects; to prevent the Apache brand name from being used by other organizations without permission.

The ASF also holds several ApacheCon conferences each year, highlighting Apache projects, related technology, and encouraging Apache developers to gather together.

History

The history of the Apache Software Foundation is linked to the Apache HTTP Server, development beginning in February, 1995. A group of eight developers started working on enhancing the NCSA HTTPd daemon. They came to be known as the Apache Group.

On March 25, 1999, the Apache Software Foundation was formed. The first official meeting of the Apache Software Foundation was held on April 13, 1999, and by general consent that the initial membership list of the Apache Software Foundation, would be: Brian Behlendorf, Ken Coar, Miguel Gonzales, Mark Cox, Lars Eilebrecht, Ralf S. Engelschall, Roy T.

Fielding, Dean Gaudet, Ben Hyde, Jim Jagielski, Alexei Kosut, Martin Kraemer, Ben Laurie, Doug MacEachern, Aram Mirzadeh, Sameer Parekh, Cliff Skolnick, Marc Slemko, William (Bill) Stoddard, Paul Sutton, Randy Terbush and Dirk-Willem van Gulik. After a series of additional meetings to elect board members and resolve other legal matters regarding incorporation, the effective incorporation date of the Apache Software Foundation was set to June 1, 1999.

The name 'Apache' was chosen from respect for the Native American Apache Nation, well known for their superior skills in warfare strategy and their inexhaustible endurance. It also makes a pun on "a patchy web server"-a server made from a series of patches-but this was not its origin. The group of developers who released this new software soon started to call themselves the "Apache Group".

Projects

Apache divides its software development activities into separate semi-autonomous areas called "top-level projects" (formally known as a "Project Management Committee" in the bylaws), some of which have a number of sub-projects. Unlike some other organizations that host FOSS projects, before a project is hosted at Apache it has to be licensed to the ASF with a grant or contributor agreement. In this way, the ASF gains the necessary intellectual property rights for the development and distribution of all its projects.

Board of directors

The ASF board of directors has responsibility for overseeing the ASF's activities and acting as a central point of contact and communication for its projects. The board assigns corporate issues, assigning resources to projects, and manages corporate services, including funds and legal issues.

It does not make technical decisions about individual projects; these are made by the individual Project Management Committees. The board is elected annually by members of the foundation and, after the May 2013 Annual Members Meeting, it consists of:

- Shane Curcuru
- Doug Cutting
- Bertrand Delacretaz
- Roy T. Fielding
- Jim Jagielski
- Chris Mattmann
- Brett Porter (chairman)
- Sam Ruby
- Greg Stein

In the 2010-11 fiscal year, the Foundation took in $539,410, almost entirely from grants and contributions with $12,349 from two ApacheCons. With no employees and 2,663 volunteers, it spent $270,846 on infrastructure, $92,364 on public relations, and $17,891 on two Apache Cons.

Eclipse

In computer programming, Eclipse is an Integrated development environment (IDE). It contains a base workspace and an extensible plug-in system for customizing the environment. Written mostly in Java, Eclipse can be used to develop applications in Java.

By means of various plug-ins, Eclipse may also be used to develop applications in other programming languages: Ada, C, C++, COBOL, Fortran, Haskell, JavaScript, Lasso, Perl, PHP, Python, R, Ruby (including Ruby on Rails framework), Scala, Clojure, Groovy, Scheme, and Erlang. It can also be used to develop packages for the software Mathematica.

Development environments include the Eclipse Java development tools (JDT) for Java and Scala, Eclipse CDT for C/C++ and Eclipse PDT for PHP, among others.

The initial codebase originated from IBM VisualAge. The Eclipse software development kit (SDK), which includes the Java development tools, is meant for Java developers. Users can extend its abilities by installing plug-ins written for the Eclipse Platform, such as development toolkits for other programming languages, and can write and contribute their own plug-in modules.

Released under the terms of the Eclipse Public License, Eclipse SDK is free and open source software (although it is incompatible with the GNU General Public License). It was one of the first IDEs to run under GNU Classpath and it runs without problems under IcedTea.

History

Eclipse began as an IBM Canada project. Object Technology International (OTI), which had previously marketed the Smalltalk-based VisualAge family of integrated development environment (IDE) products, developed the new product as a Java-based replacement. In November 2001, a consortium was formed with a board of stewards to further the development of Eclipse as open-source software. It is estimated that IBM had already invested close to $40 million by that time. The original members were Borland, IBM, Merant, QNX Software Systems, Rational Software, Red Hat, SuSE, TogetherSoft and WebGain. The number of stewards increased to over 80 by the end of 2003. In January 2004, the Eclipse Foundation was created.

Eclipse 3.0 (released on 21 June 2004) selected the OSGi Service Platform specifications as the runtime architecture.

The Association for Computing Machinery recognized Eclipse with the 2011 ACM Software Systems Award on 26 April 2012.

Licensing

The Eclipse Public License (EPL) is the fundamental license under which Eclipse projects are released. Some projects require dual licensing, for which the Eclipse Distribution License (EDL) is available, although use of this license must be applied for and is considered on a case-by-case basis.

Eclipse was originally released under the Common Public License, but was later relicensed under the Eclipse Public License. The Free Software Foundation has said that both licenses are free software licenses, but are incompatible with the GNU General Public License (GPL). Mike Milinkovich, of the Eclipse Foundation commented that moving to the GPL would be considered when version 3 of the GPL was released.

Name

According to Lee Nackman, Chief Technology Officer of IBM's Rational division (originating in 2003) at that time, the name "Eclipse" (dating from at least 2001) was not a wordplay on Sun Microsystems, as the product's primary competition at the time of naming was Microsoft Visual Studio (which it, Eclipse, was to eclipse).

Architecture

Eclipse uses plug-ins to provide all the functionality within and on top of the runtime system. Its runtime system is based on Equinox, an implementation of the OSGi core framework specification.

In addition to allowing the Eclipse Platform to be extended using other programming languages such as C and Python, the plug-in framework allows the Eclipse Platform to work with typesetting languages like LaTeX, networking applications such as telnet and database management systems. The plug-in architecture supports writing any desired extension to the environment, such as for configuration management. Java and CVS support is provided in the Eclipse SDK, with support for other version control systems provided by third-party plug-ins.

With the exception of a small run-time kernel, everything in Eclipse is a plug-in. This means that every plug-in developed integrates with Eclipse in exactly the same way as other plug-ins; in this respect, all features are "created equal". Eclipse provides plug-ins for a wide variety of features, some of which are through third parties using both free and commercial models. Examples of plug-ins include for UML, for Sequence and other UML diagrams, a plug-in for DB Explorer, and many others.

The Eclipse SDK includes the Eclipse Java development tools (JDT), offering an IDE with a built-in incremental Java compiler and a full model of the Java source files. This allows for advanced refactoring techniques and code analysis. The IDE also makes use of a workspace, in this case a set of metadata over a flat filespace allowing external file modifications as long as the corresponding workspace "resource" is refreshed afterwards.

Eclipse implements widgets through a Java toolkit called SWT, whereas most Java applications use the Java standard Abstract Window Toolkit (AWT) or Swing. Eclipse's user interface also uses an intermediate graphical user interface layer called JFace, which simplifies the construction of applications based on SWT. Language packs developing by the "Babel project" provide translations into over a dozen natural languages.

Rich Client Platform

Eclipse provides the Rich Client Platform (RCP) for developing general purpose applications. The following components constitute the rich client platform:

- Equinox OSGi - a standard bundling framework.
- Core platform - boot Eclipse, run plug-ins.
- Standard Widget Toolkit (SWT) - a portable widget toolkit.
- JFace - viewer classes to bring model view controller programming to SWT, file buffers, text handling, text editors.
- Eclipse Workbench - views, editors, perspectives, wizards.

Examples of rich client applications based on Eclipse are:

- IBM Notes 8 and 9
- Novell/NetIQ Designer for Identity Manager
- Apache Directory Studio

Server platform

Eclipse supports development for Tomcat, GlassFish and many other servers and is often capable of installing the required server (for development) directly from the IDE. It supports remote debugging, allowing the user to watch variables and step through the code of an application that is running on the attached server.

Web Tools Platform

The Eclipse Web Tools Platform (WTP) project is an extension of the Eclipse platform with tools for developing Web and Java EE applications. It includes source and graphical editors for a variety of languages, wizards and built-in applications to simplify development, and tools and APIs to support deploying, running, and testing apps.

Modeling Platform

The Modeling project contains all the official projects of the Eclipse Foundation focusing on model-based development technologies. They are all compatible with the Eclipse Modeling Framework created by IBM. Those projects are separated in several categories: Model Transformation, Model Development Tools, Concrete Syntax Development, Abstract Syntax Development, Technology and Research, and Amalgam.

Model Transformation

Model Transformation projects uses EMF based models as an input and produce either a model or text as an output. Model to model transformation projects includes ATL, an open source transformation language and toolkit used to transform a given model or to generate a new model from a given EMF model.

Model to text transformation projects contains Acceleo, an implementation of MOFM2T, a standard model to text language from the OMG.

Acceleo is an open source code generator that can generate any textual language (Java, PHP, Python, etc.) from EMF based models defined with any metamodel (UML, SysML, etc.).

Model Development Tools

Model Development Tools projects are implementations of modeling standard used in the industry like UML or OCL and their toolkit. Among those projects can be found implementation of the following standard:

- UML
- SysML
- OCL
- BPMN
- IMM
- SBVR
- XSD
- NEDA

Concrete Syntax Development

The Concrete Syntax Development project contains the Graphical Modeling Framework, an Eclipse based framework dedicated to the graphical representation of EMF based models.

Abstract Syntax Development

The Abstract Syntax Development project hosts the Eclipse Modeling Framework, core of most of the modeling project of the Eclipse Foundation and the framework available for EMF like CDO, EMF query or EMF validation.

Technology and Research

Technology and Research projects are prototypes of Modeling project, this project is used to host all the modeling projects of the Eclipse Foundation during their incubation phase.

Amalgam

Amalgam provides the packaging and integration between all the available modeling tools for the Eclipse package dedicated to modeling tools.

Extensions

Eclipse supports a rich selection of extensions, adding support for Python via pydev, Android development via Google's ADT, JavaFX support via e(fx)clipse, and many others at the Eclipse Marketplace.

Alternative Distributions

A number of alternative distributions exist in the Eclipse project.

Eclipse PDT (PHP Development Tools)

The PHP Development Tools project provides a PHP Development Tools framework for the Eclipse platform. The project encompasses all development components, including code-completion, develop PHP and facilitate extensibility. It leverages the existing Eclipse Web Tools Platform (WTP) and Dynamic Languages Toolkit (DLTK).

FREE SOFTWARE FOUNDATION

The Free Software Foundation (FSF) is a 501(c)(3) non-profit organization founded by Richard Stallman on 4 October 1985 to support the free software movement, which promotes the universal freedom to create, distribute and modify computer software, with the organization's preference for software being distributed under copyleft ("share alike") terms, such as with its own GNU General Public License. The FSF was incorporated in Massachusetts, USA, where it is also based.

From its founding until the mid-1990s, FSF's funds were mostly used to employ software developers to write free software for the GNU Project. Since the mid-1990s, the FSF's employees and volunteers have mostly worked on legal and structural issues for the free software movement and the free software community. Consistent with its goals, only free software is used on FSF's computers.

History

The Free Software Foundation was founded in 1985 as a non-profit corporation supporting free software development. It continued existing GNU projects such as the sale of manuals and tapes, and employed developers of the free software system. Since then, it has continued these activities, as well as advocating for the free software movement. The FSF is also the steward of several free software licenses, meaning they publish them and have the ability to make revisions as needed.

In March 2003, SCO filed suit against IBM alleging that IBM's contributions to various free software, including FSF's GNU, violated SCO's rights. While FSF was never a party to the lawsuit, FSF was subpoenaed on November 5, 2003. During 2003 and 2004, FSF put substantial advocacy effort into responding to the lawsuit and quelling its negative impact on the adoption and promotion of free software.

In 2007, the FSF published the third version of the GNU General Public License after significant outside input.

The FSF holds the copyrights on many pieces of the GNU system, such as GNU Compiler Collection. As holder of these copyrights, it has the authority to enforce the copyleft requirements of the GNU General Public License (GPL) when copyright infringement occurs on that software.

While other copyright holders of other software systems adopted the GPL as their license, FSF was the only organization to regularly assert its copyright interests on software so licensed until Harald Welte launched gpl-violations.org in 2004.

From 1991 until 2001, GPL enforcement was done informally, usually by Stallman himself, often with assistance from FSF's lawyer, Eben Moglen. Typically, GPL violations during this time were cleared up by short email exchanges between Stallman and the violator.

In late 2001, Bradley M. Kuhn (then Executive Director), with the assistance of Moglen, David Turner, and Peter T. Brown, formalized these efforts into FSF's GPL Compliance Labs. From 2002-2004, high profile GPL enforcement cases, such as those against Linksys and OpenTV, became frequent.GPL enforcement and educational campaigns on GPL compliance was a major focus of the FSF's efforts during this period.

In December 2008 FSF filed a lawsuit against Cisco for using GPL-licensed components shipped with Linksys products. Cisco was notified of the licensing issue in 2003 but Cisco repeatedly disregarded its obligations under the GPL. In May 2009, FSF dropped the lawsuit when Cisco agreed to make a monetary donation to the FSF and appoint a Free Software Director to conduct continuous reviews of the company's license compliance practices.

From 2003 to 2005, FSF held legal seminars to explain the GPL and the law around it. Usually taught by Bradley M. Kuhn and Daniel Ravicher, these seminars offered CLE credit and were the first effort to give formal legal education on the GPL.

Current and ongoing activities

The GNU project

The original purpose of the FSF was to promote the ideals of free software. The organization developed the GNU operating system as an example of this.

GNU licenses

The GNU General Public License (GPL) is a widely used license for free software projects. The current version (version 3) was released in June 2007. The FSF has also published the GNU Lesser General Public License (LGPL), the GNU Free Documentation License (GFDL), and the GNU Affero General Public License (AGPL).

GNU Press

The FSF's publishing department, responsible for "publishing affordable books on computer science using freely distributable licenses."

The Free Software Directory

This is a listing of software packages that have been verified as free software. Each package entry contains 47 pieces of information such as the project's homepage, developers, programming language, etc.

The goals are to provide a search engine for free software, and to provide a cross-reference for users to check if a package has been verified as being free software. FSF has received a small amount of funding from UNESCO for this project. It is hoped that the directory can be translated into many languages in the future.

Maintaining the Free Software Definition

FSF maintains many of the documents that define the free software movement.

Project hosting

FSF hosts software development projects on their Savannah website.

Political campaigns

FSF sponsors a number of campaigns against what it perceives as dangers to software freedom, including software patents, digital rights management (which the FSF has re-termed "digital restrictions management", as part of their effort to highlight their view that such technologies are "designed to take away and limit your rights,") and user interface copyright. Defective by Design is an FSF-initiated campaign against DRM. They also have a campaign to promote Ogg+Vorbis, a free alternative to proprietary formats like MP3 and AAC. They also sponsor some free software projects that are deemed to be "high-priority".

Annual awards

"Award for the Advancement of Free Software" and "Free Software Award for Projects of Social Benefit"

High priority projects

The FSF maintains a list of "high priority projects" to which the Foundation claims that "there is a vital need to draw the free software community's attention". The FSF considers these projects "important because computer users are continually being seduced into using non-free software, because there is no adequate free replacement."

Previous projects highlighted as needing work included the Free Java implementations, GNU Classpath, and GNU Compiler for Java, which ensure compatibility for the Java part of OpenOffice.org, and the GNOME desktop environment (see Java: Licensing).

The effort has been criticized for either not instigating active development or for being slow at the work being done, even after certain projects were added to the list.

Recognition

- 1999: Linus Torvalds for Open Source Computing
- 2005: Prix Ars Electronica Award of Distinction in the category of "Digital Communities"

Structure

The FSF's board of directors includes:

- Hal Abelson, Founding member, Professor of Computer Science at the Massachusetts Institute of Technology (served from inception until March 5, 1998, and rejoined circa 2005)
- Geoffery Knauth, Senior Software Engineer at SFA, Inc. (served since October 23, 1997)
- Henry Poole, Founder of CivicActions, a grassroots campaign technology consulting firm. (served since December 12, 2002)
- Richard Stallman, Founding President, launched the GNU project, author of the GNU General Public License (served as President since inception)

- Gerald Jay Sussman, Professor of Computer Science at the Massachusetts Institute of Technology (served since inception)
- Benjamin Mako Hill, graduate student at the MIT Media Lab (served since July 25, 2007)
- Bradley Kuhn, Executive Director of the Software Freedom Conservancy and FSF's former Executive Director (served since March 25, 2010)

Previous board members include:

- Lawrence Lessig, Professor of Law at Stanford University (served from March 28, 2004 until 2008)
- Robert J. Chassell, Founding Treasurer, as well as a Founding Director (served from inception until June 3, 1997)
- Len Tower Jr., Founding member, (served until September 2, 1997)
- Miguel de Icaza (served from August 1999 until February 25, 2002)

The FSF Board of Directors is elected by the Voting Membership, whose powers include at least this are outlined in the by-laws:

In addition to the right to elect Directors as provided in the by-laws and such other powers and rights as may be vested in them by law, these Articles of Organization or the by-laws, the Voting Members shall have such other powers and rights as the Directors may designate.

Articles of Amendment, Free Software Foundation, Inc. There are currently no known documents available that indicate the composition of the FSF's Voting Membership.

John Sullivan is the current FSF Executive Director. Previous members that occupied the position were Peter Brown (2005-2010) and Bradley M. Kuhn (2001-2005). At any given time, there are usually around a dozen employees. Most, but not all, work at the FSF headquarters in Boston, Massachusetts.

Eben Moglen and Dan Ravicher previously served individually as pro bono legal counsel to the FSF. Since the forming of the Software Freedom Law Center, legal services to the FSF are provided by that organization.

On November 25, 2002, the FSF launched the FSF Associate Membership program for individuals. Bradley M. Kuhn (FSF Executive Director, 2001-2005) launched the program and also signed up as the first Associate Member Associate members hold a purely honorary and funding support role to the FSF.

GNOME

The GNOME Foundation is a non-profit organization based in Cambridge, Massachusetts, United States, coordinating the efforts in the GNOME project.

Purpose

The GNOME Foundation works to further the goal of the GNOME project: to create a computing platform for use by the general public that is composed entirely of free software. It was founded on 15 August 2000 by Compaq, Eazel, Helix Code, IBM, Red Hat, Sun Microsystems and VA Linux Systems.

To achieve this goal, the Foundation coordinates releases of GNOME and determines which projects are a part of GNOME. The Foundation acts as an official voice for the GNOME project, providing a means of communication with the press and with commercial and noncommercial organizations interested in GNOME software.

The foundation produces educational materials and documentation to help the public learn about GNOME software.

In addition, it sponsors GNOME-related technical conferences, such as GUADEC, GNOME.Asia, and the Boston Summit, represents GNOME at relevant conferences sponsored by others, helps create technical standards for the project, and promotes the use and development of GNOME software.

Management

As of June 2011, Karen Sandler is the Foundation's executive director. The Executive Director is selected and hired by the GNOME Board of Directors.

Board of directors

The Foundation's Board of Directors is elected every year via elections held by the GNOME Foundation Election Committee. Current (since July 2013) Board Members are Emmanuele Bassi, Joanmarie Diggs, Ekaterina Gerasimova, Tobias Mueller, Andreas Nilsson, Sriram Ramkrishna, and Marina Zhurakhinskaya.

Notable former board members

- Nat Friedman (2001-2003)
- Jim Gettys (2000-2002)
- Miguel de Icaza (2000-2002)
- Raph Levien (2000-2001)
- Michael Meeks (2001)
- Federico Mena Quintero (2000-2001, 2004-2005)
- Havoc Pennington (2000-2001)
- Luis Villa (2002-2006, 2008-2009)

Membership

All GNOME contributors can apply for Foundation membership. All members are eligible to stand for the Board of Directors, vote in Board elections and suggest referendum for voting.

Advisory board

The Foundation's Advisory Board is a body of organizations and companies that wish to communicate and work closely with the Board of Directors and the GNOME project. Organizations may join the advisory board for an annual fee of between US$5000 and US$10000, or be invited as a non-profit. As of 2010, Advisory Board members include: Canonical Ltd., Debian, Free Software Foundation, Google, Hewlett-Packard, IBM, Igalia, Intel, Motorola, Mozilla Foundation, Nokia, Novell, OLPC, Red Hat, Software Freedom Law Center, Sugar Labs and Sun Microsystems.

KDE COMMUNITY

KDE is an international free software community producing an integrated set of cross-platform applications designed to run on Linux, FreeBSD, Solaris, Microsoft Windows, and OS X systems. It is known for its Plasma Desktop, a desktop environment provided as the default working environment on many Linux distributions, such as openSUSE, Mageia and Kubuntu and is default desktop environment on PC-BSD a BSD operating system.

The goal of the community is to provide basic desktop functions and applications for daily needs as well as tools and documentation for developers to write stand-alone applications for the system. In this regard, the KDE project serves as an umbrella project for many standalone applications and smaller projects that are based on KDE technology. These include Calligra Suite, digiKam, Rekonq, K3b, and many others.

KDE software is based on the Qt framework. The original GPL version of this toolkit only existed for the X11 platform, but with the release of Qt 4, LGPL versions are available for all platforms. This allows KDE software based on Qt 4 to also be distributed to Microsoft Windows and OS X.

History

Origins

K Desktop Environment (KDE) was founded in 1996 by Matthias Ettrich, who was then a student at the Eberhard Karls University of Tübingen. At the time, he was troubled by certain aspects of the Unix desktop. Among his concerns was that none of the applications looked, felt, or worked alike. He proposed the creation of not merely a set of applications but a desktop environment in which users could expect things to look, feel, and work consistently. He also wanted to make this desktop easy to use; one of his complaints about desktop applications of the time was that his girlfriend deemed them too complicated to use. His initial Usenet post spurred a lot of interest, and the KDE project was born.

The name KDE was intended as a wordplay on the existing Common Desktop Environment, available for Unix systems. CDE is an X11-based user environment jointly developed by HP, IBM, and Sun through the X/Open consortium, with an interface and productivity tools based on the Motif graphical widget toolkit. It was supposed to be an intuitively easy-to-use desktop computer environment. The K was originally suggested to stand for "Kool", but it was quickly decided that the K should stand for nothing in particular. The KDE initialism is therefore expanded to "K Desktop Environment".

Licensing

In November 1998, the Qt framework was dual-licensed under the free and open source Q Public License (QPL) and a commercial license for proprietary software developers. The same year, the KDE Free Qt foundation was created which guarantees that Qt would fall under a variant of the very liberal BSD license should Trolltech cease to exist or no free version of Qt be released during 12 months.

Debate continued about compatibility with the GNU General Public License (GPL), hence in September 2000 Trolltech made the Unix version of the Qt libraries available under the GPL in addition to the QPL which eliminated the concerns of the Free Software Foundation. Trolltech continued to require licenses for developing proprietary software with Qt. The core libraries of KDE are collectively licensed under the GNU LGPL but the only way for proprietary software to make use of them was to be developed under the terms of the Qt proprietary license.

Starting with Qt 4.5, Qt was also made available under the LGPL version 2.1, now allowing proprietary applications to legally use the open source Qt version.

Brand repositioning

On 24 November 2009 the KDE Marketing Team announced a rebranding of the KDE project components, motivated by the perceived shift from building a desktop environment to a complete project around a community of "people who create software". The rebranding focused on de-emphasizing the desktop environment as "just another product", and emphasizing both the community and the other technologies provided as KDE software. After the repositioning, the name KDE no longer stands for K Desktop Environment, as it now acts as an umbrella brand for software produced by the community. What would have been previously known as KDE 4 will now be referred as "KDE Software Compilation 4" (abbreviated "KDE SC 4"). Regardless, many users still refer to it as KDE 4.

Community structure

Organization

The financial and legal matters of KDE are handled by KDE e.V., which is a German non-profit organization, and help organizing the conferences and meetings of the community members is also handled by the organization. KDE e.V. helps run the servers needed by the KDE community. It owns the trademark on KDE and the logo. It pays for travel to meetings and subsidizes events. The working groups are a structure which will formalize some roles within KDE and enhance coordination within KDE and communication between parts of KDE. KDE e.V. has no influence on development. KDE e.V. logo has been contributed by David Vignoni. The three flags on top of the logo represent the three main tasks of the KDE e.V.: supporting the community, representing the community, and governing the community.

The KDE community's developer meetings, servers, and related events are frequently sponsored by individuals, universities, and businesses. The supporting members of the KDE e.V. are extraordinary members supporting the KDE through financial or material contributions. Supporting members are entitled to display the "Member of KDE" logo on their website or in printed materials. The Patron of KDE is the highest level of supporting member. The patrons of KDE also are entitled to display the exclusive "Patron of KDE" logo on their website or in printed materials. On 15 October 2006, it was announced that Mark Shuttleworth had become the first Patron of KDE. On 7 July 2007, it was announced that Intel Corporation and Novell had also become patrons of KDE. In January 2010, Google became a supporting member. On 9 June 2010, KDE e.V. launched the "Join the Game" campaign.

This campaign promotes the idea of becoming a supporting member for individuals. It is made available for those who would like to support KDE, but do not have enough time to do so. Georg Greve, founder of the Free Software Foundation Europe (FSFE) was first to 'join the game'.

Local community

In many countries, KDE has local branches. These are either informal organizations (KDE India) or like the KDE e.V., given a legal form (KDE France). The local organizations host and maintain regional websites, and organise local events, such as tradeshows, contributor meetings and social community meetings.

KDE-AR (KDE Argentina) is the group of KDE developers and users in Argentina, and was officially opened in 22 November 2008 at a meeting in an IRC channel. They organise release parties on holidays to celebrate releases of new versions of the KDE SC since 4.2. KDE-AR has an own mailing lists and an IRC channel.

KDE Brasil is composed by several local groups in Brazil, like KDE-MG, Live Blue, KDE Piauí, and KDE-RS. The main goals of local groups are regional promotion and direction of contributions of members, and still maintaining harmony with the KDE Brazil community. KDE-MG is a local group in Minas Gerais.

The idea of structuring the group has arisen during the FISL (Fórum Internacional Software Livre) 10. Live Blue is a KDE working group in Bahia. KDE Piauí is a group of users and contributors of KDE in the Piauí. The idea was born during the Software Freedom Day Teresina 2009 and has concretized during the Akademy-Br 2010, where the group was officially created. KDE-RS is a group of KDE users from Rio Grande do Sul. KDE Lovelace is a Brazilian female group of users and contributors in KDE.

KDE España was registered as an association under the Spanish law in 2009. The aim is stimulating the development and use of the KDE software in Spain. Its supreme governing body is the general assembly. Ordinary as well as extraordinary general assemblies canbe held. An ordinary general assembly is held at least once a year. Extraordinary general assemblies are held as necessary. The board consists of the president, the vice president, the secretary, the treasurer and members. In the current board are Aleix Pol i Gonzàlez (president), Alejandro Fiestas Olivares (vice president), Víctor Blázquez Francisco (secretary), and José Millán Soto (treasurer). In addition, KDE España is the official representative of KDE e.V. in Spain.

KDE.in (KDE India), founded in 2005, provides Indian KDE developers and users with a community hub to coordinate with and support each other. Besides making efforts in the internationalization and localization, a major aim is to foster the creation and adaptation of KDE applications to needs specific to India.

Japan KDE Users' Group is the Japanese local users' group of KDE. The membership types of the association are corporate members and individual members. About 15 members form the active staff. The officers include one president, two vice presidents and one accountant. Currently, president is Daisuke Kameda, vice presidents are Taiki Komoda and Satoru Sat?. The association holds an annual general assembly in December. Its activities include message translation to Japanese, making patches for multilingualization, and exchanging information about KDE/Qt.

KDE GB is a KDE community with a constitution in Britain. At their meeting in October 2010 they agreed to register as a charity. KDE-ir (????? KDE) is a Persian KDE community. Korean KDE Users Group was started in 1999. The group's work is mostly translation.

KDE România is a community founded in Romania in 2013.

Communication

Communication within the community takes place via mailing lists, IRC, blogs, forums, news announcements, wikis and conferences. The community has a Code of Conduct for acceptable behavior within the community.

The mailing lists are one of the main channels of communication. The Kde list is for user discussion and Kde-announce for version updates, security patches and other changes. The general development lists are Kde-devel, for developer communication, and Kde-core-devel, used to discuss development of the KDE Platform. Many applications have individual mailing lists.

The KDE Community Forums are actively used. "KDE Brainstorm", allows users to submit ideas to developers. The request can then be considered by other users. Every few months, the highest-voted features are submitted to developers. IRC bots that announce new threads and posts on IRC channels, by braiding forum posts into mailinglist messages and by offering RSS feeds.

KDE has three wikis: UserBase, TechBase and Community Wiki. UserBase provides documentation for end users. It contains tutorials, links to help and an application catalogue. The logo was designed by Eugene Trounev. TechBase provides technical documentation for developers and system administrators. Community Wiki coordinates community teams. It is used for publishing and sharing community-internal information.

IRC channels provide real-time discussions. Planet KDE is made from the blogs of KDE's contributors. KDE.News is the website of office news announcements. KDE Buzz tracks identi.ca, Twitter, Picasa, Flickr and

YouTube to show social media activity concerning KDE. KDE Pastebin allows for posting of source code snippets and provides syntax highlighting to ease reviewing code. Sections can be password protected. RSS notifies of new posts. KDE Bug Tracking System uses Bugzilla to manage reports and fixes. "Behind KDE" offers interviews of contributor KDE contributors.

Identity

The KDE community's mascot is a green dragon named Konqi. Konqi has a girlfriend named Katie. Konqi and Katie made their costumed appearance at the KDE 4.0 Release Event and Camp KDE 2010. Konqi also appears on the KDE software's about dialog. Kandalf the wizard was the former mascot for the KDE community during its 1.x and 2.x versions, but he was dropped owing to copyright issues (his resemblance to Gandalf).

KDE has community identity guidelines (CIG) for definitions and recommendations which help the community to establish a unique, characteristic, and appealing design. The KDE official logo displays the white trademarked K-Gear shape on a blue square with mitred corners.Copying of the KDE Logo is subject to the LGPL. Some local community logos are derivations of the official logo. The KDE software labels are used by producers of software to show that they are part of the KDE community or that they use the KDE Platform. There are three labels available. The Powered by KDE label is used to show that an application derives its strength from the KDE community and from the KDE development platform. The Built on the KDE Platform label indicates that the application uses the KDE platform. The Part of the KDE family label is used by application authors to identify themselves as being part of the KDE community.

Many KDE applications have a K in the name, mostly as an initial letter. The K in many KDE applications is obtained by spelling a word which originally begins with C or Q differently, for example Konsole and Kaffeine. Also, some just prefix a commonly used word with a K, for instance KGet. Among KDE SC 4 applications and technologies, however, the trend is not to have a K in the name at all, such as Stage and Dolphin.

Contributors

Like many free/open source software projects, KDE is primarily a volunteer effort, although various companies, such as Novell, Nokia, and Mandriva, employ developers to work on the project. Since a large number of individuals contribute to KDE in various ways (e.g. code, translation, artwork), organization of such a project is complex.

Development

The overall direction of the KDE Platform is made on the KDE Core Team. These are developers who have made significant contributions to KDE over a long period of time. This team communicates using the kde-core-devel mailing list, which is publicly archived and readable, but joining requires approval. KDE does not have a single central leader who can veto important decisions. Instead, the KDE core team consisting of several dozen contributors takes decisions. The decisions do not take a formal vote, but through discussions. The Developers also organize alongside topical teams. For example, the KDE Edu team develops free educational software. While these teams work mostly independent and do not all follow a common release schedule. Each team has its own messaging channels, both on IRC and on the mailinglists. And they have mentor program which helps beginner to get start.

Currently KDE community uses the Git repository. The KDE Projects site gives an overview of all projects within Git repository. QuickGit is another repository browser. It shows all the Git repositories. ReviewBoard site gives patch review. Commitfilter will send an email with each commit for the projects you want to watch, without either getting tons of mails or getting infrequent and redundant information. English Breakfast Network (EBN) is a collection of machines that do automated KDE source artifact quality checking. The EBN provides KDE API documentation validation, user documentation validation, source code checking. It is operated by Adriaan de Groot and Allen Winter. Commit-Digest site gives a weekly overview of the development activity. LXR indexes classes and methods used in KDE.

Season of KDE (SoK) is a program for people could not get accepted into Google Summer of Code. They will have a mentor from the KDE community to help them if any question arises or if they do not know how to continue.

On 20 July 2009, KDE announced that the one millionth commit has been made to its Subversion repository. On October 11, 2009, Cornelius Schumacher, a main developer within KDE, wrote about the estimated cost (using the COCOMO model with SLOCCount) to develop KDE software package with 4,273,291 LoC, which would be about US$175,364,716. This estimation does not include Qt, Calligra Suite, Amarok, Digikam, and other applications that are not part of KDE core.

The work can be measured in figures:

- Over 6 million lines of code. This does not include Qt.
- More than 1800 contributors help develop KDE. About 20 new developers contribute their first code each month.

- KDE is translated in over 108 languages.
- KDE has more than 114 official FTP mirrors in over 34 countries.
- The KDE community is the second largest Free Software community behind the Linux kernel community.

Other groups

The KDE community has many smaller teams working towards specific goals. The Accessibility team make KDE accessible to all users, including those with physical handicaps. The Artists team has designed most of the artwork used by the software like icons, wallpapers and themes. They have also produced graphics for t-shirts and websites. Discuss of the team is most active on the IRC channel. The Bugsquad team keeps track of incoming bugs.

They verify that a bug exists, that it is reproducible, and that the reporter has given enough information. The goal is to help developers notice valid bugs quicker, and to save their time. The Documentation team writing documentation for application. The team uses the DocBook format and custom tools to create documentation. The Localization team translate KDE software into many different languages. This team works beside the Documentation team. The Marketing and Promotion team manages marketing and promotion.

The team writes news articles, release announcements and other webpages on KDE websites. The articles of KDE.News is submitted by the team. It also has channels at social media sites for communication and promotion. They also attend conference events. The Research team is to improve the collaboration with external parties to achieve more funded research.

They support community members by providing information, navigating bureaucracies, and matching research partners. The usability team has written a Human Interface Guideline (HIG) for the developers and they do regular reviews of KDE applications. The HIG provides a standardized layout. The Web team maintains KDE's web presence. The KDE Women help women to contribute and encourage women to give talks at conferences.

The Release team defines and executes the official software releases. The Team is responsible for setting release schedules for the official releases. This includes release dates, deadlines for individual release steps and restrictions for code changes. The Release Team coordinates release dates with the marketing and press efforts of KDE. The release team is composed of Module Coordinators, Marketing Team liaison, and the people who actually do the work of tagging and creating the releases.

Activities

The two most important conferences of KDE are Akademy and Camp KDE. Each event is on a large scale, both thematically and geographically. Akademy-BR and Akademy-es are local community events.

Akademy

Akademy is the annual world summit, held each summer at varying venues in Europe. The primary goals of Akademy are to act as a community building event, to communicate the achievements of community, and to provide a platform for collaboration with community and industry partners. Secondary goals are to engage local people, and to provide space for getting together to write code. KDE e.V. assist with procedures, advice and organization. Akademy including conference, KDE e.V. general assembly, marathon coding sessions, BOFs (birds of a feather sessions) and social program. BOFs are meet to discuss specific sub-projects or issues.

The KDE community held KDE One that was first conference in Arnsberg, Germany in 1997 to discuss the first KDE release. Initially, each conference was numbered after the release, and not regular hold. Since 2003 the conferences were hold one a year. And they were named Akademy since 2004.

The yearly Akademy conference gives Akademy Awards, are awards that the KDE community gives to KDE contributors. Their purpose is to recognize outstanding contribution to KDE. There are three awards, best application, best non-application and jury's award. As always the winners are chosen by the winners from the previous year. First winners received a framed picture of Konqi signed by all attending KDE developers.

Camp KDE

Camp KDE is another annual contributor's conference of the KDE community. The event provides a regional opportunity for contributors and enthusiasts to gather and share their experiences. It's free to all participants. It is intended to ensure that KDE in the world is not simply seen as being Euro-centric. The KDE e.V. helps travel and accommodation subsidies for presenters, BoF leaders, organizers or core contributor. It is held in the North America since 2009.

In January 2008, KDE 4.0 Release Event was held at the Google headquarters in Mountain View, California, USA to celebrate the release of KDE SC 4.0. The community realized that there was a strong demand for KDE events in the Americas, therefore Camp KDE was produced.

Camp KDE 2009 was the premiere meeting of the KDE Americas, was held at the Travellers Beach Resort in Negril, Jamaica, sponsored by Google, Inte, iXsystem, KDE e.V. and Kitware. The event included 1-2 days of presentations, BoF meetings and hackathon sessions. Camp KDE 2010 took place at the University of California San Diego (UCSD) in La Jolla, USA. The schedule included presentations, BoFs, hackathons and a day trip. It started with a short introduction by Jeff Mitchell, who was the principal organizer of the conference, talked a bit of history about Camp KDE and some statistics about the KDE community.

The talks of the event were relatively well attended, and an increase over the previous year to around 70 people. On 1/19, the social event was a tour of a local brewery. Camp KDE 2011 was held at Hotel Kabuki in San Francisco, USA, was co-located with the Linux Foundation Collaboration Summit. The schedule included presentations, hackathons and a party at Noisebridge. The conference opened with an introduction spoken by Celeste Lyn Paul.

Akademy-es

Akademy-es is a conference for Spanish community since 2006, aimed at Spanish speakers. The event is organized by Spanish local organization. KDE España organizes the event since 2008. The annual KDE España Assembly took place during the event.

Akademy-es 2006 was held at Espai Jove Bocanord in Barcelona, organized by Badopi. Akademy-es 2007 was hosted by Hispalinux, Wireless Zaragoza, and the Zaragoza council.

Akademy-es 2008 was held at University of A Coruña, was organized by the KDE España and GPUL, sponsored by Oficina de Software Libre da Universidade da Coruña, Mancomun, Igalia, Qt Software and eyeOs. Akademy-es 2009 was held in the University of Las Palmas de Gran Canaria.

Akademy-es 2010 was held in the Engineering Technical School of Bilbao, was organized by KDE España and Itsas. There were approximately 80 participants. The KDE España Assembly elected the new board consists of Albert Astals Cid (president), Rafael Fernández López (vice president), Aleix Pol (secretary), and José Millán Soto (treasurer). Akademy-es 2011 was organized by KDE España, was sponsored by Google and Nokia, and was supported by the Linux and Todo-Linux magazines. The event was held in the in two different locations: the Polytechnic University of Catalunya for presentations of fist day, The School of Sant Marc de Sarrià for last two day.

Other community events

Akademy-BR is addressed to Brazilian community since 2010. The purpose of the meeting is to gather and organize ideas Brazilian developers on how to help KDE in Brazil. Akademy-BR 2010 was organized by the local group named LiveBlue. There were thirty participants from all over Brazil. Akademy-BR 2011 is organized by KDE-MG.

Akademy-BR

Year	Venue	Date
2010	Salvador	4/9-4/11
2011	São Paulo	11/12-11/15

Conf.KDE.in

Year	Venue	Date
2011	Bengaluru	3/9-3/13

conf.kde.in was the first KDE and Qt conference in India. The conference was organized by KDE India, was held at R.V. College of Engineering in Bengaluru, India. The first three days of the event had talks, tutorials and interactive sessions. The last two days were a focused code sprint. The conference was opened by its main organiser Pradeepto Bhattacharya, over 300 people were at the opening talks.

The Lighting of the Auspicious Lamp ceremony was performed to open the conference. The first session was by Lydia Pintscher who talk "So much to do - so little time". At the event, Project Neon announced return on Mar 11, 2011, provides nightly builds of the KDE Software Compilation. Closing the conference was keynote speaker and old-time KDE developer Sirtaj.

Día KDE (KDE Day) is an Argentinian event focused on KDE. It gives talks and workshops. The purpose of the event are: spread the free software movement among the population of Argentina, bringing to it the KDE community and environment developed by it, to know and strengthen KDE-AR, and generally bring the community together to have fun. The event is free.

Dia KLDE

Year	Venue	Date
2011	Rosario	8/27

Release party is a party, which celebrates released of new version of the KDE SC (twice a year). KDE also participates other conferences that around free software.

Developer Sprints

In addition to Camp KDE and Akademy there are other conferences, which is called Developer Sprints. The Developer Sprints are focused gatherings of developers to work on a specific part of KDE. Usually there are 2-3 days meetings of around 10-15 people. The Developer Sprints include core people, but also least one or two newbie quota to get fresh developers into the community. They are supported by KDE e.V. financially and organizationally. It will also provide help and advice where needed and appropriate. The results of meetings are documented on the KDE.News. They also create a sprint landing page on the community wiki, which give a brief summary of the sprint and link to relevant material.

Promo sprint

Year	Venue	Date
2009	Stuttgart, Germany	
2011	Southampton, England	5/6-5/8

KDE PIM Meeting is the annual meeting of KDE PIM team, held in Osnabrück, Germany since 2003. Akonadi Sprint is another meeting of KDE PIM team since 2007; it focus on Akonadi. Calligra Sprint is the meeting of designers and developers of Calligra Suite. Usually the meetings are held in Berlin, Germany. Krita Sprint is the meeting of Krita team since 2009. KDE Education Meeting is the meeting of KDE Edu team. KDE Marble sprint is the meeting of Marble team, held in Nürnberg, Germany. KDE Games Sprint is the meeting of KDE Games team. KDE Imaging Sprint is a sprint for KDE photography applications. Tokamak is the meeting of designers and developers of Plasma, KWin, and Oxygen since 2008. KDE Finances Sprint is the meeting of developers from KMyMoney, Kraft and Skrooge. Promo sprint is the meeting, which discuses KDE Marketing and Promo.

Technology platform

The KDE technology platform consists of three parts: KDE Development Platform, KDE Workspace and KDE Applications.

KDE Platform

KDE Platform consists of the libraries and services needed to run KDE applications. Libraries include: Solid, Nepomuk, Phonon, etc. Packages include: kdelibs, kdepimlibs and kdebase-runtime. The libraries must be licensed under one of the LGPL, BSD license, MIT License and X11 license.

While the KDE Platform is mainly written in C++, it includes bindings for other programming languages. Bindings use the following generic technologies:

- Smoke: for creating bindings for Ruby, C# and PHP;
- SIP: for creating bindings for Python;

- Kross: Embedded scripting for C++ applications, with support for Ruby, Python, JavaScript, QtScript, Falcon and Java are supported

Stable and mature bindings available for the following programming languages:

- Python
- Ruby (Korundum, built on top of QtRuby)
- C#
- Perl

Plasma Workspaces

The Plasma Workspaces provide the environment for running and managing applications. They include many components such as KWin, KDM, Plasma core libraries, Klipper, KSysguard, and System Settings. There are different available GUI environments: Plasma Desktop for desktop computers, Plasma Netbook for netbooks, and "Plasma Active" for smartphones and tablets.

KDE Applications

KDE Applications are built on top of the KDE Platform like Okular, KTorrent, Kexi and KDE Partition Manager. KDE applications can potentially be portable between operating systems and independent of a particular workspace or desktop environment. Some brands identify application suites built up from several applications, such as KDE Network, KDE Graphics and KDE Utilities. Some applications are part of the regular Software Compilation releases, others are part of Extragear and release to their own schedule.

Implementation

Most KDE software uses the Qt framework which runs on most Unix and Unix-like systems (including OS X), and Microsoft Windows. As of 2011 CMake serves as the build tool. This allows KDE to support a wider range of platforms, including Windows. GNU gettext is used for translation. Doxygen is used to generate api documentation.

- KDE Software Compilation: KDE Software Compilation (KDE SC) is the coordinated releases of new software versions, gathering elements from the previous components to build an integrated core of software. The KDE SC is not a product as a single entity.
- Calligra Suite: Integrated office suite.
- KDEWebdev: Web development tools.
- KDE-Extragear: Extragear is a collection of applications associated with KDE. Those applications are not part the official software compilation, but they are still part of the project.

- KDE-Playground: This package contains pre-release and unstable software. It is a place for applications to mature.

COLLABORATIONS WITH OTHER ORGANIZATIONS

Wikimedia

On 23 June 2005, chairman of the Wikimedia Foundation announced that the KDE community and the Wikimedia Foundation have begun efforts towards cooperation.

Fruits of that cooperation are MediaWiki syntax highlighting in Kate and accessing Wikipedia content within KDE applications, such as Amarok and Marble.

On 4 April 2008, the KDE e.V. and Wikimedia Deutschland opened shared offices in Frankfurt. In September 2009 KDE e.V. moved to shared offices with Free Software Foundation Europe in Berlin.

Free Software Foundation Europe

In May 2006, KDE e.V. became an Associate Member of the Free Software Foundation Europe (FSFE).

On 22 August 2008, KDE e.V. and FSFE jointly announced that after working with FSFE's Freedom Task Force for one and a half years KDE adopts FSFE's Fiduciary Licence Agreement. Using that, KDE developers can - on a voluntary basis - assign their copyrights to KDE e.V.

In September 2009, KDE e.V. and FSFE moved into shared offices in Berlin.

Commercial enterprises

Several companies actively contribute to KDE, like Collabora, Erfrakon, Intevation GmbH, Kolab Konsortium, Klarälvdalens Datakonsult AB (KDAB), Blue Systems, and KO GmbH.

Nokia used Calligra Suite as base for their Office Viewer application for Maemo/MeeGo. They have also been contracting KO GmbH to bring MS Office 2007 file format filters to Calligra.

Nokia also employed several KDE developers directly - either to use KDE software for MeeGo (e.g. KCal) or as sponsorship.

The software development and consulting companies Intevation GmbH of Germany and the Swedish KDAB use Qt and KDE software - especially Kontact and Akonadi for Kolab - for their services and products, therefore both employ KDE developers.

Others

KDE participates in freedesktop.org, an effort to standardize Unix desktop interoperability.

Since 2009, GNOME and KDE co-host their conferences Akademy and GUADEC every two years under the Desktop Summit label.

In December 2010 KDE e.V. became a licensee of the Open Invention Network.

Many Linux distributions and other free operating systems are involved in the development and distribution of the software, and are therefore also active in the KDE community. These include commercial distributors such as SUSE/Novell or Red Hat but also government-funded non-commercial organizations such as the Scientific and Technological Research Council of Turkey with its Linux distribution Pardus.

Notable uses

Brazil's primary school education system operates computers running KDE software, with more than 42,000 schools in 4,000 cities, thus serving nearly 52 million children. The base distribution is called Educational Linux, which is based on Kubuntu.

Besides this, thousands more students in Brazil use KDE products in their universities. KDE software is also running on computers in Portuguese and Venezuelan schools, with respectively 700,000 and one million systems reached.

Germany uses KDE software in its embassies around the world, representing around 11,000 systems.

Through use of Pardus, a local Linux distribution, many sections of the Turkish government make use of KDE software, including the Turkish Armed Forces, Ministry of Foreign Affairs, Ministry of National Defence, Turkish Police, and the SGK (Social Security Institution of Turkey), although these departments often do not exclusively use Pardus as their operating system. The CERN (European Organization for Nuclear Research) is using KDE software.

kernel.org

kernel.org is a main repository of source code for the Linux kernel, the base of the popular Linux operating system. It makes all versions of the source code available to all users. It also hosts various other projects, like Google Android. The main purpose of the site is to host a repository for Linux kernel developers and maintainers of Linux distributions.

2011 attack

On 28 August 2011, developers at www.kernel.org realized that there had been a major security breach. Hackers had gained root access to the system and added a trojan to the startup scripts. Developers reinstalled all the servers and investigated the origin of the attack. It is likely, though not yet known, whether this is related to the LinuxFoundation.org and Linux.com website hacks found shortly afterwards.

Git, a distributed (and thus open) source management system designed to guarantee the integrity of the source code is used to keep track of changes in the Linux source code. This and the fact that the source code is available to anyone and widely known makes any attempt to tamper with the source code fairly easy to detect and revert if required.

kernel.org is not the primary repository, but rather a distribution point of the kernel sources.

As of November 2011, kernel.org is completely back up with the exception of a few secondary services.

As of September 2013, the site maintainers still have not published a report of how the breach occurred.

LINUX FOUNDATION

The Linux Foundation (LF) is a non-profit technology consortium chartered to foster the growth of Linux. Founded in 2007 by the merger of the Open Source Development Labs (OSDL) and the Free Standards Group (FSG), the Linux Foundation sponsors the work of Linux creator Linus Torvalds and is supported by leading Linux and open source companies, including prominent technology corporations such as Fujitsu, HP, IBM, Intel, NEC, Oracle, Qualcomm and Samsung, and developers from around the world.

The Linux Foundation promotes, protects, and standardizes Linux "by providing a comprehensive set of services to compete effectively with closed platforms."

History

On September 11, 2011, The Linux Foundation's website was taken down due to a breach discovered 27 days prior, including but limited to all attendant subdomains of The Linux Foundation, such as Linux.com. Major parts including OpenPrinting were still offline on October 20, 2011. The restoration was complete on January 4, 2012 (although one site, the Linux Developer Network, will not be restored).

Goals

The Linux Foundation serves as a neutral spokesperson for Linux and generates original content that advances the understanding of the Linux platform. It also fosters innovation by hosting collaboration events among the Linux technical community, application developers, industry, and end users to solve pressing issues facing Linux.

Through the Linux Foundation's community programs, end users, developers, and industry members collaborate on technical, legal, and promotional issues.

In order for Linux creator Linus Torvalds and other key kernel developers to remain independent, the Linux Foundation sponsors them so they can work full-time on improving Linux. The Linux Foundation also manages the Linux trademark, offers developers legal intellectual property protection, and coordinates industry and community legal collaboration and education.

The Linux Foundation offers application developers standardization services and support that makes Linux an attractive target for their development efforts. These include: the Linux Standard Base (LSB) and the Linux Developer Network.

The Linux Foundation supports the Linux community by offering technical information and education through its annual events, such as the Linux Collaboration Summit, the Linux Kernel Developers Summit, and the general LinuxCon event inaugurated in September 2009.

The Linux Foundation also provides services to key areas of the Linux community, including an open source developer travel fund and other administrative assistance.

Through its workgroups, members and developers can collaborate on key technical areas. There is also a training program that is vendor-neutral, technically advanced, and created with the actual leaders of the Linux development community.

PUBLICATIONS

Fields of activity

Linux.com

On March 3, 2009, the Linux Foundation announced that they would take over management of Linux.com from its previous owners, SourceForge, Inc.

The site was relaunched on May 13, 2009, shifting away from its previous incarnation as a news site to become a central source for Linux tutorials, information, software, documentation and answers across the server, desktop/netbook, mobile, and embedded areas. It also includes a directory of Linux software and hardware.

Much like Linux itself, Linux.com plans to rely on the community to create and drive the content and conversation.

Linux Videos

The Linux Foundation hosts a Linux video forum where users, developers and vendors can create and share Linux video tutorials. It also includes videos from recent Linux Foundation events, as well as other industry forums. It is the home for the annual Linux Foundation Video Contest. The Linux Foundation plans to add commissioned series of Linux video tutorials on Linux.com in the months ahead.

Linux Developer Network

The Linux Developer Network is an online community for Linux application developers and independent software vendors who want to start or continue to develop applications for the Linux platform. The Linux Developer Network's goal is to empower developers to target the Linux platform. One of the ways the Linux Developer Network helps developers accomplish this is to help them build portable Linux applications.

The Linux Developer Network also gives developers tools to create the best Linux apps possible, no matter which platform developers want to work with.

Training

The Linux Foundation Training Program features instructors and content straight from the leaders of the Linux developer community.

Attendees receive Linux training that is vendor-neutral, technically advanced and created with the actual leaders of the Linux development community themselves. The Linux Foundation Linux training courses, both online and in-person, give attendees the broad, foundational knowledge and networking needed to thrive in their careers.

Linux Standard Base

The Linux Standard Base, or LSB, is a joint project by several Linux distributions under the organizational structure of the Linux Foundation to standardize the software system structure, or filesystem hierarchy, used with Linux operating system. The LSB is based on the POSIX specification, the Single UNIX Specification, and several other open standards, but extends them in certain areas.

According to the LSB:

The goal of the LSB is to develop and promote a set of open standards that will increase compatibility among Linux distributions and enable software applications to run on any compliant system even in binary form. In addition, the LSB will help coordinate efforts to recruit software vendors to port and write products for Linux Operating System.

The LSB compliance may be certified for a product by a certification procedure.

The LSB specifies for example: standard libraries, a number of commands and utilities that extend the POSIX standard, the layout of the file system hierarchy, run levels, the printing system, including spoolers such as CUPS and tools like Foomatic and several extensions to the X Window System.

OpenPrinting

The OpenPrinting workgroup is a website belonging to the Linux Foundation which provides documentation and software support for printing under Linux. Formed as LinuxPrinting.org, in 2006 it became part of the Free Standards Group.

They developed a database that lists a wide variety of printers from various manufacturers. The database allows people to give a report on the support and quality of each printer, and they also give a report on the support given to Linux by each printer vendor. They have also created a foomatic (formerly cupsomatic) script which plugs into the Common Unix Printing System (CUPS).

Collaborative Projects

Linux Foundation Collaborative Projects. As of October 2013, the following "Collaborative Projects" were founded (alphabetical order)

Code Aurora Forum

Code Aurora Forum is a consortium of companies with projects serving the mobile wireless industry. Software projects it concerns itself with are e.g. Android for MSM, Femto Linux Project, LLVM, MSM WLAN and Linux-MSM.

FOSSBazaar

FOSSBazaar is an open community of technology and industry leaders who are collaborating to accelerate adoption of free and open-source software in the enterprise.

MeeGo

MeeGo was project to build a Linux kernel-based operating system for mobile devices and IVI. It was replaced by Tizen.

Open Virtualization Alliance (OVA)

The consortium was founded 2011. At the LinuxCon 2013 it was announced, that it has become a Linux Foundation Collaborative Project. Kernel-based Virtual Machine and oVirt.

bel

The Biological Expression Language (BEL) is a language for representing scientific findings in the life sciences in a computable form. OpenBEL powers SBVImprover Challenge 3. The goal of the Challenge is to perform peer review of a massive number of networks for lung biology. The key is using OpenBEL to represent the biology in a consistent open format that can be turned into a computationally tractable model

OpenDaylight

OpenDaylight is a community-led, open, industry-supported framework, for accelerating adoption, fostering new innovation, reducing risk and creating a more transparent approach to Software-Defined Networking

OpenMama

OpenMAMA (Open Middleware Agnostic Messaging API) is a lightweight vendor-neutral integration layer for systems built on top of a variety of message orientated middlewares.

Tizen

Tizen is a free and open-source, standards-based software platform supported by leading mobile operators, device manufacturers, and silicon suppliers for multiple device categories such as smartphones, tablets, netbooks, in-vehicle infotainment devices, and smart TVs.

Xen Project

The Xen Project team is a global open source community that develops the Xen Hypervisor, contributes to the Linux PVOPS framework, the Xen® Cloud Platform and Xen® ARM.

yocto Project

The Yocto Project is an open source collaboration project that provides templates, tools and methods to help you create custom Linux-based systems for embedded products regardless of the hardware architecture. It was founded in 2010 as a collaboration among many hardware manufacturers, open-source operating systems vendors, and electronics companies to bring some order to the chaos of embedded Linux development.

Members

By the end of April 2013, there are more than 180 corporate members who identify with the ideals & mission of the Linux Foundation:

1. Platinum Members (8), who each donate US$500,000 annually, incl. (listed alphabetically) Fujitsu Ltd, Hewlett-Packard Development Co. LP, Intel Corp., IBM Corp., NEC Corp., Oracle Corp., Qualcomm Innovation Center Inc. and Samsung Electronics Co. Ltd

2. Gold Members (14), who each donate US$100,000 annually, incl. (listed alphabetically) Advanced Micro Devices Inc., China Mobile Ltd, Cisco Systems Inc., Citrix Systems, Electronics and Telecommunications Research Inst., Google Inc., Hitachi Ltd, Huawei, Motorola Solutions Inc., NetApp Inc., NYSE Technologies, Panasonic Corp., SUSE and Toyota Motor Corp.

3. Silver Members (157), who each donate US$5,000-20,000 (scaling with number of employees) annually, e.g. (listed alphabetically) Adobe Systems Inc., ARM Holdings PLC, Broadcom Corp., Canonical Ltd, Dell Inc., DreamWorks Animation LLC, EMC Corp., Igalia S.L., Inktank, Lexmark International, Inc., LG Electronics Inc., MIPS Technologies Inc., Protecode Inc., Red Hat Inc., Renesas Electronics Corp., Siemens AG, Sony Corp., Texas Instruments Inc., Tieto, Twitter, Toshiba Corp., VMware Inc., et al.

Funding

Its funding comes primarily from its Platinum Members: Fujitsu, HP, IBM, Intel, NEC, Oracle, Qualcomm, and Samsung and for many years Hitachi. These nine each having a representative on the Board of Directors, they hold a majority on the 16-person board.

THE MOZILLA FOUNDATION

The Mozilla Foundation is a non-profit organization that exists to support and lead the open source Mozilla project. Founded in July 2003, the organization sets the policies that govern development, operates key infrastructure and controls Mozilla trademarks and copyrights. It owns a taxable subsidiary: the Mozilla Corporation, which employs many Mozilla developers and coordinates releases of the Mozilla Firefox web browser and Mozilla Thunderbird email client. The subsidiary is 100% owned by the parent, and therefore follows the same non-profit principles. The Mozilla Foundation was founded by the Netscape-affiliated Mozilla Organization, and is funded almost exclusively by Google Inc.

The organization is currently based in the Silicon Valley city of Mountain View, California, USA. The Mozilla Foundation describes itself as "a non-profit organization that promotes openness, innovation and participation on the Internet." The Mozilla Foundation is guided by the Mozilla Manifesto, which lists 10 principles which Mozilla believes "are critical for the Internet to continue to benefit the public good as well as commercial aspects of life."

History

On February 23, 1998, Netscape created the Mozilla Organization to co-ordinate the development of the Mozilla Application Suite. When AOL (Netscape's parent) drastically scaled back its involvement with Mozilla Organization, the Mozilla Foundation was launched on July 15, 2003 to ensure Mozilla could survive without Netscape. AOL assisted in the initial creation of the Mozilla Foundation, transferring hardware and intellectual property to the organization, employed a three-person team for the first three months of its existence to help with the transition, and donated $2 million to the Foundation over two years.

Initially, the remit of the Mozilla Foundation grew to become much wider than that of mozilla.org, with the organization taking on many tasks that were traditionally left to Netscape and other vendors of Mozilla technology. As part of a wider move to target end-users, the foundation made deals with commercial companies to sell CDs containing Mozilla software and provide telephone support.

In both cases, the group chose the same suppliers as Netscape for these services. The Mozilla Foundation also became more assertive over its intellectual property, with policies put in place for the use of Mozilla trademarks and logos. New projects such as marketing were also started.

With the formation of the Mozilla Corporation, the Mozilla Foundation delegated all their development and business-related activities to the new subsidiary. The Mozilla Foundation now focuses solely on governance and policy issues, though it also continues to oversee the projects that have not been "productized", such as Camino and SeaMonkey. The Mozilla Foundation owns the Mozilla trademarks and other intellectual property, which it licenses to the Mozilla Corporation. It also controls the Mozilla source code repository and decides who is allowed to check code in.

Subsidiaries

Mozilla Corporation

On 3 August 2005, the Mozilla Foundation announced the creation of Mozilla Corporation, described as "a taxable subsidiary that serves the non-profit, public benefit goals of its parent, the Mozilla Foundation, and that will be responsible for product development, marketing and distribution of Mozilla products." It also handles relationships with businesses, many of which generate income.

Unlike the Mozilla Foundation, the Mozilla Corporation is a tax-paying entity, which gives it much greater freedom in the revenue and business activities it can pursue. The majority of the revenues comes from Google Inc., which is the default search engine on Mozilla Firefox.

Beijing Mozilla Online Ltd

Beijing Mozilla Online Ltd, a.k.a. Mozilla China, is a wholly owned subsidiary of the Mozilla Corporation with its headquarters in Beijing.

Financing

The Mozilla Foundation is funded by donations and "search royalties". Since 2005, the vast majority of funds have come from Google Inc.

Initial funding in 2003 came from AOL, who donated US$2 million, and from Mitch Kapor who donated US$300,000. The group has tax-exempt status under section 501(c)(3) of the U.S. tax code, though the Mozilla Corporation subsidiary is taxable.

In 2006, the Mozilla Foundation received US$66.8 million in revenues, of which US$61.5 million is attributed to "search royalties" from Google.

The foundation has an ongoing deal with Google to make Google search the default in the Firefox browser search bar and hence send it search referrals; a Firefox themed Google search site has also been made the default home page of Firefox.

The original contract expired in November 2006. However, Google renewed the contract until November 2008 and again through 2011. On 20 December 2011 Mozilla announced that the contract was once again renewed for at least three years to November 2014, at three times the amount previously paid, or nearly US$300 million annually. Approximately 85% of Mozilla's revenue for 2006 was derived from this contract.

People

The Mozilla Foundation Board of Directors has six members:

- Mitchell Baker (Chair)
- Brian Behlendorf
- Brendan Eich
- Joichi Ito
- Bob Lisbonne
- Cathy Davidson

Originally, Christopher Blizzard had a seat on the board, but he moved to the Mozilla Corporation Board of Directors when it was established; Joichi Ito joined the Mozilla Foundation board at that time. Bob Lisbonne and Carl Malamud were elected to the board in October 2006.

The Mozilla Corporation also has a number of employees, many of whom worked for the foundation before the establishment of the corporation.

The Mozilla project has traditionally been overseen by a committee known as mozilla.org staff; some individuals on that committee later became Foundation or Corporation board members or employees.

Donations

In 2006, after a request from Theo de Raadt of OpenBSD for funding from corporate entities which make a profit through the use of OpenSSH in their packaged distributions, the Mozilla Foundation donated US$10,000 to de Raadt and OpenBSD for OpenSSH development.

The funds donated came from money earned through the income provided by Google. While the target of this request were corporations such as Cisco, IBM, HP, and Red Hat (which all sell operating systems containing OpenSSH but have not donated to its continued development before), the Mozilla Foundation found that without OpenSSH, much of the work done by developers would be through insecure and unsafe methods and thus gave the funds as a thank you.

At the end of 2010, the Mozilla Foundation partnered with Knoxville Zoo in an effort to raise awareness about endangered red pandas. Two red pandas (a.k.a. Firefox) cubs born at the Knoxville Zoo have officially become a part of the Mozilla community. The cubs are named Spark and Ember by online voters and Mozilla broadcast a 24 hour live video stream of the cubs for several months.

NetBSD

NetBSD is an open-source Unix-like operating system descended from Berkeley Software Distribution (BSD), a Unix derivative developed at the University of California, Berkeley. It was the second open-source BSD descendant to be formally released, after 386BSD, and it continues to be actively developed. The NetBSD project is primarily focused on high-quality design, stability and performance of the system. Due to its portability and Berkeley-style license, NetBSD is often used in embedded systems.

The current stable release of NetBSD is version 6.1.2 (30 September 2013).

History

NetBSD was originally derived from the 4.3BSD release of the Berkeley Software Distribution from the Computer Systems Research Group of the University of California, Berkeley, via their Net/2 source code release and the 386BSD project. The NetBSD project began as a result of frustration within the 386BSD developer community with the pace and direction of the operating system's development.

The four founders of the NetBSD project, Chris Demetriou, Theo de Raadt, Adam Glass and Charles Hannum, felt that a more open development model would be beneficial to the project: one which was centered on portable, clean, correct code. Their aim was to produce a unified, multi-platform, production-quality, BSD-based operating system. The name "NetBSD" was suggested by de Raadt, based on the importance and growth of networks such as the Internet at that time, and the distributed, collaborative nature of its development.

The NetBSD source code repository was established on 21 March 1993 and the first official release, NetBSD 0.8, was made in April, 1993. This was derived from 386BSD 0.1 plus the version 0.2.2 unofficial patchkit, with several programs from the Net/2 release missing from 386BSD re-integrated, and various other improvements.

The first multi-platform release, NetBSD 1.0, was made in October 1994. Also in 1994, for disputed reasons, one of the founders, Theo de Raadt, left the project. He later founded a new project, OpenBSD, from a forked version of NetBSD 1.0 near the end of 1995. In 1998, NetBSD 1.3 introduced the pkgsrc packages collection.

Until 2004, NetBSD 1.x releases were made at roughly annual intervals, with minor "patch" releases in between. From release 2.0 onwards, each major NetBSD release corresponds to an incremented major version number, i.e. the major releases following 2.0 are 3.0, 4.0 and so on. The previous minor releases are now divided into two categories: x.y "stable" maintenance releases and x.y.z releases containing only security and critical fixes.

Features

Portability

As the project's motto ("Of course it runs NetBSD") suggests, NetBSD has been ported to a large number of 32- and 64-bit architectures. These range from VAX minicomputers to Pocket PC PDAs. As of 2009, NetBSD supports 57 hardware platforms (across 15 different processor architectures). The NetBSD distribution supports more platforms than any single GNU/Linux distribution.

The kernel and userland for these platforms are all built from a central unified source-code tree managed by CVS. Currently, unlike other kernels such as ?Clinux, the NetBSD kernel requires the presence of an MMU in any given target architecture.

NetBSD's portability is aided by the use of hardware abstraction layer interfaces for low-level hardware access such as bus input/output or DMA. Using this portability layer, device drivers can be split into "machine-independent" and "machine-dependent" components.

This allows a single driver to be easily used on several platforms by hiding details of exactly how the driver accesses the hardware, and reduces the amount of work needed to port it to a new architecture.

This enables, for instance, a driver for a specific PCI card to work whether that card is in a PCI slot on an IA-32, Alpha, PowerPC, SPARC, or other architecture with a PCI bus. Also, a single driver for a specific device can operate via several different buses, for example ISA, PCI, PC card, etcetera.

In comparison, Linux device driver code often needs to be reworked for every new architecture. As a consequence, in porting efforts by NetBSD and Linux developers, NetBSD has taken much less time to port to new hardware.

This platform independence aids the development of embedded systems, particularly since NetBSD 1.6, when the entire toolchain of compilers, assemblers, linkers, and other tools fully support cross-compiling.

In 2005, as a demonstration of NetBSD's portability and suitability for embedded applications, Technologic Systems, a vendor of embedded systems hardware, designed and demonstrated a NetBSD-powered kitchen toaster.

Commercial ports to embedded platforms, including the AMD Geode LX800, Freescale PowerQUICC processors, Marvell Orion, AMCC 405 family of PowerPC processors, Intel XScale IOP and IXP series, were available from and supported by Wasabi Systems.

Portable build framework

The NetBSD cross-compiling framework (also known as "build.sh") allows a complete NetBSD system for an architecture to be built from another system of different architecture (usually faster or with more hardware resources), even on a different operating system, since the framework supports most POSIX-compliant systems.

Several embedded systems using NetBSD have required no additional software development other than toolchain and target rehost.

The pkgsrc packages collection

NetBSD features pkgsrc (short for "package source"), a framework for building and managing third-party application software packages. The pkgsrc collection consists of more than 12000 packages as of October 2012. Building and installing packages such as KDE, GNOME, the Apache HTTP server or Perl is performed through the use of a system of makefiles.

This can automatically fetch the source code, unpack, patch, configure, build and install the package such that it can be removed again later. An alternative to compiling from source is to use a precompiled binary package. In either case, any prerequisites/dependencies will be installed automatically by the package system, without need for manual intervention.

pkgsrc supports not only the hardware platforms that run NetBSD, but also several other Unix-like operating systems, such as Linux, other BSD variants like FreeBSD, Solaris, Darwin/Mac OS X, IRIX, Interix and others. pkgsrc has also been adopted as the official package management system for DragonFly BSD.

Symmetric multiprocessing

NetBSD has had support for SMP since the NetBSD 2.0 release in 2004, which was initially implemented using the giant lock approach. During the development cycle of the NetBSD 5 release, major work was done to improve SMP support; most of the kernel subsystems were modified to be MP safe and use the fine-grained locking approach. New synchronization primitives were implemented and scheduler activations was replaced with a 1:1 threading model in February 2007. A scalable M2 thread scheduler was implemented, though the old 4.4BSD scheduler still remains the default but was modified to scale with SMP.

Threaded software interrupts were implemented to improve synchronization. The virtual memory system, memory allocator and trap handling were made MP safe. The file system framework, including the VFS and major file systems were modified to be MP safe. Since April, 2008 the only subsystems running with a giant lock are the network protocols and most device drivers.

Security

NetBSD provides various features in the security area. The Kernel Authorization framework (or Kauth) is a subsystem managing all authorization requests inside the kernel, and used as system-wide security policy. It allows external modules to plug-in the authorization process. NetBSD also incorporates exploit mitigation features, ASLR, MPROTECT and Segvguard from PaX project, and GCC Stack Smashing Protection (SSP, or also known as ProPolice, enabled by default since NetBSD 6.0) compiler extensions.

Verified Executables (or Veriexec) is an in-kernel file integrity subsystem in NetBSD. It allows the user to set digital fingerprints (hashes) of files, and take a number of different actions if files do not match their fingerprints. For example, one can allow Perl to run only scripts that match their fingerprints. The cryptographic device driver (CGD) allows using disks or partitions (including CDs and DVDs) for encrypted storage.

Virtualization

The Xen virtual-machine monitor has been supported in NetBSD since release 3.0. The use of Xen requires a special pre-kernel boot environment that loads a Xen-specialized kernel as the "host OS" (Dom0). Any number of "guest OSes" (DomU) virtualized computers, with or without specific Xen/DomU support, can be run in parallel with the appropriate hardware resources.

The need for a third-party boot manager, such as GRUB, was eliminated with NetBSD 5's Xen-compatible boot manager. NetBSD 6 as a Dom0 has been benchmarked comparably to Linux, with better performance than Linux in some tests.

User-space virtualization such as VirtualBox and QEMU are also supported on NetBSD.

NetBSD 5.0 introduced rump (Runnable Userspace Meta Programs), an architecture to run drivers in user-space by emulating kernel-space calls. The anykernel architecture allows adding support of NetBSD drivers to other kernel architectures, ranging from Exokernels to Monolithic kernels.

Storage

NetBSD includes many enterprise features like iSCSI, a journaling filesystem, logical volume management and the ZFS filesystem.

The WAPBL journaling filesystem, an extension of the BSD FFS filesystem, was contributed by Wasabi Systems in 2008.

The NetBSD Logical Volume Manager is based on a BSD reimplementation of a device-mapper driver and a port of the Linux Logical Volume Manager tools. It was mostly written during the Google Summer of Code 2008.

The ZFS filesystem developed by Sun Microsystems was imported into the NetBSD base system in 2009. Currently, the NetBSD ZFS port is based on ZFS version 13.

The CHFS Flash memory filesystem was imported into NetBSD in November 2011. CHFS is a file system developed at the Department of Software Engineering, University of Szeged, Hungary, and is the first open source Flash-specific file system written for NetBSD.

Compatibility with other operating systems

At the source code level, NetBSD is very nearly entirely compliant with POSIX.1 (IEEE 1003.1-1990) standard and mostly compliant with POSIX.2 (IEEE 1003.2-1992).

NetBSD also provides system call-level binary compatibility on the appropriate processor architectures with several UNIX-derived and UNIX-like operating systems, including Linux, other BSD variants like FreeBSD, Apple's Darwin, Solaris and SunOS 4. This allows NetBSD users to run many applications that are only distributed in binary form for other operating systems, usually with no significant loss of performance.

A variety of "foreign" disk filesystem formats are also supported in NetBSD, including FAT, NTFS, Linux ext2fs, Mac OS X UFS, RISC OS FileCore/ADFS, AmigaOS Fast File System, IRIX EFS and many more through FUSE.

Licensing

All of the NetBSD kernel and most of the core userland source code is released under the terms of the BSD License (two, three, and four-clause variants). This essentially allows everyone to use, modify, redistribute or sell it as they wish, as long as they do not remove the copyright notice and license text (the four-clause variants also include terms relating to publicity material). Thus, the development of products based on NetBSD is possible without having to make modifications to the source code public. In contrast, the GPL stipulates that changes to source code of a product must be released to the product recipient when products derived from those changes are released.

On 20 June 2008, the NetBSD Foundation announced a transition to the two clause BSD license, citing concerns with UCB support of clause 3 and industry applicability of clause 4.

NetBSD also includes the GNU development tools and other packages, which are covered by the GPL and other open source licenses. As is the case for the other BSD projects, NetBSD separates those in its base source tree, in order to make removal of code under more restrictive licenses easier. As for packages, the installed software licenses may be controlled by modifying the list of allowed licenses in the pkgsrc configuration file (mk.conf).

Logo

The NetBSD "flag" logo, designed by Grant Bissett, was introduced in 2004 and is an abstraction of their older logo, designed by Shawn Mueller in 1994. Mueller's version was based on the famous World War II photograph Raising the Flag on Iwo Jima, which some perceived as culturally insensitive and inappropriate for an international project.

The NetBSD Foundation

The NetBSD Foundation is the legal entity that owns the intellectual property and trademarks associated with NetBSD, and on 22 January 2004, became a 501(c)3 tax-exempt non-profit organization. The members of the foundation are developers who have CVS commit access. The NetBSD Foundation has a Board of Directors, elected by the voting of members for two years.

Examples of use

NetBSD's clean design, high performance, scalability, and support for many architectures has led to its use in embedded devices and servers, especially in networking applications.

A commercial real-time operating system, QNX, uses a network stack which is based on NetBSD code, and provides various drivers ported from NetBSD.

Dell Force10 uses NetBSD as the underlying operating system that powers FTOS (the Force10 Operating System), which is used in high scalability switch/routers. Force10 also made a donation to the NetBSD Foundation in 2007 to help further research and the open development community.

Wasabi Systems provides a commercial Wasabi Certified BSD product based on NetBSD with proprietary enterprise features and extensions, which are focused on embedded, server and storage applications.

NetBSD was used in NASA's SAMS-II Project of measuring the microgravity environment on the International Space Station, and for investigations of TCP for use in satellite networks.

In 2004, SUNET used NetBSD to set the Internet2 Land Speed Record. NetBSD was chosen "due to the scalability of the TCP code".

NetBSD is also used in Apple's AirPort Extreme and Time Capsule products, instead of their own Mac OS X (which uses FreeBSD's userland) platform. The operating system of the T-Mobile Sidekick LX 2009 smartphone is based on NetBSD.

The Minix operating system uses a mostly NetBSD userland as well as its pkgsrc packages infrastructure since version 3.2.

Hosting

Hosting for the project is provided primarily by the Internet Systems Consortium Inc, Columbia University, and Western Washington University. Mirrors for the project are spread around the world and provided by volunteers and supporters of the project.

OASIS

The Organization for the Advancement of Structured Information Standards (OASIS) is a global consortium that drives the development, convergence, and adoption of e-business and web service standards. With its headquarters in the United States, members of the consortium decide how and what work is undertaken through an open, democratic process.

Technical work is carried out under the following categories: Web Services, e-Commerce, Security, Law & Government, Supply Chain, Computing Management, Application Focus, Document-Centric, XML Processing, Conformance/Interop, and Industry Domains.

History

OASIS was first formed as SGML Open in 1993 as a trade association of SGML tool vendors to cooperatively promote the adoption of SGML through mainly educational activities, though some amount of technical activity was also pursued including an update of the CALS Table Model specification and specifications for fragment interchange and entity management.

In 1998, with the movement of the high tech industry to XML, SGML Open changed its emphasis from SGML to XML, and changed its name to OASIS Open to be inclusive of XML and any future structured information standards. The focus of the consortium's activities also moved from promoting adoption (as XML was getting lots of attention on its own) to developing technical specifications. In July 2000 a new technical committee process was approved. With the adoption of the process the manner in which technical committees were created, operated, and progressed their work was regularized. At the adoption of the process there were five technical committees; by 2004 there were nearly 70.

During 1999 OASIS was approached by UN/CEFACT, the committee of the United Nations dealing with standards for business, to jointly develop a new set of specifications for electronic business. The joint initiative, called "ebXML" and which first met in November 1999, was chartered for a three-year period. At the final meeting under the original charter, in Vienna, UN/CEFACT and OASIS agreed to divide the remaining work between the two organizations and to coordinate the completion of the work through a coordinating committee. In 2004 OASIS submitted its completed ebXML specifications to ISO TC154 where they were approved as ISO 15000.

Standards under development

The following standards are under development by OASIS technical committees:

- AMQP - Advanced Message Queuing Protocol, an application layer protocol for message-oriented middleware.
- BCM - Business Centric-Methodology, BCM is a comprehensive approach and proven techniques that enable a service-oriented architecture (SOA) and support enterprise agility and interoperability.

- CAP - Common Alerting Protocol, is an XML-based data format for exchanging public warnings and emergencies between alerting technologies.
- CAM - Content Assembly Mechanism, is a generalized assembly mechanism for using templates of XML business transaction content and the associated rules. CAM templates augment schema syntax and provide implementers with the means to specify interoperable interchange patterns.
- CAMP - Cloud Application Management for Platforms, is an API for managing public and private cloud applications.
- CMIS - Content Management Interoperability Services, is a domain model and Web services standard for working with Enterprise content management repositories and systems.
- CIQ - Customer Information Quality, is an XML Specifications for defining, representing, interoperating and managing party information (e.g. name, address).
- DocBook - DocBook, a markup language for technical documentation. It was originally intended for authoring technical documents related to computer hardware and software but it can be used for any other sort of documentation.
- DITA - Darwin Information Typing Architecture, a modular and extensible XML-based language for topic-based information, such as for online help, documentation, and training.
- EML - Election Markup Language, End to End information standards and processes for conducting democratic elections using XML-based information recording.
- EDXL - Emergency Data Exchange Language, Suite of XML-based messaging standards that facilitate emergency information sharing between government entities and the full range of emergency-related organizations
- GeoXACML - Geospatial eXtensible Access Control Markup Language, a geo-specific extension to XACML Version 2.0, mainly the geometric data-type urn:ogc:def:dataType:geoxacml:1.0:geometry and several geographic functions such as topological, bag, set, geometric and conversion functions.
- KMIP - The Key Management Interoperability Protocol tries to establish a single, comprehensive protocol for the communication between enterprise key management systems and encryption systems.
- Legal XML LegalDocumentML (Akoma Ntoso), LegalRuleML, Electronic Court Filing, and eNotarization standards.
- oBIX - open Building Information Exchange, an extensible XML specification for enterprise interaction with building-based (or other)

control systems, including HVAC, Access Control, Intrusion Detection, and many others.

- OpenDocument - OASIS Open Document Format for Office Applications, an open document file format for saving office documents such as spreadsheets, memos, charts, and presentations.
- OSLC - Open Services for Lifecycle Collaboration, (OSLC) develops standards that make it easy and practical for software lifecycle tools to share data with one another. See the OSLC community web site (http://open-services.net) for more details.
- SAML - Security Assertion Markup Language, a standard XML-based framework for the secure exchange of authentication and authorization information.
- SDD - Solution Deployment Descriptor, a standard XML-based schema defining a standardized way to express software installation characteristics required for lifecycle management in a multi-platform environment.
- SPML - Service Provisioning Markup Language, a standard XML-based protocol for the integration and interoperation of service provisioning requests.
- TOSCA - Topology and Orchestration Specification for Cloud Applications, a Standard to describe cloud services, the relationships between parts of the service, and the operational behavior of the services.
- UBL - Universal Business Language, National effort to define a royalty-free library of standard electronic XML business documents. All invoices to the Danish government have to be in UBL electronic format since February 2005.
- UDDI - Universal Description Discovery and Integration, a platform-independent, XML-based registry for companies and individuals to list Web Services.
- WebCGM - Web Computer Graphics Metafile, a profile of Computer Graphics Metafile (CGM), which adds Web linking and is optimized for Web applications in technical illustration, electronic documentation, geophysical data visualization, and similar fields.
- WS-BPEL - Web Services Business Process Execution Language
- WSDM - Web Services Distributed Management
- XACML - eXtensible Access Control Markup Language, a standard XML-based protocol for access control policies.
- XDI - XRI Data Interchange, a standard for sharing, linking, and synchronizing data ("dataweb") across multiple domains and applications using XML documents, eXtensible Resource Identifiers (XRIs), and a new method of distributed data control called a link contract.

- XLIFF - XML Localization Interchange File Format, a XML-based format created to standardize localization.
- XRI - eXtensible Resource Identifier, a URI-compatible scheme and resolution protocol for abstract identifiers used to identify and share resources across domains and applications.

Patent disclosure controversy

Like many bodies producing open standards, OASIS has a patent disclosure policy requiring participants to disclose intent to apply for software patents for technologies under consideration in the standard. Like the W3C, which requires participants to offer royalty-free licenses to anyone using the resulting standard, OASIS offers a similar Royalty Free on Limited Terms mode, along with a Royalty Free on RAND Terms mode and a RAND (reasonable and non-discriminatory) mode for its committees.

Controversy has arisen because this licensing allows publication of standards requiring licensing fee payments to patent holders, the use of which would effectively eliminate the possibility of free/open source implementations of these standards. Further, contributors could initially offer royalty-free use of their patent, later imposing per-unit fees, after the standard becomes accepted.

Supporters of OASIS point out this could occur anyway since an agreement would not be binding on non-participants, discouraging contributions from potential participants.

Supporters further argue that IBM and Microsoft shifting standardization efforts from the W3C to OASIS is evidence this is already occurring.

Criticism

Doug Mahugh - while working for Microsoft (a promoter of Office Open XML, a Microsoft document format competing with OASIS's ISO/IEC 26300, i.e. OpenDocument) as a Senior Product Manager specializing in Office client interoperability - claimed that "many countries have expressed frustration about the pace of OASIS's responses to defect reports that have been submitted on ISO/IEC 26300 and the inability for SC 34 members to participate in the maintenance of ODF."

However, Rob Weir, co-chair of the OASIS ODF Technical Committee noted that at the time, "the ODF TC had received zero defect reports from any ISO/IEC national body other than Japan", and that the one report that was submitted by them was handled promptly and to the satisfaction of the submitter.

OPEN INVENTION NETWORK

The Open Invention Network (OIN) is a company that acquires patents and licenses them royalty free to entities which, in turn, agree not to assert their own patents against Linux and Linux-related systems and applications.History

Based in Durham, NC, the company was founded on November 10, 2005 by IBM, Novell, Philips, Red Hat, and Sony. NEC subsequently became a member. Canonical and Google are Associate Members. Keith Bergelt is the chief executive of the company.

Bergelt had previously served as President and CEO of Paradox Capital, LLC

Open Invention Network has more than 600 U.S. and international patents and patent applications. It holds the Commerce One Web services patents (previously acquired by Novell for $15.5 million), which cover several fundamentals of current business-to-business e-commerce practice. OIN's founders intend for these patents to encourage others to join, and to discourage legal threats against Linux and Linux-related applications. As of October 2013, OIN had more than 600 licensees.

The list of key applications considered by OIN, according to Red Hat's Mark Webbink, includes Apache, Eclipse, Evolution, Fedora Directory Server, Firefox, GIMP, GNOME, KDE, Mono, Mozilla, MySQL, Nautilus, OpenLDAP, OpenOffice.org, Open-Xchange, Perl, PostgreSQL, Python, Samba, SELinux, Sendmail, and Thunderbird.

On March 26, 2007, Oracle licensed OIN's portfolio, thus agreeing not to assert patents against the GNU/Linux-based environment, including competitors MySQL and PostgreSQL when used as part of a GNU/Linux system. On August 7, 2007, Google also joined OIN as a licensee. On October 2, 2007, Barracuda Networks joined OIN as a licensee. On March 23, 2009 TomTom joined OIN as a licensee. In May 2011, the European Open Source software manufacturer Univention joined OIN as a licensee.

Countering Microsoft strategy for feeding patent trolls

In early September 2009, Open Invention Network acquired 30 patents, from Allied Security Trust, another defensive patent management organization, that had been acquired from Microsoft through a private auction. Microsoft's sale appeared dubious because the patents were marketed as relating to Linux. If the patents had been acquired by patent trolls, they might have caused financial obstacles to Linux developers, distributors and users. OIN was able to avert this issue with the patent acquisition.

Ways to participate with Open Invention Network

Open Invention Network has three levels of participation, each of which helps to promote open source as a modality for invention and ensure ongoing freedom of action for GNU/Linux community members:

- Founding Members - Open Invention Network comprises six forward-looking organizations that originally created OIN with a mission of enabling and protecting Linux-based systems as it relates to IP rights. OIN's Founding Members include IBM, NEC, Novell, Philips, Red Hat and Sony.
- Associate Members - Associate Members are recruited from Linux-related companies, including those that are leaders in advancing Linux-based migration into emerging growth markets. Associate Members make a commitment to the Linux Community by virtue of their commitments to and membership in OIN and help to ensure that patent issues do not impair growth of Linux-based systems.
- Licensees - Any company or organization that agrees to refrain from using its patent portfolio against the Linux System may become an OIN licensee. Licensees benefit from royalty-free access to a valuable and growing portfolio of strategic patents, as well as from ongoing communication with OIN concerning Linux-related patent issues. In so doing, licensees facilitate their access to OIN resources such as Linux Defenders, which is designed to address patent issues with the potential to impact Linux. OIN licensees, be they founding members, associate members or licensees, contribute to an ever expanding community of companies that share a common goal of ensuring freedom of action in and across the GNU/Linux ecosystem. Through their unified commitment to Linux, they limit the negative effect of patent-based challenges mounted by companies antagonistic to Linux and open source innovation.

On June 22, 2010, OIN announced a new Associate Member program and the recruitment of Canonical (previously an OIN licensee) as its first associate member. The announcement drew criticism from anti-software-patent activist and a European lobbyist Florian Müller, who had previously criticized the OIN for a lack of transparency and for defining arbitrarily the scope of the patent protection it offers. Florian Mueller's credibility in attacking OIN has been called into question due to his paid relationship with Microsoft.

Linux defenders

In addition to its Linux protection activities through intellectual property acquisition and royalty-free licensing, OIN offers and sponsors free services that eliminate low-quality patents-the food stuffs of aggressive strategics and patent trolls. Designed to eliminate poor quality patents and ensure that only high-quality patents issue, the Linux Defenders program enables individuals and organizations to efficiently contribute to:

- "Defensive Publications" that codify 'known' inventions that have not previously been patented so that they can be brought to the attention of the patent office to ensure that later developed patent applications claiming such inventions do not issue. In general, defensive publications are a vehicle which allows the Linux and broader open source community to create valuable prior art that enables Linux and freedom of action/freedom to operate for those active in utilizing Linux to drive innovation in products, services, and applications.
- "Peer to Patent" which solicits prior art contributions from the Linux and broader open source community to ensure patent examiners are aware of prior art relevant to published applications that are currently under review. In this way, the patent office is alerted to relevant prior art and only the most innovative and novel ideas are actually patented.
- "Post-Issue Peer to Patent" which solicits prior art contribution from Linux and the broader open source community to permit the invalidation of previously issued patents that were issued in error because of the patent office's lack of awareness of relevant prior art.

Use of Linux Defenders is free of charge to contributors and the hosting of Defensive Publications on databases accessible by patent and trademark office examiners around the world is borne by the program's sponsors.

Python Software Foundation

The Python Software Foundation (PSF), is a non-profit organization devoted to the Python programming language, launched on March 6, 2001.

The mission of the foundation is to foster development of the Python community and is responsible for various processes within the Python community, including developing the core Python distribution, managing intellectual rights, developer conferences including PyCon, and raising funds.

In 2005, the Python Software Foundation received the prestigious Computerworld Horizon Award for "cutting-edge" technology.

4

Predicting the Future of Open Source

The Open Source community is large. When many people work on solving a problem, it gets solved. The technology is used for enabling the business, it has become a backbone of the business, and it is even at the front and center of the business.

Open source software is software with basis code that anyone can examine, modify, and enhance. Open source software is different from other. A software for which the original source code is made willingly available. And may be redistributed and revised according to the requirement of the users.

Open source software is when the source code is usually accessible for improvement or enhancement by anyone for reusability and accessibility. Open source code is the portion of software that mostly users don't ever notice. Anyone can manipulate and change a portion of software so that the program or application can work.

Programmers who have access to a computer program source code can enhance a program by expanding features to it or repairing parts that don't always work correctly.

From Linux to the Cloud

One of the first big successes of Open Source was in Operating Systems: Linux. Today you see many mission-critical platforms and workloads running on Linux. Nowadays we talk of Open Hybrid Cloud. There is no lock-in: It gives you freedom and offers you choices. During the pandemic, there was a need for flexibility and agility. That led to more acceptance of the cloud. There was a lot of public cloud infrastructure that was built in the country. On top of the cloud, in order to accelerate Digital Transformation, there was a need to build modern applications, what we call cloud-native applications. A lot of innovation happened around the cloud. All this change had to be managed by automation. In the cloud, the Kubernetes container was a big thing that evolved. That gave you the acceleration to build your say smartphone app and a lot of flexibility.

What Red Hat does here is work with communities. We take up some projects and kind of convert them into a product as an enterprise software with scalability, a clear roadmap, providing security with innovation.

The future is Open Source

Look at the very vibrant startup ecosystem in India. All of them are using technology whether they want to deliver goods or want to build products. Even in the government. We as citizens use a lot of services like Aadhaar and taxation. Everywhere at a platform level, you will find Open Source.

No one knows what the future holds. It is changing rapidly with the advent of 5G, Edge, and Industry 4.0. There is continuous innovation happening. There are millions of developers who are part of the community. They are trying to solve many complex challenges. Whatever new technology and innovation are happening, take blockchain or AI-ML, all the pillars of Digital Transformation, people are building on top of Open Source and are thus differentiating their businesses.

Improving and Collaborating

OSS allows programmers to improve the software by finding and fixing errors in the code, updating the software to work with new technology, and creating new features.

Last week, Microsoft's blog post touched on four important lessons that open source can teach us this year, including how different perspectives make better software and finding the perfect balance between policy and autonomy.

"We strongly believe that most of the hard (and, by that we mean interesting) problems of today will take a team or the whole industry to solve. This means we all need to be trustworthy and (corporately) self-aware participants in open source," wrote Sarah Novotny, Microsoft's open-source lead for the Azure Office of the chief technology officer, in a blog post.

Novotny added that "companies are working together more frequently, and the amount of cross-industry work we're able to accomplish is accelerating."

But we are very much already in an open-source world, since many of the things we use daily are run by open-source programs, including Android, Wordpress' content management system, Linux operating systems, and even Twitter.

Aside from the more popular platforms and programs we use every day, there's practically an open-source program for everything from video editing to writing music.

And, since the global pandemic has forced most of the workforce into a remote-first culture, moving to open source to communicate and collaborate only makes sense, even as we enter a post-pandemic world.

" gives businesses peace of mind because they have guaranteed access to their own data regardless of what happens with the source of the software," Nousiainen said. "It gives businesses agility without having to invest a lot of time."

Part of the foundation of open source is building on one another's achievements, and Nousiainen said that is critical to driving innovation for the future.

"Being able to fix and improve upon what others have done is really important," he said.

However, Nousiainen said that the key to making open-source the future of the software industry is actually investing in these open source communities and making them a priority.

Growth

Very bright; Docker has radically changed the way OSS is consumed, and now it's very simple to distribute OSS to a wider audience.

It will continue to accelerate and be integrated in different ways to solve problems and achieve results. Start caring about upgrades. Data shows people don't upgrade and this results in tremendous liability. Some companies have an effort to look inside and start licensing components by hand to look at risk and to know what's going on. Security and legal need to work together to assess risk.

Open source business models evolve to address the challenge of monetization. MuleSoft has done this with their terms of use so they are compensated if someone generates revenue from their solution. The proliferation of frameworks will continue. Open source will play an even larger role as unique business logic is layered on top.

There will be an uptick in adoption of open-source tools. More companies will offer proprietary services with an open-sourced core (open-core model). Open source software will start focusing on usability and adoption by the mainstream as opposed to focusing on innovation.

I expect the importance of open source software to continue to grow. I see more and more companies recognize the value in open sourcing architecture components they develop and then sharing the maintenance and enhancement of those components with the community. The commercial opportunities that arise from providing services in these products are also widely recognized, which actually increases the incentive to open source as companies see an opportunity to get someone else to invest in improving the technology they rely on.

It's definitely growing rapidly. All of the big players are joining the OSI. Someone needs to take ownership of the solutions to the problems. If someone doesn't take ownership I'm not sure it will continue to grow. Google has made a lot of contributions. Perhaps they'll take it over?

I see three renditions of what's needed. Communities are islands. Docker with open orchestration into microservices with Kubernetes. There's a true Russian doll architecture of how code bases work together with dependencies across the board. Centers of gravity as people use all three elements together in solutions. Commingling of data and AI to act on the information. Spark and TensorFlow result in much open source activity.

Open source will continue to grow and make developers stronger touching all aspects of our lives.

The future of open source software is bright. In the past year, more software companies have started adopting the use of open source technology, and it has been identified as a viable business model. Part of this can be attributed to the fact that it brings transparency, encourage innovation and improves the work environment.

It's a mechanism for large companies to collaborate on non-differentiating software that will continue to grow.

Continue to grow and get bigger. How to make money from open source? Sell the services around the open source project. UI Orbit is in the cloud and host for customers. Hosted service, hosted UI, hosted management platforms.

1) When open source first emerged two decades ago, it was mostly alternatives to commercial applications that were created by — sometimes quite idealistic — lone wolves. While some of these projects grew a community and became successful, the vast majority suffered from a lack of commercial support, which inevitably led to a lack of attention in the

long run and therefore a discontinued maintenance and development. (2) Today, the viability of open source has fundamentally changed because there is a commercially justified interest in continuous investments. At least two proven models for not just consuming, but in fact creating, open source technology have emerged: As a side effect of internal innovation; or, as a strategic element of a business model. (3) This evolution has led to the sustainability and predictability of open source projects, which fuels adoption by even the most conservative companies across all industries. This has worked especially for "infrastructure" technology like databases, middleware or workflow automation. (4) I expect open source will be increasingly relevant for infrastructure components and basically end the dominance of big software companies in this market. I don't expect to see this trend happen with end-user applications because much of what has driven the adoption of open source is missing there, especially the element of "developers creating something that is used by other developers."

However, I do believe that end-user applications will continue to move into the cloud, and those SaaS products will be heavily based on open source components like databases, workflow engines, etc.

Innovation

Open source will be a key driver of innovation. For example, tools like TensorFlow have helped to democratize machine learning by making machine learning something that is implementable within an enterprise. We will continue to see open source as a means to enable innovation and more and more enterprises will begin to look toward open source to drive their future roadmaps.

The future is largely here. Customers benefit every day from work being done somewhere else. Facebook just released a computer vision object detection framework which is built on their previously released machine learning library. This isn't to say we'll use that, but it very well might be something that might make our products better. Meanwhile, we already use advanced Machine Learning technologies developed as part of Spark and other projects. The future of open source is the place where advanced cutting-edge technologies are developed. This is where the real geeks and even everyday people come together and make computers do everything from think to make things.

We expect to see the broadest impact around AI and machine learning. Open source will democratize AI and create a community of more innovation. We'll also see major advancements in containers like Docker and Kubernetes as they are the future of Open Source.

The future of open source software is bright. More and more vendors will contribute new open source software. Nontraditional software companies like Capital One, which are on the move to become akin to a software company, will continue to develop new open standards and contribute open source software. More and more open source software will be written in the AI/Blockchain/IoT domain. Open source organizations like Apache Foundation will continue to drive new projects in the open source space and new innovative open source communities like openai.com will be established.

We believe that open source will always exist. It's a great place to innovate and develop projects quickly due to the opportunities to "crowdsource" from great minds to solve major problems in our industry. However, we believe that the software produced by open source often only solve a singular problem for most companies when they are actually trying to solve greater issues and achieve business outcomes.

With every new language, a slew of new developers comes along and creates a whole new ecosystem and community around that language. We'll see the open source world continue to expand, with more new and innovative projects released every year.

I believe we'll also see more corporate sponsorship and backing of open source projects, which will allow for more open source projects to flourish. We'll also see communities begin taking security more seriously.

Open Source Surpasses Commercial

The future is brilliant as the ecosystem continues to grow. Open source has won the battle of the software landscape.

We're well beyond the tipping point where open source software has become critical to organizations of all shapes and sizes. We expect to see complete platforms that include both open source and proprietary components coming to the market, taking full advantage of what open source has to offer while making it easy for companies to quickly adopt the technologies.

Just part of how software is done. You're expecting the new project is probably open source backed. New frontiers like open source hardware. Stay vigilant on security with lots of contributions people need to think about dependencies.

Open source software will maintain, if not broaden, its central role in the broad software ecosystem. Domains dominated by proprietary software will continue to be invaded by open source and more and more large companies (e.g., Microsoft) will invest heavily in open source, releasing both existing and new software under open source licenses. As more software gets consumed as a service rather than as a source, it will be interesting to see how open source principles keep pace.

Open source principles are also moving out into other fields, related or not: open source hardware is growing rapidly and allowing for an entire ecosystem of hardware development never seen before. Open collaboration in academia is on the rise, allowing researchers in all sorts of fields, not just computer science, to share information in ways that are speeding up discoveries by leaps and bounds.

Open Source has won, and in many cases will become, the default model for most software projects. I wouldn't be surprised to see a movement back to Copyleft-based licenses as more companies move to SaaS. While many new components are licensing under non-Copyleft open source licenses, the fact that SaaS-based companies aren't required to share their improvements or customizations, the community may respond in a way to require this. A license much like the LGPL, but for the SaaS distribution model, would encourage this sharing of modifications (e.g. a LAGPL)

Open source as a movement has conquered the IT industry and academia. 20 years ago, it was hard not to be laughed at by bringing Linux as an alternative to SCO or HP/UX. The future of open source is to keep on innovating and to become commonplace across operating systems - even on Windows environments (who could have predicted that?)

Other

There's a push by Google and other big players. I expect barriers in licensing will increase. More big companies are just developing code and restricting use. It's a little sad.

Barriers to creating software have declined. There will be increasing luminaries that help companies navigate the landscape. Opportunity for people and organizations to provide advice to companies to make sense of the landscape. Gartner, Forrester, IDC value of an advisory service. A greater way for individual contributors to open source to have more of a voice on the future of their projects.

For most developers, the next twelve months will look a lot like the last twelve months, which is to say, more people are going to be using the front-end library React to build web applications, more people are going to be installing things with our package manager, and more people are going to be learning to write JavaScript. Those are what our statistical trends would project, using the data from the billions of software downloads that happen on our package manager every week. Beyond that, there will probably be a new framework entering the mix, and everyone will be very suspicious of this and claim, "We don't need it" for a while, but then they'll adopt it wholeheartedly when they understand the use case it solves problems for.

The future promises to be one where developers have a huge buffet of choices. While it's great to have options, some developers will suffer from a "paradox of choice" and fear of making the wrong bet, thus we see them starting to flock towards solutions that have broad backing in the market rather than necessarily choosing ones that are fit to purpose. Unfortunately, this threatens to reduce the size of Eric Raymond's "bazaar" to projects sponsored or run by well-capitalized large players. It's going to be increasingly tough for small, point-solution projects (or vendors) to survive.

Open source software is now at the core of our web browsers, operating systems, and many other aspects of our everyday life. We will continue to see open source proliferate in common, everyday tasks as IoT and wearables continue to grow in popularity. Coupled with the open standards designed to facilitate open communication between them, these will be the areas of focus for open source software in the future.

The Return of Open Source Computing

So in the midst of UNIX wars, browser wars and commercial competition, the emergence of open source software as a more and more accepted part of the computing environment comes as something of a surprise. The catalyst is Microsoft, or rather the reaction of Microsoft's Silicon Valley competitors to the Seattle-based company's monopolistic practices. The problem for Silicon Valley firms, despite the pride in the geography-driven technology innovation of the region, is that such proximity does not automatically create the standards that propel economic growth, especially in the absence of a firm alliance with government. Technology firms have tried to create substitutes for government through private consortia like CommerceNet and other standards bodies, but none have the core of public-interested officials that government can wield to transcend particularistic company concerns in favor of the public interest.

The reality is that despite the Internet's success, many of the firms in the region continually struggle with the danger of proprietary technologies upsetting the trust needed to sustain the collaborative model that has fueled the growth of firms in the region. At the top of the list of dangers is of, course, Microsoft. Microsoft used a combination of its early alliance with IBM and hardball tactics to build its proprietary operating system monopoly on the desktop. From that base, Microsoft would extend its proprietary standards into the market for large-scale business computing, formerly the province of mainframes or UNIX-based network servers. While the Internet at first appeared as a danger to Microsoft, even a dagger at its throat, Microsoft also saw that success in molding those standards in a proprietary direction could extend the company's control throughout the whole world of corporate computing.

Microsoft responded with a combination of in-house software applications and developer tools optimized for its proprietary standards, creating an all-pervasive computing environment that promised any corporation that its needs would be met. The Microsoft solution might be less innovative than any particular competitor, but Microsoft's very completeness and pervasiveness across all sectors of computing would make up for its rigidity.

In fact, Microsoft's rigidity could be an advantage when compared to the weak standards that pervaded the UNIX corporate environment by the 1990s. After the heyday of the 80s when government purchasing requirements had enforced a broad UNIX standard on the industry, the industry had divided into warring UNIX camps and left customers uncertain that their needs would be met in the fragmented UNIX environment. By 1997 Microsoft NT computer servers were outselling UNIX servers. It was clear that in the absence of strong standards and government support for such standards, proprietary models had a decided advantage in yielding the market stability and monopoly rents that a company like Microsoft could reap.

Even as Silicon Valley firms sought to finesse innovation from the economic pressure of Windows competition, the UNIX wars made clear that strong open standards were the key to the region competing economically against proprietary steamrollers like Microsoft. Consortia like CommerceNet built around Internet standards were the first step in the process, but companies like Sun and Netscape saw the need for broader solutions that would expand open standards from the operating system to the tools used by programmers. The Java language, with its promise that any program would be able to run on any computer, no matter its hardware or operating system, became a part of that strategy.

With the need to generate stronger global support for its standards, Netscape took the unprecedented step in March 1998 of publicly revealing its browser source code--the usually top-secret guts of any program. Netscape invited developers to modify the code and even resell their own version as long as any modifications to the code were republished publicly and made according to the terms of their license, and subject to coordination by the development team at Mozilla.org. Faced with the onslaught of Microsoft's proprietary approach, Netscape decided that the regional commercial commitment to developing standards was insufficient. It needed to marshal the resources of the global programming community, and it needed to open its code to gain the kind of trust needed to ensure their support.

The idea, harking back to the original ARPANET vision, was to invite the participation of the whole Net community in developing the tools and standards embedded in the browser software. "It's no longer Netscape alone, pushing the client software forward, but now it's really the whole Net," said Bob Lisbonne, Netscape's senior vice president for client products at the time. "For Netscape, this gives us a way to engage the creative, innovative abilities of literally orders of magnitude more people than we could ever--really any commercial software company could ever afford to just put on their payroll." With hacker enthusiasts lauding the decision, thousands of developers would download the source code within the first day and major modifications of Navigator were released onto the Net within weeks by independent developers from all over the country.

The idea was that Netscape could release existing modifications in its continual upgrades of both browser and server software. What it lost by giving up control of its code, it would make up through selling customized business versions and server software, and by preventing Microsoft's control of standards which would be Netscape's deathnell.

Netscape's action highlights the continued importance of public-interest-oriented software development. This type of software has survived much of the privatization of the Internet. Most dramatically, despite the focus on the Microsoft-Netscape rivalry, the most popular Web server on the Internet was neither company's but rather a free, open source server called Apache. After the NCSA developed its Mosaic browser software and its original server software, the NSCA as part of the government privatization had ceased aggressively updating its software.

Instead, a geographically dispersed group of software programmers, some at universities and some in private business, began collaborating in 1995 to update the NCSA server to increase its power and manageability. Most of the programmers participated out of altruism. The result was a Web server that in 1997 was used in 44 percent of Internet sites, compared to just 16 percent that used Microsoft and 12 percent using Netscape's software. And that list of sites included McDonalds, UUNET Technologies, HotWired, Yahoo Inc., CSB, the FBI and IBM, which passed over its own Lotus Domino server in favor of Apache when it put its "Big Blue-Gary Kasparov" chess match on the Internet.

Similarly, one of the favorite Web programming languages is a free and open language named perl which has similarly been modified and improved through a global network of collaborators coordinated by programmer Larry Wall.

Netscape also announced that it would begin making all its software applications available in the Linux operating system, a freeware version of UNIX that has become the fastest expanding operating system in the world with three to nine million copies on computers around the world. Linux was described by Wired magazine in 1997 as "[Window] NT's most serious competitor, the only viable alternative to the Microsoft monoculture."

Adoption of open source will continue to advance

The growth we saw throughout 2020 has set the pace for open source adoption to soar throughout the remainder of this year, particularly as cloud services continue to permeate our society and facilitate digital transformation. Meanwhile, any barriers blockading the widespread adoption of open source are being met with innovative solutions from industry leaders, opening up a pathway for open source ingenuity.

For example, one of the biggest concerns around open source is security. To overcome this barrier, tech giants such as Microsoft, Google and IBM have launched the Open Source Security Foundation – hosted by the Linux Foundation – to implement initiatives and protocols that will improve security in the industry. The foundation will initially focus on issues such as security tooling, digital identity attestation and vulnerability disclosures.

The open source community has also started to dedicate time and effort to resolving some of the world's most life-threatening challenges. When the COVID-19 pandemic hit, the open source community quickly distributed data to create apps and dashboards that could follow the evolution of the virus.

Tech leaders like Apple and Google came together to build upon this technology to provide an open API that could facilitate the development of standard and applications by health organisations around the world, and open hardware designs for ventilators and other critical medical equipment that was in high demand.

During lockdown last year, the open source community also launched projects to tackle the climate crisis an increasingly important issue that world leaders are under ever-more pressure to address. One of the most notable developments was the launch of the Linux Foundation Climate Finance Foundation, which aims to provide more funding for game-changing solutions through open source applications.

Cloud will evolve

The huge growth of public cloud infrastructure over the past 18 months has been driven by the rapid adoption of public cloud usage by organisations throughout the pandemic, much of which can be attributed to the business agility benefits associated with cloud and digital transformation. As a result of such growth, I'm interested to see what innovative strategies from the likes of IBM and OVH arise to challenge industry leaders like AWS and Azure, both of which most likely will continue to dominate the market.

Equally, other digital technologies will continue to flourish. Dependent on where sensors are able to be placed and what data can be collected, solutions like IoT and smart devices will grow exponentially over the coming years as investment soars to mirror the growth of digital developments.

Going forward, it's safe to assume our smarter and more connected world will require advanced analytical capabilities to quantify the masses of data being collected in order to produce actionable insights.

3. Demand for made-to-measure databases and managed services will grow

As well as analytic tools, the influx of data will also mandate made-to-measure databases. Of the current options available, time-series databases are already one of the most popular and fastest-growing and will remain secure in its place until the end of this year.

Similarly, as digital transformation trends pick up more speed and organisations continue to adapt and evolve to the changing landscape, managed service providers will be an increasingly popular option for those that want to maximise the potential of open source and cloud solutions without implementing themselves. Avoiding the time, money and effort involved in installing and maintaining these technologies will allow businesses to focus on what they do best while supporting them in managing their data.

An eye to the future

In accordance with the rise in adoption of cloud and open source, a combination of investment, expertise and demand will push open source and cloud technologies in an exciting direction.

As industry leaders tackle barriers to progress, the open source community can continue to develop futuristic solutions to modern problems. With the right infrastructure in place and the resources to drive innovation, technology will continue to serve as a platform for life-altering developments.

Advantage And Disadvantage of Open Source

The advantages of open source are enormous and have increased huge popularity in the field of IT in current years. This is mainly because the advantages of open-source software are that it's independent to use, its most significant benefit. As a non-profit organization develops it.

The main disadvantage of open-source software is not being straightforward to use.

Open-source operating systems like Linux cannot be understood in a day. They need effort and possibly training from your side before you are able to comprehend them. You may require to employ a trained person to make things easier.

Open source products are free to use and could also be customized based on the requirement by making changes in their source code.

The best part of these products is, they can work the same way are the other paid products that perform the same task. It is preferred by the professional and the companies in their early stage due to its being available easily for free. If you want to perform any task, you can give a try to check if the software to do that work is available as open source. That could help you to save some bucks or reduce the project cost.

5

Open-source Intelligence

Open-source intelligence (OSINT) is the collection and analysis of data gathered from open sources (overt and publicly available sources) to produce actionable intelligence. OSINT is primarily used in national security, law enforcement, and business intelligence functions and is of value to analysts who use non-sensitive intelligence in answering classified, unclassified, or proprietary intelligence requirements across the previous intelligence disciplines.

OSINT sources can be divided up into six different categories of information flow:

Media, print newspapers, magazines, radio, and television from across and between countries.

Internet, online publications, blogs, discussion groups, citizen media (i.e. – cell phone videos, and user created content), YouTube, and other social media websites (i.e. – Facebook, Twitter, Instagram, etc.). This source also outpaces a variety of other sources due to its timeliness and ease of access.

Public government data, public government reports, budgets, hearings, telephone directories, press conferences, websites, and speeches. Although this source comes from an official source they are publicly accessible and may be used openly and freely.

Professional and academic publications, information acquired from journals, conferences, symposia, academic papers, dissertations, and theses.

Commercial data, commercial imagery, financial and industrial assessments, and databases.

Grey literature, technical reports, preprints, patents, working papers, business documents, unpublished works, and newsletters.

OSINT is distinguished from research in that it applies the process of intelligence to create tailored knowledge supportive of a specific decision by a specific individual or group.

Definition

OSINT is defined by both the U.S. Director of National Intelligence and the U.S. Department of Defense (DoD), as intelligence "produced from publicly available information that is collected, exploited, and disseminated in a timely manner to an appropriate audience for the purpose of addressing a specific intelligence requirement." As defined by NATO, OSINT is intelligence "derived from publicly available information, as well as other unclassified information that has limited public distribution or access."

According to political scientist Jeffrey T. Richelson, "open source acquisition involves procuring verbal, written, or electronically transmitted material that can be obtained legally. In addition to documents and videos available via the Internet or provided by a human source, others are obtained after U.S. or allied forces have taken control of a facility or site formerly operated by a foreign government or terrorist group."

Security researcher Mark M. Lowenthal defines OSINT as "any and all information that can be derived from overt collection: all types of media, government reports and other documents, scientific research and reports, commercial vendors of information, the Internet, and so on. The main qualifiers to open-source information are that it does not require any type of clandestine collection techniques to obtain it and that it must be obtained through means that entirely meet the copyright and commercial requirements of the vendors where applicable."

OSINT in the United States traces its origins to the creation of the Foreign Broadcast Monitoring Service (FBMS), an agency responsible for the monitoring of foreign broadcasts. An example of their work is reflected in the application of the correlation of changes in the price of oranges in Paris with that of railway bridges being bombed successfully.

The Aspin-Brown Commission stated in 1996 that US access to open sources was "severely deficient" and that this should be a "top priority" for both funding and DCI attention.

In July 2004, following the September 11 attacks, the 9/11 Commission recommended the creation of an open-source intelligence agency. In March 2005, the Iraq Intelligence Commission recommended the creation of an open-source directorate at the CIA.

Following these recommendations, in November 2005 the Director of National Intelligence announced the creation of the DNI Open Source Center. The Center was established to collect information available from "the Internet, databases, press, radio, television, video, geospatial data, photos and commercial imagery." In addition to collecting openly available information, it would train analysts to make better use of this information. The center absorbed the CIA's previously existing Foreign

Broadcast Information Service (FBIS), originally established in 1941, with FBIS head Douglas Naquin named as director of the center. Then, following the events of 9/11 the Intelligence Reform and Terrorism Prevention Act merged FBIS and other research elements into the Office of the Director of National Intelligence creating the Open Source Enterprise.

Furthermore, the private sector has invested in tools which aid in OSINT collection and analysis. Specifically, In-Q-Tel, a Central Intelligence Agency supported venture capital firm in Arlington, VA assisted companies develop web-monitoring and predictive analysis tools.

In December 2005, the Director of National Intelligence appointed Eliot A. Jardines as the Assistant Deputy Director of National Intelligence for Open Source to serve as the Intelligence Community's senior intelligence officer for open source and to provide strategy, guidance and oversight for the National Open Source Enterprise. Mr. Jardines has established the National Open Source Enterprise and authored intelligence community directive 301. In 2008, Mr. Jardines returned to the private sector and was succeeded by Dan Butler who is ADDNI/OS and previously Mr. Jardines' Senior Advisor for Policy.

The Dark Side of Open Source Intelligence

At this point, it's time to address the second major issue with open source intelligence: if something is readily available to intelligence analysts, it's also readily available to threat actors.

Threat actors use open source intelligence tools and techniques to identify potential targets and exploit weaknesses in target networks. Once a vulnerability is identified, it is often an extremely quick and simple process to exploit it and achieve a variety of malicious objectives.

This process is the main reason why so many small and medium-sized enterprises get hacked each year. It isn't because threat groups specifically take an interest in them, but rather because vulnerabilities in their network or website architecture are found using simple open source intelligence techniques. In short, they are easy targets.

And open source intelligence doesn't only enable technical attacks on IT systems and networks. Threat actors also seek out information about individuals and organizations that can be used to inform sophisticated social engineering campaigns using phishing (email), vishing (phone or voicemail), and SMiShing (SMS). Often, seemingly innocuous information shared through social networks and blogs can be used to develop highly convincing social engineering campaigns, which in turn are used to trick well-meaning users into compromising their organization's network or assets.

This is why using open source intelligence for security purposes is so important — It gives you an opportunity to find and fix weaknesses in your organization's network and remove sensitive information before a threat actor uses the same tools and techniques to exploit them.

Open Source Intelligence Techniques

Now that we've covered the uses of open source intelligence (both good and bad) it's time to look at some of the techniques that can be used to gather and process open source information.

First, you must have a clear strategy and framework in place for acquiring and using open source intelligence. It's not recommended to approach open source intelligence from the perspective of finding anything and everything that might be interesting or useful — as we've already discussed, the sheer volume of information available through open sources will simply overwhelm you. Instead, you must know exactly what you're trying to achieve — for example, to identify and remediate weaknesses in your network — and focus your energies specifically on accomplishing those goals. Second, you must identify a set of tools and techniques for collecting and processing open source information. Once again, the volume of information available is much too great for manual processes to be even slightly effective.

Broadly speaking, collection of open source intelligence falls into two categories: passive collection and active collection.

Passive collection often involves the use of threat intelligence platforms (TIPs) to combine a variety of threat feeds into a single, easily accessible location. While this is a major step up from manual intelligence harvesting, the risk of information overload is still significant. More advanced threat intelligence solutions like Recorded Future solve this problem by using artificial intelligence, machine learning, and natural language processing to automate the process of prioritizing and dismissing alerts based on an organization's specific needs.

In a similar manner, organized threat groups often use botnets to collect valuable information using techniques like traffic sniffing and keylogging.

On the other hand, active collection is the use of a variety of techniques to search for specific insights or information. For security professionals, this type of collection work is usually done for one of two reasons:

A passively collected alert has highlighted a potential threat and further insight is required.

The focus of an intelligence gathering exercise is very specific, such as a penetration testing exercise.

Open Source Intelligence Tools

To close things out, we'll take a look at some of the most commonly used tools for collecting and processing open source intelligence.

While there are many free and useful tools available to security professionals and threat actors alike, some of the most commonly used (and abused) open source intelligence tools are search engines like Google — just not as most of us know them.

As we've already explained, one of the biggest issues facing security professionals is the regularity with which normal, well-meaning users accidentally leave sensitive assets and information exposed to the internet. There are a series of advanced search functions called "Google dork" queries that can be used to identify the information and assets they expose.

Google dork queries are based on the search operators used by IT professionals and hackers on a daily basis to conduct their work. Common examples include "filetype:", which narrows search results to a specific file type, and "site:", which only returns results from a specified website or domain.

The Public Intelligence website offers a more thorough rundown of Google dork queries, in which they give the following example search:

"sensitive but unclassified" filetype:pdf site:publicintelligence.net

If you type this search term into a search engine, it returns only PDF documents from the Public Intelligence website that contain the words "sensitive but unclassified" somewhere in the document text.

As you can imagine, with hundreds of commands at their disposal, security professionals and threat actors can use similar techniques to search for almost anything.

Moving beyond search engines, there are literally hundreds of tools that can be used to identify network weaknesses or exposed assets. For example, you can use Wappalyzer to identify which technologies are used on a website, and combine the results with Sploitus or the National Vulnerability Database to determine whether any relevant vulnerabilities exist.

Taking things a step further, you could use a more advanced threat intelligence solution like Recorded Future to determine whether a vulnerability is being actively exploited, or is included in any active exploit kits.

Of course, the examples given here are just a tiny fraction of what is possible using open source intelligence tools. There are a huge number of free and premium tools that can be used to find and analyze open source information, with common functionality including:

- Metadata search
- Code search
- People and identity investigation
- Phone number research
- Email search and verification
- Linking social media accounts
- Image analysis
- Geospatial research and mapping
- Wireless network detection and packet analysis

Start With the End in Mind

Whatever your goals, open source intelligence can be tremendously valuable for all security disciplines. Ultimately, though, finding the right combination of tools and techniques for your specific needs will take time, as well as a degree of trial and error. The tools and techniques you need to identify insecure assets are not the same as those that would help you follow up on a threat alert or connect data points across a variety of sources.

The most important factor in the success of any open source intelligence initiative is the presence of a clear strategy — once you know what you're trying to accomplish and you've set objectives accordingly, identifying the most useful tools and techniques will be much more achievable.

Value

OSINT is valuable because it has less rigorous processing and exploitation processes and timelines than more technical intelligence disciplines such as HUMINT, SIGINT, MASINT, GEOINT, etc. Additionally, OSINT collects a valuable variety of opinions because it encompasses a great variety of sources.

According to the Commission on the Intelligence Capabilities of the United States Regarding Weapons of Mass Destruction report submitted in March 2005, OSINT must be included in the all-source intelligence process for the following reasons (as stated in the report):

The ever-shifting nature of intelligence needs compels the IC (Intelligence Community) to quickly and easily understand a wide range of foreign countries and cultures. – ... today's threats are rapidly changing and geographically diffuse; an intelligence analyst may be forced to shift rapidly from one topic to the next. Increasingly, IC professionals need to quickly assimilate social, economic, and cultural information about a country—information often detailed in open sources.

Open-source information provides a base for understanding classified materials. Despite large quantities of classified material produced by the IC, the amount of classified information produced on any one topic can be quite limited, and may be taken out of context if viewed only from a classified-source perspective. A notable example relates to terrorism, where open-source information can fill gaps and create links that allow analysts to better understand fragmented intelligence, rumored terrorist plans, possible means of attack, and potential targets.

Open-source materials can protect sources and methods. Sometimes an intelligence judgment that is actually informed with sensitive, classified information can be defended on the basis of open-source reporting. This can prove useful when policy-makers need to explain policy decisions or communicate with foreign officials without compromising classified sources.

Only open source can store history. A robust open-source program can, in effect, gather data to monitor the world's cultures and how they change with time. This is difficult, if not impossible, using the snapshots provided by classified collection methods.

Process

OSINT is a highly diverse form of intelligence collection and analysis. It does not have its own agency, however, units are scattered within the Department of Defense and the State Department. Most OSINT collectors need to take precautions while collecting information from the Internet. This can come in the form of using a VPN to anonymize their identity and collect information more discreetly. This is where evaluating sources becomes important to the overall OSINT collection and analysis process. An OSINT analyst needs intelligence evaluation to determine a true process or expose a false process that would affect predicting the future. Finally, the analysts need to find use of the evaluated intelligence so that it can be incorporated into a finished classified, unclassified, or proprietary intelligence product.

See also: Big Data

Information collection in OSINT is generally a different problem from collection in other intelligence disciplines where obtaining the raw information to be analyzed may be the major difficulty, particularly if it is to be obtained from non-cooperative targets. In OSINT, the chief difficulty is in identifying relevant, reliable sources from the vast amount of publicly available information. However, this is not as great a challenge for those who know how to access local knowledge and how to leverage human experts who can create new tailored knowledge on the fly.

Open Source Intelligence analysis software

There are several categories of tools intended for OSINT analysis. The first category includes open source tools to query multiple search engines simultaneously such as federated search engines and both proprietary and open source software projects which exploit the APIs of both free and paywalled open source and publicly available information (PIA) sources. This category also includes social media search engines and search engines of domains and people such as data aggregator services (sometimes referred to as data brokers or information brokers). The ecosystem of bespoke OSI gathering, collection and analysis tools includes specialized functions related to the following (partial) list of data types and categories as illustrated in the open-source project, OSINT Framework:

- Username
- Email Address
- Domain Name
- IP Address
- Images
- Videos
- Documents
- Instant messaging
- Telephone Numbers
- Public Records
- Business Records
- Transportation
- Geolocation Tools / Maps
- Forums / Blogs / IRC
- Archives
- Metadata
- Dark Web
- Digital Currency

The second category is designed for big data analytics platforms such as Palantir, DataWalk, i2 as well as node-based graph tools such as Maltego which combine OSINT insight with local, internal data for further visual analysis and to conduct link analysis to identify connections across a large volume of records.

Tools

The web browser is a powerful OSINT tool that provides access to numerous websites and both open source and proprietary software tools that are either purpose-built for open source information collection or which can be exploited for the purposes of either gathering of open source information or to facilitate analysis and validation to provide intelligence.

A cottage industry of both for-profit and not-for-profit investigative and educational groups such as Bellingcat, IntelTechniques SANS and others offer indices, books, podcasts and video training materials on OSINT tools and techniques. Books such as Michael Bazzell's Open Source Intelligence Techniques serve as indices to resources across mulitple domains but according the author, due to the rapidly changing information landscape, some tools and techniques change or become obsolete frequently, hence it is imperative for OSINT researchers to study, train and survey the landscape of source material regularly.

A guide by Ryan Fedasiuk, an analyst at the Center for Security and Emerging Technology, lists six tools open-source analysts can use to stay safe and utlize operational security (OPSEC) when conducting online investigations. These include VPNs, cached webpages, digital archive services, URL and file scanners, browser sandbox applications, and antivirus software.

Numerous lists of aggregated OSINT content are available on the web. The OSINT Framework contains over 30 primary categories of tools and is maintained as an open source project on GitHub. A sample list of some tools used for collecting open source intelligence:

- Whois
- Nslookup
- SpiderFoot
- Maltego
- OpenCorporates
- Shodan
- SunCalc
- TinEye Reverse Image Search
- OSINT community disciplines
- United States
- Government

There are a large number of open-source activities taking place throughout the US Government. Frequently, these open-source activities are described as "media monitoring", "media analysis", "internet research" and "public surveys" but are open source nonetheless.

The Library of Congress sponsors the Federal Research Division (FRD) which conducts a great deal of tailored open-source research on a fee-for-service basis for the executive branch.

Intelligence

The US Intelligence Community's open-source activities (known as the National Open Source Enterprise) are dictated by Intelligence Community Directive 301 promulgated by the Director of National Intelligence. The Directive establishes the authorities and responsibilities of the Assistant Deputy Director of National Intelligence for Open Source (ADDNI/OS), the DNI's Open Source Center and the National Open Source Committee.

Prior to the establishment of the National Open Source Enterprise, the Foreign Broadcast Information Service (FBIS), established in 1941, was the government's primary open-source unit, transcribing and translating foreign broadcasts. It absorbed the Defense Department's Joint Publications Research Service (JPRS), which did a similar function with foreign printed materials, including newspapers, magazines, and technical journals.

Armed forces

The former Under-Secretary of Defense for Intelligence, Dr. Stephen Cambone encouraged in part by the Defense Science Board reports on strategic communication and transition to and from hostilities, created the Defense Open Source Program (DOSP). The current under-secretary of defense for intelligence is assigned executive agency for this program to the Defense Intelligence Agency.

- U.S. military offices that engage in OSINT activities include:
- Unified combatant command
- Defense Intelligence Agency
- National Geospatial-Intelligence Agency
- US Army Foreign Military Studies Office
- EUCOM JAC Molesworth

Foreign media monitoring in support of information operations, U.S. Strategic Command

Homeland Security

The Department of Homeland Security has an active open-source intelligence unit. In congressional testimony before the House Homeland Security Committee's Intelligence, Information Sharing and Terrorism Risk Assessment Subcommittee, Undersecretary of Homeland Security Charles

Allen indicated on February 14, 2007, that he had established the "Domestic Open Source Enterprise" to support the Department's OSINT needs and that of state, local,? and tribal partners.

Law enforcement

The law enforcement OSINT community applies open-source intelligence (OSINT) to the prediction, prevention, investigation, and prosecution of criminals including terrorists. Additionally, fusion centers around the US are increasingly utilizing OSINT to support their intelligence generation and investigations.

Examples of successful law enforcement OSINT include Scotland Yard OSINT; Royal Canadian Mounted Police (RCMP) OSINT.

INTERPOL and EUROPOL experimented with OSINT units for a time, but they appear to have atrophied with the departure of their individual champions.

New York Police Department (NYPD) is known to have an OSINT unit, as does the Los Angeles County Sheriff's Department, housed within the Emergency Operations Bureau and affiliated with the LA Joint Regional Intelligence Center.

Business

Business OSINT encompasses Commercial Intelligence, Competitor Intelligence, and Business Intelligence, and is often a chief area of practice of private intelligence agencies.

Businesses may use information brokers and private investigators to collect and analyze relevant information for business purposes which may include the media, deep web, web 2.0 and commercial content.

Private specialized business

Another related business group within the United States that relies upon OSINT is the commercial bail-bond industry. This related industry, servicing the court system, is apart from the above Business Intelligence sector. OSINT is useful to bail-bond agencies that employ a private fugitive recovery agency to locate and apprehend their absent client; i.e., a criminal defendant who has failed to appear for court and subsequently a warrant for arrest was issued. OSINT is the first method of discovery to help locate the defendant when initial interviewing of the bond co-signers, defendant's relatives and friends is lacking. OSINT gathering leads the investigator to discover an alternate hypothesis to analyze and then match relevant data for making a prediction regarding the fugitive's location; e.g., data is scrubbed from web access on Facebook entries, Twitter messages, and Snapchat.

Should those methods fail, the next step is to seek the specialized behavioral intelligence services that reference OSINT to aid in establishing the veracity of subjects during the forensic interview and is used to create a behavioral profile. OSINT data is correlated with interview data to include a variety behavioral patterns; e.g., a list of daily personal contacts, habits of activities, visited places of interest, vehicles used, favorite group involvements, etc. According to the director, psychologist and forensic interviewer at MN-Behavioral Intelligence Agency, (2016) OSINT data base has to be critically filtered and analyzed before it can be applied within investigative interviewing and interrogation.

Risks for practitioners

A main hindrance to practical OSINT is the volume of information it has to deal with ("information explosion"). The amount of data being distributed increases at a rate that it becomes difficult to evaluate sources in intelligence analysis. To a small degree the work has sometimes been done by amateur crowd-sourcing.

Accredited journalists have some protection in asking questions, and researching for recognized media outlets. Even so, they can be imprisoned, even executed, for seeking out OSINT. Private individuals illegally collecting data for a foreign military or intelligence agency is considered espionage in most countries. Of course, espionage that is not treason (i.e. betraying one's country of citizenship) has been a tool of statecraft since ancient times.

The scientific scope of the action covers both computer science and computational linguistics, specifically in the domain of Internet technologies, information extraction and analysis in a multilingual environment, applied to massive data setsThe action is continuously enhancing its expertise and capacity in developing and applying technological solutions relevant to operational crisis management and to effective EU policy-making in general.

The overall strategy of the action is to improve its scientific achievements in the areas of Computational Linguistics and Information Technology by directly applying these achievements in an operational context. This strategy has proven to be effective because of the positive feedback resulting from the immediate validation of the scientific results in a real-world environment. Furthermore, it is only because of the clear demonstration of the operational validity of these methods, as shown on the actions public website, that the action has been able to attract the attention of organizations like Council#s Secretariat General (EU Joint

Situation Centre), the African Union, the various UN agencies, EU law enforcement and counter-terrorism authorities, and agencies like FRONTEX and the U.S. Department Of Defence Joint Information Operations Centre.

The action focuses on developing and testing pragmatic solutions to extract value from Open Source information in order to enhance decision-making in crisis management (from risk reduction/prevention and preparedness to early warning and response) and the monitoring and understanding of trends and impacts in EU policy making.The solutions are typically tested and applied in environments like media monitoring, operational law enforcement, counter-terrorism, as well as in crisis management and related decision making. The solutions consist of early warning and alerting systems as well as automated open source monitoring, mining and analysis systems, which combine the action#s R+D and expertise in web, information and language technologies.

The action is engaged in research developments in the following specific application areas:

- Monitoring and early warning alerting systems to support crisis management: monitoring and early warning systems are useful in shortening the decision-making time and enhancing crisis preparedness, alert and response to crisis outbreaks. One example is the Medical Health Intelligence System (MEDISYS) which is undergoing improvement to rapidly identify reporting on potential public health threats including infectious diseases and CBRN threats. Another example is the Continental early warning system (CEWS) for anticipating potential conflict and instability, currently being developed for the African Union. A third example is ODIN, the system developed for Council#s SitCen which is being upgraded with the latest research results.
- Open source mining, intelligence and analysis systems for law enforcement, organised crime and intelligence (counter-terrorism): open source mining and analysis is an increasingly active area of research with many applications in the security field particularly as regards activities concerned with counter-terrorism and fight against organised crime. The importance of open sources for providing information useful for identifying patterns and events, for identifying relationships between entities and between events, and for monitoring purposes is recognised in the law enforcement, intelligence and other security related communities. However, the increasingly fast growth of multi-lingual information in open sources and the increasing complexity of the variety of open sources (media, blogs, discussion

forums, chat rooms,#), implies that we also increasingly need advanced techniques for automatically mining, extracting, analysing and monitoring relevant information and knowledge from these open sources. The OSINT suite, currently under development, attempts to bring together the necessary tools in a complete package that can be used by an investigator as a stand-alone tool on a personal computer. Other examples are the EMM derived systems in use by 2 EU law enforcement and counter-terrorism authorities.

- Open source mining, intelligence and analysis systems for policy impact analysis: open sources also provide a wealth of information that can serve the purposes of monitoring trends and impact in policies and political affaires, be they European, African, International or others. Relevant open sources can provide information on key political/policy issues of interest to the citizen and emerging trends, on speculation surrounding policies (including EU), on negative and positive publicity and on opinion related to policies and political leaders in the EU and other levels. Such information can serve to improve EU (and African and other) policy-making, can help political institutions better understand public and other opinion as well as awareness of EU and other issues. Advanced tools are needed to be able to extract and monitor relevant information that can provide answers to the above requirements.

The action is actively engaged in developing tools that can automatically mine unstructured information from multi-lingual sources, that can classify and understand what the extracted information is talking about, and that can even detect and monitor the tonality of the extracted information. The tools are being applied in European open source monitoring and analysis systems (e.g. EMM) serving a number of Commission services including DG COMM who is the main driver of these developments. In the future, these developments will be extended to the Pan-African parliament. This extension is referenced in the AU-EU TP.

Challenges

The challenges faced by the Optima action in developing these systems are common to all of the above research developments and can be roughly divided into the 3 areas of expertise of the action:

- Internet/Web technology: a huge amount of information is harvested from the Internet. The way data is being published on the Internet is constantly changing however and this means that the techniques and tools necessary to harvest this data are also subject to constant change. As the Internet is moving towards Web 3.0 the level of interaction between the client (in this case the harvesting software) and the server (where the data is located) becomes more and more interactive and the data can no longer be guaranteed to be available as a static resource like an HTML page.

- Computational Linguistics: all of the solutions are applied in a multi lingual environment. This poses extra challenges to any of the problems the action attempts to solve. The algorithms and techniques used for the recognition of keywords, entities and place names have to be devised in such a way that they are as much as possible language #agnostic#. When however there is an inescapable need for semantic analysis of the document content, as is the case for event extraction, the algorithms have to guarantee a minimal dependency on language specific resources.
- Computer Science: for any of the solutions devised to be effective, the information derived has to be available in a timely manner. Especially in the field of crisis monitoring and early warning/alerting systems, it is mandatory that the required analysis is carried out immediately after the underlying information is published. Given the amount of information published and processed this means that any chosen solution has to be inherently capable of dealing with large data quantities in near real time. This leads to the use of fundamental comp

Open sources for intelligence

OSINT includes a wide variety of information and sources:

- Media: newspapers, magazines, radio, television, and computer-based information.
- Web-based communities and user-generated content: social-networking sites, video sharing sites, wikis, blogs, and folksonomies.
- Public data: government reports, official data such as budgets, demographics, hearings, legislative debates, press conferences, speeches, marine and aeronautical safety warnings, environmental impact statements and contract awards.
- Observation and reporting: amateur airplane spotters, radio monitors and satellite observers among many others have provided significant information not otherwise available. The availability of worldwide satellite photography, often of high resolution, on the Web (e.g., Google Earth) has expanded open-source capabilities into areas formerly available only to major intelligence services.
- Professional and academic (or grey literature): conferences, symposia, professional associations, academic papers, and subject matter experts.

- Most information has geospatial dimensions, but many often overlook the geospatial side of OSINT: not all open-source data is unstructured text. Examples of geospatial open source include hard and softcopy maps, atlases, gazetteers, port plans, gravity data, aeronautical data, navigation data, geodetic data, human terrain data (cultural and economic), environmental data, commercial imagery, LIDAR, hyper and multi-spectral data, airborne imagery, geo-names, geo-features, urban terrain, vertical obstruction data, boundary marker data, geospatial mashups, spatial databases, and web services. Most of the geospatial data mentioned above is integrated, analyzed, and syndicated using geospatial software like a Geographic Information System (GIS) not a browser per se.

OSINT is distinguished from research in that it applies the process of intelligence to create tailored knowledge supportive of a specific decision by a specific individual or group.

Definers for OSINT

OSINT is defined by both the U.S. Director of National Intelligence and the U.S. Department of Defense (DoD), as "produced from publicly available information that is collected, exploited, and disseminated in a timely manner to an appropriate audience for the purpose of addressing a specific intelligence requirement."

OSINT is, as of 2005, defined by the U.S. Office of Management and Budget under the category of "Forces And Direct Support" and specifically for the DoD under Commercial Code M320 as

Open-source intelligence (OSINT) collection/processing

A wide variety of vendors sell information products specifically within this category.

Open-source intelligence under one name or another has been around for hundreds of years. The significance today of OSINT in the USA is the conflict between military, government, and the private sector as to how the bulk of intelligence should be obtained. With the Internet, instant communications, and advanced media search the bulk of actionable and predictive intelligence can be obtained from public, unclassified sources. Government agencies have been slow to embrace OSINT, or believe they already have suitable information feeds from the media, academia and public records.

OSINT is especially helpful in addressing global coverage, a term encompassing all of the countries and topics that are not considered by the secret or national security worlds to be "vital."

Competitive intelligence

In the private sector, competitive intelligence has become a tool for marketing strategies that focus on strategically prepared information under the direction of private companies or individuals who sell organized information to specific security, law enforcement and military industries, amongst other strategic applications, often on a contractual basis. Governments and civilians both use open source intelligence, both legitimately and illegitimately, the latter being the case with criminals who use information to gain an edge in planning and conducting criminal activities.

There are still opportunities for small and medium businesses to compete in niche markets, but this too is being consolidated by major information providers (e.g.?). OSINT is not a novel concept in media where everyday operations of traditional newsroom methods of operations engage in useful strategies towards obtaining information for unique and original content through investigations of story leads, absent of reliance on formal methods of obtaining inside information through legal documents or basic interview techniques.

Investigative journalists use searches, databases, primary interviews, original sources, and leaks (informants/witnesses) who come forward either anonymously or openly, as direct contributors of inside information for journalists. Investigative journalists use specific strategies to obtain information. Sometimes informants come forward on their own to contribute original information that might not otherwise be made available, which often directly contributes to the publication of original feature stories. Such has been the case with regard to many whistle blowers in politics, government, law enforcement and also in commercial, financial and private sectors.

Risks for practitioners

Accredited journalists have some protection in asking questions, and researching for recognized media outlets. Even so they can be imprisoned, even executed, for seeking out OSINT. Private individuals illegally collecting data for a foreign military or intelligence agency is considered espionage in most countries. Of course, espionage that is not treason (i.e. betraying one's country of citizenship) has been a tool of statecraft since ancient times, is widely engaged in by nearly all countries, and is considered an honorable trade. Most countries recognize this, and if their counterintelligence agencies capture a foreign spy, that spy is usually unceremoniously deported or traded back to their homeland (for other spies) after a hostile debriefing; actual execution or refusal to trade back foreign spies with non-official cover would result in consequences in bilateral relations of the gravest possible magnitude, being an extraordinarily hostile act, even if those consequences were unofficially and extrajudicially imposed.

Value

According to the Commission on the Intelligence Capabilities of the United States Regarding Weapons of Mass Destruction report submitted in March 2005, OSINT must be included in the all-source intelligence process for the following reasons (as stated in the report):

1. The ever-shifting nature of our intelligence needs compels the IC to quickly and easily understand a wide range of foreign countries and cultures. - ... today's threats are rapidly changing and geographically diffuse; it is a fact of life that an intelligence analyst may be forced to shift rapidly from one topic to the next. Increasingly, IC professionals need to quickly assimilate social, economic, and cultural information about a country-information often detailed in open sources.

2. Open-source information provides a base for understanding classified materials. Despite large quantities of classified material produced by the IC, the amount of classified information produced on any one topic can be quite limited, and may be taken out of context if viewed only from a classified-source perspective. Perhaps the most important example today relates to terrorism, where open-source information can fill gaps and create links that allow analysts to better understand fragmented intelligence, rumored terrorist plans, possible means of attack, and potential targets.

3. Open-source materials can protect sources and methods. Sometimes an intelligence judgment that is actually informed with sensitive, classified information can be defended on the basis of open-source reporting. This can prove useful when policy-makers need to explain policy decisions or communicate with foreign officials without compromising classified sources.

4. Only open source can store history. A robust open-source program can, in effect, gather data to monitor the world's cultures and how they change with time. This is difficult, if not impossible, using the snapshots provided by classified collection methods.

History

The Foreign Broadcast Information Service (FBIS) was created in 1941 to access and exploit OSINT in relation to World War II. A classic example of their value and success is reflected in the price of oranges in Paris as an indicator of whether railroad bridges had been bombed successfully.

The recent history of OSINT began in 1988 when General Alfred M. Gray, Jr., Commandant of the Marine Corps, called for a redirection of US intelligence away from the collapsing Soviet Union and toward non-state actors and Third World zones of instability. Additionally, he pointed out that most of the intelligence which needs to be known could be obtained via OSINT, and recommended a substantive increase in resources for this aspect of the intelligence collection spectrum of sources.

In the fall of 1992, Senator David Boren, then Chairman of the Senate Select Committee on Intelligence, sponsored the National Security Act of 1992, attempting to achieve modest reform in the U.S. Intelligence Community. His counterpart on the House Permanent Select Committee on Intelligence was Congressman Dave McCurdy. The House version of the legislation included a separate open-source office, at the suggestion of Larry Prior, a Marine Reservist familiar with the MCIC experience and then serving on the House Permanent Select Committee on Intelligence staff.

The Aspin-Brown Commission stated in 1996 that US access to open sources was "severely deficient" and that this should be a "top priority" for both funding and DCI attention.

In issuing its July 2004 report, the 9/11 Commission recommended the creation of an open-source intelligence agency, but without further detail or comment. Subsequently, the WMD Commission (also known as the Robb-Silberman Commission) report in March 2005 recommended the creation of an open-source directorate at the CIA.

Following these recommendations, in November 2005 the Director of National Intelligence announced the creation of the DNI Open Source Center. The Center was established to collect information available from "the Internet, databases, press, radio, television, video, geospatial data, photos and commercial imagery." In addition to collecting openly available information, it would train analysts to make better use of this information. The Center absorbed the CIA's previously existing Foreign Broadcast Information Service (FBIS), originally established in 1941, with FBIS head Douglas Naquin named as director of the Center.

In December 2005, the Director of National Intelligence appointed Eliot A. Jardines as the Assistant Deputy Director of National Intelligence for Open Source to serve as the Intelligence Community's senior intelligence officer for open source and to provide strategy, guidance and oversight for the National Open Source Enterprise. Mr. Jardines has established the National Open Source Enterprise and authored Intelligence Community Directive 301. In 2008, Mr. Jardines returned to the private sector and was succeeded by Dan Butler who is ADDNI/OS and previously Mr. Jardines' Senior Advisor for Policy.

6

History of Free and Open-source Software

In the 1950s and 1960s, computer operating software and compilers were delivered as a part of hardware purchases without separate fees. At the time, source code, the human-readable form of software, was generally distributed with the software providing the ability to fix bugs or add new functions. Universities were early adopters of computing technology. Many of the modifications developed by universities were openly shared, in keeping with the academic principles of sharing knowledge, and organizations sprung up to facilitate sharing. As large-scale operating systems matured, fewer organizations allowed modifications to the operating software, and eventually such operating systems were closed to modification. However, utilities and other added-function applications are still shared and new organizations have been formed to promote the sharing of software.

Sharing techniques before software

The concept of free sharing of technological information existed long before computers. For example, in the early years of automobile development, one enterprise owned the rights to a 2-cycle gasoline engine patent originally filed by George B. Selden. By controlling this patent, they were able to monopolize the industry and force car manufacturers to adhere to their demands, or risk a lawsuit. In 1911, independent automaker Henry Ford won a challenge to the Selden patent. The result was that the Selden patent became virtually worthless and a new association (which would eventually become the Motor Vehicle Manufacturers Association) was formed. The new association instituted a cross-licensing agreement among all US auto manufacturers: although each company would develop technology and file patents, these patents were shared openly and without the exchange of money between all the manufacturers. By the time the US entered World War 2, 92 Ford patents and 515 patents from other companies were being shared between these manufacturers, without any exchange of money (or lawsuits).

Free software before the 1980s

In the 1950s and into the 1960s almost all software was produced by academics and corporate researchers working in collaboration, often shared as public-domain software. As such, it was generally distributed under the principles of openness and cooperation long established in the fields of academia, and was not seen as a commodity in itself. Such communal behavior later became a central element of the so-called hacking culture (a term with a positive connotation among open-source programmers). At this time, source code, the human-readable form of software, was generally distributed with the software machine code because users frequently modified the software themselves, because it would not run on different hardware or OS without modification, and also to fix bugs or add new functions. [failed verification]

The first example of free and open-source software is believed to be the A-2 system, developed at the UNIVAC division of Remington Rand in 1953, which was released to customers with its source code. They were invited to send their improvements back to UNIVAC. Later, almost all IBM mainframe software was also distributed with source code included. User groups such as that of the IBM 701, called SHARE, and that of Digital Equipment Corporation (DEC), called DECUS, were formed to facilitate the exchange of software. The SHARE Operating System, originally developed by General Motors, was distributed by SHARE for the IBM 709 and 7090 computers. Some university computer labs even had a policy requiring that all programs installed on the computer had to come with published source-code files.

In 1969 the Advanced Research Projects Agency Network (ARPANET), a transcontinental, high-speed computer network was constructed. The network (later succeeded by the Internet) simplified the exchange of software code.

Some free software which was developed in the 1970s continues to be developed and used, such as TeX (developed by Donald Knuth) and SPICE.

Initial decline of free software

By the late 1960s change was coming: as operating systems and programming language compilers evolved, software production costs were dramatically increasing relative to hardware. A growing software industry was competing with the hardware manufacturers' bundled software products (the cost of bundled products was included in the hardware cost), leased machines required software support while providing no revenue for software, and some customers, able to better meet their own needs, did not want the costs of manufacturer's software to be bundled with hardware product costs. In the United States vs.

IBM antitrust suit, filed 17 January 1969, the U.S. government charged that bundled software was anticompetitive. While some software continued to come at no cost, there was a growing amount of software that was for sale only under restrictive licenses.

In the early 1970s AT&T distributed early versions of Unix at no cost to government and academic researchers, but these versions did not come with permission to redistribute or to distribute modified versions, and were thus not free software in the modern meaning of the phrase. After Unix became more widespread in the early 1980s, AT&T stopped the free distribution and charged for system patches. As it is quite difficult to switch to another architecture, most researchers paid for a commercial license.

Software was not considered copyrightable before the 1974 US Commission on New Technological Uses of Copyrighted Works (CONTU) decided that "computer programs, to the extent that they embody an author's original creation, are proper subject matter of copyright". Therefore, software had no licenses attached and was shared as public-domain software, typically with source code.

The CONTU decision plus later court decisions such as Apple v. Franklin in 1983 for object code, gave computer programs the copyright status of literary works and started the licensing of software and the shrink-wrap closed source software business model.

In the late 1970s and early 1980s, computer vendors and software-only companies began routinely charging for software licenses, marketing software as "Program Products" and imposing legal restrictions on new software developments, now seen as assets, through copyrights, trademarks, and leasing contracts. In 1976 Bill Gates wrote an essay entitled "Open Letter to Hobbyists", in which he expressed dismay at the widespread sharing of Microsoft's product Altair BASIC by hobbyists without paying its licensing fee. In 1979, AT&T began to enforce its licenses when the company decided it might profit by selling the Unix system. In an announcement letter dated 8 February 1983 IBM inaugurated a policy of no longer distributing sources with purchased software.

To increase revenues, a general trend began to no longer distribute source code (easily readable by programmers), and only distribute the executable machine code that was compiled from the source code. One person especially distressed by this new practice was Richard Stallman. He was concerned that he could no longer study or further modify programs initially written by others. Stallman viewed this practice as ethically wrong.

In response, he founded the GNU Project in 1983 so that people could use computers using only free software. He established a non-profit organization, the Free Software Foundation, in 1985, to more formally organize the project. He invented copyleft, a legal mechanism to preserve the "free" status of a work subject to copyright, and implemented this in the GNU General Public License. Copyleft licenses allow authors to grant a number of rights to users (including rights to use a work without further charges, and rights to obtain, study and modify the program's complete corresponding source code) but requires derivatives to remain under the same license or one without any additional restrictions. Since derivatives include combinations with other original programs, downstream authors are prevented from turning the initial work into proprietary software, and invited to contribute to the copyleft commons. Later, variations of such licenses were developed by others.

1980s and 1990s

Informal software sharing continues

However, there were still those who wished to share their source code with other programmers and/or with users on a free basis, then called "hobbyists" and "hackers". Before the introduction and widespread public use of the internet, there were several alternative ways available to do this, including listings in computer magazines (like Dr. Dobb's Journal, Creative Computing, SoftSide, Compute!, Byte, etc.) and in computer programming books, like the bestseller BASIC Computer Games. Though still copyrighted, annotated source code for key components of Atari 8-bit family system software was published in mass market books, including The Atari BASIC Source Book (full source for Atari BASIC) and Inside Atari DOS (full source for Atari DOS).

SHARE program library

The SHARE users group, founded in 1955, began collecting and distributing free software. The first documented distribution from SHARE was dated 17 October 1955. The "SHARE Program Library Agency" (SPLA) distributed information and software, notably on magnetic tape.

DECUS tapes

In the early 1980s, the so-called DECUS tapes were a worldwide system for transmission of free software for users of DEC equipment. Operating systems were usually proprietary software, but many tools like the TECO editor, Runoff text formatter, or List file listing utility, etc. were developed to make users' lives easier, and distributed on the DECUS tapes. These utility packages benefited DEC, which sometimes incorporated them into new releases of their proprietary operating system. Even compilers could be distributed and for example Ratfor (and Ratfiv) helped researchers to move from Fortran coding to structured programming (suppressing the GO TO statement). The 1981 Decus tape was probably the most innovative by bringing the Lawrence Berkeley Laboratory Software Tools Virtual Operating System which permitted users to use a Unix-like system on DEC 16-bit PDP-11s and 32-bit VAXes running under the VMS operating system. It was similar to the current cygwin system for Windows. Binaries and libraries were often distributed, but users usually preferred to compile from source code.

Online software sharing communities in the 1980s

In the 1980s, parallel to the free software movement, software with source code was shared on BBS networks. This was sometimes a necessity; software written in BASIC and other interpreted languages could only be distributed as source code, and much of it was freeware. When users began gathering such source code, and setting up boards specifically to discuss its modification, this was a de facto open-source system.

One of the most obvious examples of this is one of the most-used BBS systems and networks, WWIV, developed initially in BASIC by Wayne Bell. A culture of "modding" his software, and distributing the mods, grew up so extensively that when the software was ported to first Pascal, then C++, its source code continued to be distributed to registered users, who would share mods and compile their own versions of the software. This may have contributed to it being a dominant system and network, despite being outside the Fidonet umbrella that was shared by so many other BBS makers.

Meanwhile, the advent of Usenet and UUCPNet in the early 1980s further connected the programming community and provided a simpler way for programmers to share their software and contribute to software others had written.

Launch of the free software movement

In 1983, Richard Stallman launched the GNU Project to write a complete operating system free from constraints on use of its source code.

Particular incidents that motivated this include a case where an annoying printer couldn't be fixed because the source code was withheld from users. Stallman also published the GNU Manifesto in 1985 to outline the GNU Project's purpose and explain the importance of free software. Another probable inspiration for the GNU project and its manifesto was a disagreement between Stallman and Symbolics, Inc. over MIT's access to updates Symbolics had made to its Lisp machine, which was based on MIT code. Soon after the launch, he used[clarification needed] the existing term "free software" and founded the Free Software Foundation to promote the concept. The Free Software Definition was published in February 1986.

In 1989, the first version of the GNU General Public License was published. A slightly updated version 2 was published in 1991. In 1989, some GNU developers formed the company Cygnus Solutions. The GNU project's kernel, later called "GNU Hurd", was continually delayed, but most other components were completed by 1991. Some of these, especially the GNU Compiler Collection, had become market leaders[clarification needed] in their own right. The GNU Debugger and GNU Emacs were also notable successes.

Linux (1991–present)

The Linux kernel, started by Linus Torvalds, was released as freely modifiable source code in 1991. The license was not a free software license, but with version 0.12 in February 1992, Torvalds relicensed the project under the GNU General Public License. Much like Unix, Torvalds' kernel attracted attention from volunteer programmers.

Until this point, the GNU project's lack of a kernel meant that no complete free software operating systems existed. The development of Torvalds' kernel closed that last gap. The combination of the almost-finished GNU operating system and the Linux kernel made the first complete free software operating system.

Among Linux distributions, Debian GNU/Linux, begun by Ian Murdock in 1993, is noteworthy for being explicitly committed to the GNU and FSF principles of free software. The Debian developers' principles are expressed in the Debian Social Contract. Since its inception, the Debian project has been closely linked with the FSF, and in fact was sponsored by the FSF for a year in 1994–1995. In 1997, former Debian project leader Bruce Perens also helped found Software in the Public Interest, a non-profit funding and support organization for various free software projects.

Since 1996, the Linux kernel has included proprietary licensed components, so that it was no longer entirely free software. Therefore, the Free Software Foundation Latin America released in 2008 a modified version of the Linux-kernel called Linux-libre, where all proprietary and non-free components were removed.

Many businesses offer customized Linux-based products, or distributions, with commercial support. The naming remains controversial. Referring to the complete system as simply "Linux" is common usage. However, the Free Software Foundation, and many others, advocate the use of the term "GNU/Linux", saying that it is a more accurate name for the whole operating system.

Linux adoption grew among businesses and governments in the 1990s and 2000s. In the English-speaking world at least, Ubuntu and its derivatives became a relatively popular group of Linux distributions.

The free BSDs (1993–present)

When the USL v. BSDi lawsuit was settled out of court in 1993, FreeBSD and NetBSD (both derived from 386BSD) were released as free software. In 1995, OpenBSD forked from NetBSD. In 2004, Dragonfly BSD forked from FreeBSD.

The dot-com years (late 1990s)

In the mid to late 90s, when many website-based companies were starting up, free software became a popular choice for web servers. The Apache HTTP Server became the most-used web-server software, a title that still holds as of 2015. Systems based on a common "stack" of software with the Linux kernel at the base, Apache providing web services, the MySQL database engine for data storage, and the PHP programming language for providing dynamic pages, came to be termed LAMP systems. In actuality, the programming language that predated PHP and dominated the web in the mid and late 1990s was Perl. Web forms were processed on the server side through Common Gateway Interface scripts written in Perl.

The term "open source," as related to free software, was in common use by 1995. Other recollection have it in use during the 1980s.

The launch of Open Source

In 1997, Eric S. Raymond published "The Cathedral and the Bazaar", a reflective analysis of the hacker community and free software principles. The paper received significant attention in early 1998 and was one factor in motivating Netscape Communications Corporation to release their popular Netscape Communicator Internet suite as free software.

Netscape's act prompted Raymond and others to look into how to bring free software principles and benefits to the commercial-software industry. They concluded that FSF's social activism was not appealing to companies like Netscape, and looked for a way to rebrand the free software movement to emphasize the business potential of the sharing of source code.

The label "open source" was adopted by some people in the free software movement at a strategy session held at Palo Alto, California, in reaction to Netscape's January 1998 announcement of a source code release for Navigator. The group of individuals at the session included Christine Peterson who suggested "open source", Todd Anderson, Larry Augustin, Jon Hall, Sam Ockman, Michael Tiemann, and Eric S. Raymond. Over the next week, Raymond and others worked on spreading the word. Linus Torvalds gave an all-important sanction the following day. Phil Hughes offered a pulpit in Linux Journal.

Richard Stallman, pioneer of the free software movement, flirted with adopting the term, but changed his mind. Those people who adopted the term used the opportunity before the release of Navigator's source code to free themselves of the ideological and confrontational connotations of the term "free software". Netscape released its source code under the Netscape Public License and later under the Mozilla Public License.

The term was given a big boost at an event organized in April 1998 by technology publisher Tim O'Reilly. Originally titled the "Freeware Summit" and later named the "Open Source Summit", the event brought together the leaders of many of the most important free and open-source projects, including Linus Torvalds, Larry Wall, Brian Behlendorf, Eric Allman, Guido van Rossum, Michael Tiemann, Paul Vixie, Jamie Zawinski of Netscape, and Eric Raymond.

At that meeting, the confusion caused by the name free software was brought up. Tiemann argued for "sourceware" as a new term, while Raymond argued for "open source".

The assembled developers took a vote, and the winner was announced at a press conference that evening. Five days later, Raymond made the first public call to the free software community to adopt the new term. The Open Source Initiative was formed shortly thereafter. According to the OSI Richard Stallman initially flirted with the idea of adopting the open source term. But as the enormous success of the open source term buried Stallman's free software term and his message on social values and computer users' freedom, later Stallman and his FSF strongly objected to the OSI's approach and terminology.

Due to Stallman's rejection of the term "open-source software", the FOSS ecosystem is divided in its terminology; see also Alternative terms for free software. For example, a 2002 FOSS developer survey revealed that 32.6% associated themselves with OSS, 48% with free software, and 19.4% in between or undecided. Stallman still maintained, however, that users of each term were allies in the fight against proprietary software.

On 13 October 2000, Sun Microsystems released the StarOffice office suite as free software under the GNU Lesser General Public License. The free software version was renamed OpenOffice.org, and coexisted with StarOffice.

By the end of the 1990s, the term "open source" gained much traction in public media and acceptance in software industry in context of the dotcom bubble and the open-source software driven Web 2.0.

Desktop (1984–present)

The X Window System was created in 1984, and became the de facto standard window system in desktop free software operating systems by the mid-1990s. X runs as a server, and is responsible for communicating with graphics hardware on behalf of clients (which are individual software applications). It provides useful services such as having multiple virtual desktops for the same monitor, and transmitting visual data across the network so a desktop can be accessed remotely.

Initially, users or system administrators assembled their own environments from X and available window managers (which add standard controls to application windows; X itself does not do this), pagers, docks and other software. While X can be operated without a window manager, having one greatly increases convenience and ease of use.

Two key "heavyweight" desktop environments for free software operating systems emerged in the 1990s that were widely adopted: KDE and GNOME. KDE was founded in 1996 by Matthias Ettrich. At the time, he was troubled by the inconsistencies in the user interfaces of UNIX applications. He proposed a new desktop environment. He also wanted to make this desktop easy to use. His initial Usenet post spurred a lot of interest.

Ettrich chose to use the Qt toolkit for the KDE project. At the time, Qt did not use a free software license. Members of the GNU project became concerned with the use of such a toolkit for building a free software desktop environment. In August 1997, two projects were started in response to KDE: the Harmony toolkit (a free replacement for the Qt libraries) and GNOME (a different desktop without Qt and built entirely on top of free software). GTK+ was chosen as the base of GNOME in place of the Qt toolkit.

In November 1998, the Qt toolkit was licensed under the free/open source Q Public License (QPL) but debate continued about compatibility with the GNU General Public License (GPL). In September 2000, Trolltech made the Unix version of the Qt libraries available under the GPL, in addition to the QPL, which has eliminated the concerns of the Free Software Foundation. KDE has since been split into KDE Plasma Workspaces, a desktop environment, and KDE Software Compilation, a much broader set of software that includes the desktop environment.

Both KDE and GNOME now participate in freedesktop.org, an effort launched in 2000 to standardize Unix desktop interoperability, although there is still competition between them.

Since 2000, software written for X almost always uses some widget toolkit written on top of X, like Qt or GTK.

In 2010, Canonical released the first version of Unity, a replacement for the prior default desktop environment for Ubuntu, GNOME. This change to a new, under-development desktop environment and user interface was initially somewhat controversial among Ubuntu users.

In 2011, GNOME 3 was introduced, which largely discarded the desktop metaphor in favor of a more mobile-oriented interface. The ensuing controversy led Debian to consider making the Xfce environment default on Debian 7. Several independent projects were begun to keep maintaining the GNOME 2 code.

Fedora did not adopt Unity, retaining its existing offering of a choice of GNOME, KDE and LXDE with GNOME being the default, and hence Red Hat Enterprise Linux (for which Fedora acts as the "initial testing ground") did not adopt Unity either. A fork of Ubuntu was made by interested third-party developers that kept GNOME and discarded Unity. In March 2017, Ubuntu announced that it will be abandoning Unity in favour or GNOME 3 in future versions, and ceasing its efforts in developing Unity-based smartphones and tablets.

When Google built the Linux-based Android operating system, mostly for phone and tablet devices, it replaced X with the purpose-built SurfaceFlinger.

Open-source developers also criticized X as obsolete, carrying many unused or overly complicated elements in its protocol and libraries, while missing modern functionality, e.g., compositing, screen savers, and functions provided by window managers.

Several attempts have been made or are underway to replace X for these reasons, including:

The Y Window System, which had ceased development by 2006.

The Wayland project, started in 2008.

The Mir project, started in 2013 by Canonical Ltd. to produce a replacement windowing system for Ubuntu.

Microsoft, SCO and other attacks (1998–2014)

As free software became more popular, industry incumbents such as Microsoft started to see it as a serious threat. This was shown in a leaked 1998 document, confirmed by Microsoft as genuine, which came to be called the first of the Halloween Documents.

Steve Ballmer once compared the GPL to "a cancer", but has since stopped using this analogy. Indeed, Microsoft has softened its public stance towards open source in general, with open source since becoming an important part of the Microsoft Windows ecosystem. However, at the same time, behind the scenes, Microsoft's actions have been less favourable toward the open-source community.

SCO v. IBM and related bad publicity (2003–present)

In 2003, a proprietary Unix vendor and former Linux distribution vendor called SCO alleged that Unix intellectual property had been inappropriately copied into the Linux kernel, and sued IBM, claiming that it bore responsibility for this. Several related lawsuits and countersuits followed, some originating from SCO, some from others suing SCO.

However, SCO's allegations lacked specificity, and while some in the media reported them as credible, many critics of SCO believed the allegations to be highly dubious at best.

Over the course of the SCO v. IBM case, it emerged that not only had SCO been distributing the Linux kernel for years under the GPL, and continued to do so (thus rendering any claims hard to sustain legally), but that SCO did not even own the copyrights to much of the Unix code that it asserted copyright over, and had no right to sue over them on behalf of the presumed owner, Novell.

This was despite SCO's CEO, Darl McBride, having made many wild and damaging claims of inappropriate appropriation to the media, many of which were later shown to be false, or legally irrelevant even if true.

The blog Groklaw was one of the most forensic examiners of SCO's claims and related events, and gained its popularity from covering this material for many years.

SCO suffered defeat after defeat in SCO v. IBM and its various other court cases, and filed for Chapter 11 bankruptcy in 2007. However, despite the courts finding that SCO did not own the copyrights (see above), and SCO's lawsuit-happy CEO Darl McBride no longer running the company, the bankruptcy trustee in charge of SCO-in-bankruptcy decided to press on with some portions he claimed remained relevant in the SCO v. IBM lawsuit. He could apparently afford to do this because SCO's main law firm in SCO v. IBM had signed an agreement at the outset to represent SCO for a fixed amount of money no matter how long the case took to complete.

In 2004, the Alexis de Tocqueville Institution (ADTI) announced its intent to publish a book, Samizdat: And Other Issues Regarding the 'Source' of Open Source Code, showing that the Linux kernel was based on code stolen from Unix, in essence using the argument that it was impossible to believe that Linus Torvalds could produce something as sophisticated as the Linux kernel. The book was never published, after it was widely criticised and ridiculed, including by people supposedly interviewed for the book. It emerged that some of the people were never interviewed, and that ADTI had not tried to contact Linus Torvalds, or ever put the allegations to him to allow a response. Microsoft attempted to draw a line under this incident, stating that it was a "distraction".

Many suspected that some or all of these legal and fear, uncertainty and doubt (FUD) attacks against the Linux kernel were covertly arranged by Microsoft, although this has never been proven. Both ADTI and SCO, however, received funding from Microsoft.

European Commission v. Microsoft (2004–2007)

In 2004 the European Commission found Microsoft guilty of anti-competitive behaviour with respect to interoperability in the workgroup software market. Microsoft had formerly settled United States v. Microsoft in 2001, in a case which charged that it illegally abused its monopoly power to force computer manufacturers to preinstall Internet Explorer.

The Commission demanded that Microsoft produce full documentation of its workgroup protocols to allow competitors to interoperate with its workgroup software, and imposed fines of 1.5 million euros per day for Microsoft's failure to comply. The commission had jurisdiction because Microsoft sells the software in question in Europe.

Microsoft, after a failed attempt to appeal the decision through the Court of Justice of the European Union, eventually complied with the demand, producing volumes of detailed documentation.

The Samba project, as Microsoft's sole remaining competitor in the workgroup software market, was the key beneficiary of this documentation.

ISO OOXML controversy (2008–present)

In 2008 the International Organization for Standardization published Microsoft's Office Open XML as an international standard, which crucially meant that it, and therefore Microsoft Office, could be used in projects where the use of open standards were mandated by law or by policy. Critics of the standardisation process, including some members of ISO national committees involved in the process itself, alleged irregularities and procedural violations in the process, and argued that the ISO should not have approved OOXML as a standard because it made reference to undocumented Microsoft Office behaviour.

As of 2012, no correct open-source implementation of OOXML exists, which validates the critics' remarks about OOXML being difficult to implement and underspecified. Presently, Google cannot yet convert Office documents into its own proprietary Google Docs format correctly. This suggests that OOXML is not a true open standard, but rather a partial document describing what Microsoft Office does, and only involving certain file formats.

Microsoft's contributions to open source and acquisition of related projects

In 2006 Microsoft launched its CodePlex open source code hosting site, to provide hosting for open-source developers targeting Microsoft platforms. In July 2009 Microsoft even open sourced some Hyper-V-supporting patches to the Linux kernel, because they were required to do so by the GNU General Public License, and contributed them to the mainline kernel. Note that Hyper-V itself is not open source. Microsoft's F# compiler, created in 2002, has also been released as open source under the Apache license. The F# compiler is a commercial product, as it has been incorporated into Microsoft Visual Studio, which is not open source.

Microsoft representatives have made regular appearances at various open source and Linux conferences for many years.

In 2012, Microsoft launched a subsidiary named Microsoft Open Technologies Inc., with the aim of bridging the gap between proprietary Microsoft technologies and non-Microsoft technologies by engaging with open-source standards. This subsidiary was subsequently folded back into Microsoft as Microsoft's position on open source and non-Windows platforms became more favourable.

In January 2016 Microsoft released Chakra as open source under the MIT License; the code is available on GitHub.

Microsoft's stance on open source has shifted as the company began endorsing more open-source software. In 2016, Steve Balmer, former CEO of Microsoft, has retracted his statement that Linux is a malignant cancer. In 2017, the company became a platinum supporter of the Linux Foundation. By 2018, shortly before acquiring GitHub, Microsoft led the charts in the number of paid staff contributing to open-source projects there. While Microsoft may or may not endorse the original philosophy of free software, data shows that it does endorse open source strategically.[original research?]

Critics have noted that, in March 2019, Microsoft sued Foxconn's subsidiary over a 2013 patent contract; in 2013, Microsoft had announced a patent agreement with Foxconn related to Foxconn's use of the Linux-based Android and Chrome OS.

Open source and programming languages

The vast majority of programming languages in use today have a free software implementation available.

Since the 1990s, the release of major new programming languages in the form of open-source compilers and/or interpreters has been the norm, rather than the exception. Examples include Python in 1991, Ruby in 1995, and Scala in 2003. In recent times, the most notable exceptions have been Java, ActionScript, C#, and Apple's Swift until version 2.2 was proprietary. Partly compatible open-source implementations have been developed for most, and in the case of Java, the main open-source implementation is by now very close to the commercial version.

Java

Since its first public release in 1996, the Java platform had not been open source, although the Java source code portion of the Java runtime was included in Java Development Kits (JDKs), on a purportedly "confidential" basis, despite it being freely downloadable by the general public in most countries. Sun later expanded this "confidential" source code access to include the full source code of the Java Runtime Environment via a separate program which was open to members of the public, and later made the source of the Java compiler javac available also. Sun also made the JDK source code available confidentially to the Blackdown Java project, which was a collection of volunteers who ported early versions of the JDK to Linux, or improved on Sun's Linux ports of the JDK.

However, none of this was open source, because modification and redistribution without Sun's permission were forbidden in all cases. Sun stated at the time that they were concerned about preventing forking of the Java platform.

However, several independent partial reimplementations of the Java platform had been created, many of them by the open-source community, such as the GNU Compiler for Java (GCJ). Sun never filed lawsuits against any of the open source clone projects. GCJ notably caused a bad user experience for Java on free software supporting distributions such as Fedora and Ubuntu which shipped GCJ at the time as their Java implementation. How to replace GCJ with the Sun JDK was a frequently asked question by users, because GCJ was an incomplete implementation, incompatible and buggy.

In 2006 Jonathan I. Schwartz became CEO of Sun Microsystems, and signalled his commitment to open source. On 8 May 2007, Sun Microsystems released the Java Development Kit as OpenJDK under the GNU General Public License. Part of the class library (4%) could not be released as open source due to them being licensed from other parties and were included as binary plugs. Because of this, in June 2007, Red Hat launched IcedTea to resolve the encumbered components with the equivalents from GNU Classpath implementation. Since the release, most of the encumbrances have been solved, leaving only the audio engine code and colour management system (the latter is to be resolved using Little CMS).

Distributed version control (2001–present)

The first open-source distributed revision control system (DVCS) was 'tla' in 2001 (since renamed to GNU arch); however, it and its successors 'baz' and 'bzr' (Bazaar) never became very popular, and GNU arch was discontinued, although Bazaar still continues and is used by Canonical.

However, other DVCS projects sprung up, and some started to get significant adoption.

Git (2005–present)

Git, the most popular DVCS, was created in 2005. Some developers of the Linux kernel started to use a proprietary DVCS called BitKeeper, notably Linux founder Linus Torvalds, although some other kernel developers never used it due to its proprietary nature. The unusual situation whereby Linux kernel development involved the use by some of proprietary software "came to a head" when Andrew Tridgell started to reverse-engineer BitKeeper with the aim of producing an open-source tool which could provide some of the same functionality as the commercial version. BitMover, the company that developed BitKeeper, in response, in 2005 revoked the special free of-charge license it had granted to certain kernel developers.

As a result of the removal of the BitKeeper license, Linus Torvalds decided to write his own DVCS, called git, because he thought none of the existing open-source DVCSs were suitable for his particular needs as a kernel maintainer (which was why he had adopted BitKeeper in the first place).

A number of other developers quickly jumped in and helped him, and git over time grew from a relatively simple "stupid content tracker" (on which some developers developed "porcelain" extensions) into the sophisticated and powerful DVCS that it is today. Torvalds no longer maintains git himself, however; it has been maintained by Junio Hamano for many years, and has continued receiving contributions from many developers.

The increasing popularity of open-source DVCSs such as git, and then, later, DVCS hosting sites, the most popular of which is GitHub (founded 2008), incrementally reduced the barriers to participation in free software projects still further. With sites like GitHub, no longer did potential contributors have to do things like hunt for the URL for the source code repository (which could be in different places on each website, or sometimes tucked away in a README file or developer documentation), or work out how to generate a patch, and if necessary subscribe to the right mailing list so that their patch email would get to the right people. Contributors can simply fork their own copy of a repository with one click, and issue a pull request from the appropriate branch when their changes are ready.

GitHub has become the most popular hosting site in the world for open-source software, and this, together with the ease of forking and the visibility of forks has made it a popular way for contributors to make changes, large and small.

Recent developments

While copyright is the primary legal mechanism that FOSS authors use to ensure license compliance for their software, other mechanisms such as legislation, software patents, and trademarks have uses also. In response to legal issues with patents and the DMCA, the Free Software Foundation released version 3 of its GNU Public License in 2007 that explicitly addressed the DMCA's digital rights management (DRM) provisions and patent rights.

After the development of the GNU GPLv3, as copyright holder of many pieces of the GNU system, such as the GNU Compiler Collection (GCC) software, the FSF updated most of the GNU programs' licenses from GPLv2 to GPLv3. Apple, a user of GCC and a heavy user of both DRM and patents, decided to switch the compiler in its Xcode IDE from GCC to Clang, another FOSS compiler, but which is under a permissive license.

LWN speculated that Apple was motivated partly by a desire to avoid GPLv3. The Samba project also switched to GPLv3, which Apple replaced in their software suite with a closed-source, proprietary software alternative.

Recent mergers have affected major open-source software. Sun Microsystems (Sun) acquired MySQL AB, owner of the popular open-source MySQL database, in 2008.

Oracle in turn purchased Sun in January 2010, acquiring their copyrights, patents, and trademarks. This made Oracle the owner of both the most popular proprietary database and the most popular open-source database (MySQL). Oracle's attempts to commercialize the open-source MySQL database have raised concerns in the FOSS community.

Partly in response to uncertainty about the future of MySQL, the FOSS community forked the project into new database systems outside of Oracle's control. These include MariaDB, Percona, and Drizzle. All of these have distinct names; they are distinct projects and cannot use the trademarked name MySQL.

Android (2008–present)

In September 2008, Google released the first version of Android, a new smartphone operating system, as open source (some Google applications that are sometimes but not always bundled with Android are not open source). Initially, the operating system was given away for free by Google, and was eagerly adopted by many handset makers; Google later bought Motorola Mobility and produced its own "vanilla" Android phones and tablets, while continuing to allow other manufacturers to use Android. Android is now the world's most popular mobile platform.

Because Android is based on the Linux kernel, this means that Linux is now the dominant kernel on both mobile platforms (via Android), and supercomputers, and a key player in server operating systems too.

Oracle v. Google.

In August 2010, Oracle sued Google claiming that its use of Java in Android infringed on Oracle's copyrights and patents. The initial Oracle v. Google trial ended in May 2012, with the finding that Google did not infringe on Oracle's patents, and the trial judge ruled that the structure of the Java application programming interfaces (APIs) used by Google was not copyrightable.

The jury found that Google made a trivial ("de minimis") copyright infringement, but the parties stipulated that Google would pay no damages, because it was so trivial. However, Oracle appealed to the Federal Circuit, and Google filed a cross-appeal on the literal copying claim. The Federal Circuit ruled that the small copyright infringement acknowledged by Google was not de minimis, and sent the fair use issue back to the trial judge for reconsideration. In 2016, the case was retried and a jury found for Google, on the grounds of fair use.

Chromium OS (2009–present)

Until recently, Linux was still a relatively uncommon choice of operating system for desktops and laptops. However, Google's Chromebooks, running Chrome OS which is essentially a thin client, have captured 20–25% of the sub-$300 US laptop market. Chrome OS is built from the open-source Chromium OS, which is based on Linux, in much the same way that versions of Android shipped on commercially available phones are built from the open source version of Android.

7

Open Source Licenses

An open-source license is a type of license for computer software and other products that allows the source code, blueprint or design to be used, modified and/or shared under defined terms and conditions. This allows end users to review and modify the source code, blueprint or design for their own customization, curiosity or troubleshooting needs. Open-source licensed software is mostly available free of charge, though this does not necessarily have to be the case. Licenses which only permit non-commercial redistribution or modification of the source code for personal use only are generally not considered as open-source licenses. However, open-source licenses may have some restrictions, particularly regarding the expression of respect to the origin of software, such as a requirement to preserve the name of the authors and a copyright statement within the code, or a requirement to redistribute the licensed software only under the same license (as in a copyleft license). One popular set of open-source software licenses are those approved by the Open Source Initiative (OSI) based on their Open Source Definition (OSD).

Comparisons

The Free Software Foundation has a related but distinct critera for evaluating whether or not a license qualifies software as free software. All free software licenses are also considered open-source software licenses. In the same way, the Debian project has its own criteria, the Debian Free Software Guidelines, on which the Open Source Definition is based. Open-source license criteria focuses on the availability of the source code and the ability to modify and share it, while free software licenses focuses on the users freedom to use the program, to modify it, and to share it.

There are also shared source licenses which have some similarities with open source, such as the Microsoft Reciprocal License (MS-RL). They are mainly used by Microsoft and can range from extremely restrictive to comparable with free open-source software.

OSL FOR COMPUTER SOFTWARES

Apache License

The Apache License /??pæt?i/ is a free software license written by the Apache Software Foundation (ASF). The Apache License requires preservation of the copyright notice and disclaimer. Like any free software license, the Apache License allows the user of the software the freedom to use the software for any purpose, to distribute it, to modify it, and to distribute modified versions of the software, under the terms of the license, without concern for royalties.

All software produced by the ASF or any of its projects or subjects is licensed according to the terms of the Apache License. Some non-ASF software is also licensed using the Apache License. In October 2012, 8708 projects located at SourceForge.net were available under the terms of the Apache License. In a blog post from May 2008, Google mentioned that 25,000 out of the 100,000 projects then hosted on Google Code were using the Apache License, including the Android operating system.

Version history

The Apache License 1.0 was the original Apache License which applies only to older versions of Apache packages (such as version 1.2 of the Web server).

The Apache License 1.1 was approved by the ASF in 2000: The primary change from the 1.0 license is in the 'advertising clause' (section 3 of the 1.0 license); derived products are no longer required to include attribution in their advertising materials, but only in their documentation.

The ASF adopted the Apache License 2.0 in January 2004. The stated goals of the license included making the license easier for non-ASF projects to use, improving compatibility with GPL-based software, allowing the license to be included by reference instead of listed in every file, clarifying the license on contributions, and requiring a patent license on contributions that necessarily infringe a contributor's own patents.

Licensing conditions

The Apache License is widely, but not universally, considered permissive in that it does not require a derivative work of the software, or modifications to the original, to be distributed using the same license (unlike copyleft licenses - see comparison). It still requires application of the same license to all unmodified parts and, in every licensed file, any original copyright, patent, trademark, and attribution notices in redistributed code must be preserved (excluding notices that do not pertain to any part of the derivative works); and, in every licensed file changed, a notification must be added stating that changes have been made to that file.

If a NOTICE text file is included as part of the distribution of the original work, then derivative works must include a readable copy of these notices within a NOTICE text file distributed as part of the derivative works, within the source form or documentation, or within a display generated by the derivative works (wherever such third-party notices normally appear).

The contents of the NOTICE file do not modify the license, as they are for informational purposes only, and adding more attribution notices as addenda to the NOTICE text is permissible, provided that these notices cannot be understood as modifying the license.

Modifications may have appropriate copyright notices, and may provide different license terms for the modifications.

Unless explicitly stated otherwise, any contributions submitted by a licensee to a licensor will be under the terms of the license without any terms and conditions, but this does not preclude any separate agreements with the licensor regarding these contributions.

GPL compatibility

The Apache Software Foundation and the Free Software Foundation both agree that the Apache License 2.0 is a free software license, compatible with version 3 of the GNU General Public License (GPL), meaning that code under GPL version 3 and Apache License 2.0 can be combined, as long as the resulting software is licensed under the GPL version 3.

The Free Software Foundation considers all versions of the Apache License (as of 2013) to be incompatible with the previous GPL versions 1 and 2 and, furthermore, considers Apache License versions before v2.0 incompatible with GPLv3.

BSD LICENSES

BSD licenses are a family of permissive free software licenses, imposing minimal restrictions on the redistribution of covered software. This is in contrast to copyleft licenses, which have reciprocity share-alike requirements.

The original BSD license was used for its namesake, the Berkeley Software Distribution (BSD), a Unix-like operating system. The original version has since been revised and its descendants are more properly termed modified BSD licenses.

Two variants of the license, the New BSD License/Modified BSD License (3-clause), and the Simplified BSD License/FreeBSD License (2-clause) have been verified as GPL-compatible free software licenses by the Free Software Foundation, and have been vetted as open source licenses by the Open Source Initiative, while the original, 4-clause license has not been accepted as an open source license and, although the original is considered to be a free software license by the FSF, the FSF does not consider it to be compatible with the GPL due to the advertising clause.

Terms

Besides the original license used in BSD, there are several derivative licenses that are commonly referred to as a "BSD license". Today, the typical BSD license is the 3-clause version, which is revised from the original 4-clause version.

Note that: In all BSD licences as following, <organization> is the organization of the <copyright holder> or just the <copyright holder>, and <year> is the year of the copyright. As published in BSD, <copyright holder> is "Regents of the University of California", and <organization> is "University of California, Berkeley".

Previous license

Some releases of BSD prior to the adoption of the 4-clause BSD license used a license that is clearly ancestral to the 4-clause BSD license. These releases include 4.3BSD-Tahoe (1988) and Net/1 (1989). Though largely replaced by the 4-clause license, this license can be found in 4.3BSD-Reno, Net/2, and 4.4BSD-Alpha.

Copyright (c) <year> <copyright holder>.

All rights reserved.

Redistribution and use in source and binary forms are permitted provided that the above copyright notice and this paragraph are duplicated in all such forms and that any documentation, advertising materials, and other materials related to such distribution and use acknowledge that the software was developed by the <organization>.

The name of the <organization> may not be used to endorse or promote products derived from this software without specific prior written permission.

This software is provided ``as is'' and without any express or Implied warranties, including, without limitation, the implied Warranties of merchantability and fitness for a particular purpose.

4-clause license (original "BSD License")

The original BSD license contained a clause not found in later licenses, known as the "advertising clause". This clause eventually became controversial, as it required authors of all works deriving from a BSD-licensed work to include an acknowledgment of the original source in all advertising material. This was clause number 3 in the original license text:

Copyright (c) <year>, <copyright holder>

All rights reserved.

Redistribution and use in source and binary forms, with or without modification, are permitted provided that the following conditions are met:

1. Redistributions of source code must retain the above copyright notice, this list of conditions and the following disclaimer.

2. Redistributions in binary form must reproduce the above copyright notice, this list of conditions and the following disclaimer in the documentation and/or other materials provided with the distribution.

3. All advertising materials mentioning features or use of this software must display the following acknowledgement:

This product includes software developed by the <organization>.

4. Neither the name of the <organization> nor the names of its contributors may be used to endorse or promote products derived from this software without specific prior written permission.

This software is provided by <copyright holder> "as is" and any Express or implied warranties, including, but not limited to, the implied Warranties of merchantability and fitness for a particular purpose are Disclaimed. In no event shall <copyright holder> be liable for any Direct, indirect, incidental, special, exemplary, or consequential damages (Including, but not limited to, procurement of substitute goods or services; Loss of use, data, or profits; or business interruption) however caused and On any theory of liability, whether in contract, strict liability, or tort (Including negligence or otherwise) arising in any way out of the use of this Software, even if advised of the possibility of such damage.

This clause was objected to on the grounds that as people changed the license to reflect their name or organization it led to escalating advertising requirements when programs were combined together in a software distribution-every occurrence of the license with a different name required a separate acknowledgment. In arguing against it, Richard

Stallman has stated that he counted 75 such acknowledgments in a 1997 version of NetBSD. In addition, the clause presented a legal problem for those wishing to publish BSD-licensed software which relies upon separate programs using the more-restrictive GNU GPL: the advertising clause is incompatible with the GPL, which does not allow the addition of restrictions beyond those it already imposes; because of this, the GPL's publisher, the Free Software Foundation, recommends developers not use the license, though it states there is no reason not to use software already using it.

Today, this original license is now sometimes called "BSD-old" or "4-clause BSD".

3-clause license ("Revised BSD License", "New BSD License", or "Modified BSD License")

The advertising clause was removed from the license text in the official BSD on 22 July 1999 by William Hoskins, Director of the Office of Technology Licensing for UC Berkeley. Other BSD distributions removed the clause, but many similar clauses remain in BSD-derived code from other sources, and unrelated code using a derived license.

While the original license is sometimes referred to as "BSD-old", the resulting 3-clause version is sometimes referred to by "BSD-new." Other names include "New BSD", "revised BSD", "BSD-3", or "3-clause BSD". This version has been vetted as an Open source license by the OSI as the "The BSD License".

The Free Software Foundation, which refers to the license as the "Modified BSD License", states that it is compatible with the GNU GPL.

The FSF encourages users to be specific when referring to the license by name (i.e. not simply referring to it as "a BSD license" or "BSD-style") to avoid confusion with the original BSD license.

This version allows unlimited redistribution for any purpose as long as its copyright notices and the license's disclaimers of warranty are maintained. The license also contains a clause restricting use of the names of contributors for endorsement of a derived work without specific permission.

Copyright (c) <year>, <copyright holder>

All rights reserved.

Redistribution and use in source and binary forms, with or without modification, are permitted provided that the following conditions are met:

- Redistributions of source code must retain the above copyright notice, this list of conditions and the following disclaimer.
- Redistributions in binary form must reproduce the above copyright notice, this list of conditions and the following disclaimer in the documentation and/or other materials provided with the distribution.
- Neither the name of the <organization> nor the names of its contributors may be used to endorse or promote products derived from this software without specific prior written permission.

This software is provided by the copyright holders and contributors "as is" and Any express or implied warranties, including, but not limited to, the implied Warranties of merchantability and fitness for a particular purpose are Disclaimed. In no event shall <copyright holder> be liable for any Direct, indirect, incidental, special, exemplary, or consequential damages (Including, but not limited to, procurement of substitute goods or services; Loss of use, data, or profits; or business interruption) however caused and On any theory of liability, whether in contract, strict liability, or tort (Including negligence or otherwise) arising in any way out of the use of this Software, even if advised of the possibility of such damage.

2-clause license ("Simplified BSD License" or "FreeBSD License")

An even more simplified version has come into use, primarily known for its usage in FreeBSD. The primary difference between it and the New BSD (3-clause) License is that it omits the non-endorsement clause. It also adds a further disclaimer about views and opinions expressed in the software. The Free Software Foundation, which refers to the license as the FreeBSD License, states that it is compatible with the GNU GPL. In addition, the FSF encourages users to be specific when referring to the license by name (i.e. not simply referring to it as "a BSD license" or "BSD-style"), as it does with the modified/new BSD license, to avoid confusion with the original BSD license.

Copyright (c) <YEAR>, <OWNER>

All rights reserved.

Redistribution and use in source and binary forms, with or without modification, are permitted provided that the following conditions are met:

1. Redistributions of source code must retain the above copyright notice, this list of conditions and the following disclaimer.

2. Redistributions in binary form must reproduce the above copyright notice, this list of conditions and the following disclaimer in the documentation and/or other materials provided with the distribution.

This software is provided by the copyright holders and contributors "as is" and Any express or implied warranties, including, but not limited to, the implied Warranties of merchantability and fitness for a particular purpose are Disclaimed. In no event shall the copyright owner or contributors be liable for Any direct, indirect, incidental, special, exemplary, or consequential damages (Including, but not limited to, procurement of substitute goods or services; Loss of use, data, or profits; or business interruption) however caused and On any theory of liability, whether in contract, strict liability, or tort (Including negligence or otherwise) arising in any way out of the use of this Software, even if advised of the possibility of such damage.

The views and conclusions contained in the software and documentation are those of the authors and should not be interpreted as representing official policies, either expressed or implied, of the FreeBSD Project.

Other projects, such as NetBSD, use a similar 2-clause license, but without the additional disclaimer. This version has been vetted as an Open source license by the OSI as the "Simplified BSD License."

Proprietary software licenses compatibility

The BSD License allows proprietary use and allows the software released under the license to be incorporated into proprietary products. Works based on the material may be released under a proprietary license as closed source software.

GNU GENERAL PUBLIC LICENSE

The GNU General Public License (GNU GPL or GPL) is the most widely used free software license, which guarantees end users (individuals, organizations, companies) the freedoms to use, study, share (copy), and modify the software. Software that ensures that these rights are retained is called free software. The license was originally written by Richard Stallman of the Free Software Foundation (FSF) for the GNU project.

The GPL grants the recipients of a computer program the rights of the Free Software Definition and uses copyleft to ensure the freedoms are preserved whenever the work is distributed, even when the work is changed or added to. The GPL is a copyleft license, which means that derived works can only be distributed under the same license terms. This is in distinction to permissive free software licenses, of which the BSD licenses are the standard examples. GPL was the first copyleft license for general use.

As of August 2007, the GPL accounted for nearly 65% of the 43,442 free software projects listed on Freecode, and as of January 2006, about 68% of the projects listed on SourceForge.net. Similarly, a 2001 survey of Red Hat Linux 7.1 found that 50% of the source code was licensed under the GPL and a 1997 survey of MetaLab, then the largest free software archive, showed that the GPL accounted for about half of the software licensed therein. Prominent free software programs licensed under the GPL include the Linux kernel and the GNU Compiler Collection (GCC). Some other free software programs (MySQL is a prominent example) are dual-licensed under multiple licenses, often with one of the licenses being the GPL.

It is believed that the copyleft provided by the GPL was crucial to the success of Linux-based systems, giving the programmers who contributed to the kernel the assurance that their work would benefit the whole world and remain free, rather than being exploited by software companies that would not have to give anything back to the community.

On 29 June 2007, the third version of the license (GNU GPLv3) was released to address some perceived problems with the second version (GNU GPLv2) that were discovered during its long-time usage. To keep the license up to date the GPL license includes an optional "any later version" clause, allowing users to choose between the original terms or the terms in new versions as updated by the FSF. Developers can omit it when licensing their software; for instance the Linux kernel is licensed under GPLv2 without the "any later version" clause.

History

The GPL was written by Richard Stallman in 1989 for use with programs released as part of the GNU project. The original GPL was based on a unification of similar licenses used for early versions of GNU Emacs, the GNU Debugger and the GNU C Compiler. These licenses contained similar provisions to the modern GPL, but were specific to each program, rendering them incompatible, despite being the same license. Stallman's goal was to produce one license that could be used for any project, thus making it possible for many projects to share code.

The second version of the license, version 2, was released in 1991. Over the following 15 years, members of the FOSS (Free and Open Source Software) community became concerned over problems in the GPLv2 license which allowed GPL-licensed software to be exploited in ways that were contrary to the intentions of the license. These problems included tivoization (the inclusion of GPL-licensed software in hardware that will refuse to run modified versions of its software); incompatibility issues like with the Affero General Public License; and patent deals between Microsoft and distributors of free and open source software, which were viewed as an attempt to use patents as a weapon against the FOSS community.

Version 3 was developed to attempt to address these concerns and was officially released on 29 June 2007.

Version 1

Version 1 of the GNU GPL, released on 25 February 1989, prevented what were then the two main ways that software distributors restricted the freedoms that define free software. The first problem was that distributors may publish binary files only-executable, but not readable or modifiable by humans. To prevent this, GPLv1 said that any vendor distributing binaries must also make the human-readable source code available under the same licensing terms (Sections 3a and 3b of the license).

The second problem was the distributors might add additional restrictions, either by adding restrictions to the license, or by combining the software with other software which had other restrictions on its distribution. If this was done, then the union of the two sets of restrictions would apply to the combined work, thus unacceptable restrictions could be added. To prevent this, GPLv1 said that modified versions, as a whole, had to be distributed under the terms in GPLv1 (Sections 2b and 4 of the license). Therefore, software distributed under the terms of GPLv1 could be combined with software under more permissive terms, as this would not change the terms under which the whole could be distributed, but software distributed under GPLv1 could not be combined with software distributed under a more restrictive license, as this would conflict with the requirement that the whole be distributable under the terms of GPLv1.

Version 2

According to Richard Stallman, the major change in GPLv2 was the "Liberty or Death" clause, as he calls it - Section 7. This section says that if somebody has restrictions imposed that prevent him or her from distributing GPL-covered software in a way that respects other users' freedom (for example, if a legal ruling states that he or she can only distribute the software in binary form), he or she cannot distribute it at all. The hope is, that this will make it less tempting for companies to use patent threats to require a fee from the free software developers.

By 1990, it was becoming apparent that a less restrictive license would be strategically useful for the C library and for software libraries that essentially did the job of existing proprietary ones; when version 2 of the

GPL (GPLv2) was released in June 1991, therefore, a second license - the Library General Public License - was introduced at the same time and numbered with version 2 to show that both were complementary. The version numbers diverged in 1999 when version 2.1 of the LGPL was released, which renamed it the GNU Lesser General Public License to reflect its place in the philosophy.

Version 3

In late 2005, the Free Software Foundation (FSF) announced work on version 3 of the GPL (GPLv3). On 16 January 2006, the first "discussion draft" of GPLv3 was published, and the public consultation began. The public consultation was originally planned for nine to fifteen months but finally stretched to eighteen months with four drafts being published. The official GPLv3 was released by FSF on 29 June 2007. GPLv3 was written by Richard Stallman, with legal counsel from Eben Moglen and the Software Freedom Law Center.

According to Stallman, the most important changes are in relation to software patents, free software license compatibility, the definition of "source code", and hardware restrictions on software modification ("tivoization"). Other changes relate to internationalization, how license violations are handled, and how additional permissions can be granted by the copyright holder. It also adds a provision that 'strips' DRM of its legal value, so people can break the DRM on GPL software without breaking laws like the DMCA.

The public consultation process was coordinated by the Free Software Foundation with assistance from Software Freedom Law Center, Free Software Foundation Europe, and other free software groups. Comments were collected from the public via the gplv3.fsf.org web portal. That portal runs purpose-written software called stet. During the public consultation process, 962 comments were submitted for the first draft. By the end, a total of 2,636 comments had been submitted.

The third draft was released on 28 March 2007. This draft included language intended to prevent patent-related agreements like the controversial Microsoft-Novell patent agreement and restricts the anti-tivoization clauses to a legal definition of a "User" or "consumer product". It also explicitly removed the section on "Geographical Limitations", whose probable removal had been announced at the launch of the public consultation.

The fourth discussion draft, which was the last, was released on 31 May 2007. It introduced Apache License compatibility, clarified the role of outside contractors, and made an exception to avoid the perceived problems of a Microsoft-Novell style agreement, saying in Section 11 paragraph 6 that

You may not convey a covered work if you are a party to an arrangement with a third party that is in the business of distributing software, under which you make payment to the third party based on the extent of your activity of conveying the work, and under which the third party grants, to any of the parties who would receive the covered work from you, a discriminatory patent license [...]

This aims to make future such deals ineffective. The license is also meant to cause Microsoft to extend the patent licenses it grants to Novell customers for the use of GPLv3 software to all users of that GPLv3 software; this is possible only if Microsoft is legally a "conveyor" of the GPLv3 software.

Also, early drafts of GPLv3 allowed licensors to add an Affero-like requirement which would have plugged the ASP loophole in the GPL. As there were concerns expressed about the administrative costs of checking code for this additional requirement, it was decided to keep the GPL and the Affero license separated.

Others, notably some high-profile developers of the Linux kernel, commented to the mass media and made public statements about their objections to parts of discussion drafts 1 and 2.

GPLv3 improves compatibility with several open source software licenses such as Apache License, version 2.0, and the GNU Affero General Public License which GPLv2 could not be combined with, but GPLv3 software can only be combined with GPLv2 software if the GPLv2 version has the optional "or later" clause of the GPL. "GPLv2 or any later version" is considered by FSF as the most common form of licensing GPLv2 software. while for example Toybox developer Rob Landley described it as a lifeboat clause. Software projects which are licensed with the optional "or later" clause include the GNU Project, while a prominent example without the clause is the Linux kernel. The final version of the license text was published on 29 June 2007.

Adoption

According to Black Duck Software, the website data show that the GPL license family is used 54%, GPLv2 33%, GPLv3 12%, LGPL 2.1 6%, and LGPL 3.0 3% by open source software projects.

In a web blog post by 451 Group analyst Matthew Aslett, Aslett argued that "copyleft" licenses went into decline and permissive licenses increased, based on statistics from Black Duck Software. However, a later study showed that software licensed under the GPL license family has increased, and that even the data from Black Duck Software have shown a total increase of software projects licensed under GPL. The study used public information gathered from repositories of the Debian Project, and the study criticized Black Duck Software for not publishing their methodology used in collecting statistics. Daniel German, Professor in the Department of Computer Science at the University of Victoria in Canada, presented a talk in 2013 about the methodological challenges in determining which are the most widely used FOSS licenses, and showed how he could not replicate the result from Black Duck Software.

In 2011, four years after the release of the GPLv3, according to Black Duck Software data, 6.5% of all open-source license projects are GPLv3 while 42.5% are GPLv2. Google open-source programs office manager Chris DiBona reported that the number of open-source projects licensed software that had moved to GPLv3 from GPLv2 was 50% in 2009, counting the projects hosted at Google Code.

Terms and conditions

The terms and conditions of the GPL must be made available to anybody receiving a copy of the work that has a GPL applied to it ("the licensee"). Any licensee who adheres to the terms and conditions is given permission to modify the work, as well as to copy and redistribute the work or any derivative version. The licensee is allowed to charge a fee for this service, or do this free of charge. This latter point distinguishes the GPL from software licenses that prohibit commercial redistribution. The FSF argues that free software should not place restrictions on commercial use, and the GPL explicitly states that GPL works may be sold at any price.

The GPL additionally states that a distributor may not impose "further restrictions on the rights granted by the GPL". This forbids activities such as distributing of the software under a non-disclosure agreement or contract. Distributors under the GPL also grant a license for any of their patents practiced by the software, to practice those patents in GPL software.

The fourth section for version 2 of the license and the seventh section of version 3 require that programs distributed as pre-compiled binaries are accompanied by a copy of the source code, a written offer to distribute the source code via the same mechanism as the pre-compiled binary, or the written offer to obtain the source code that the user got when they received the pre-compiled binary under the GPL. The second section of version 2 and the fifth section of version 3 also require giving "all recipients a copy of this License along with the Program". Version 3 of the license allows making the source code available in additional ways in fulfillment of the seventh section. These include downloading source code from an adjacent network server or by peer-to-peer transmission, provided that is how the compiled code was available and there are "clear directions" on where to find the source code.

The FSF does not hold the copyright for a work released under the GPL, unless an author explicitly assigns copyrights to the FSF (which seldom happens except for programs that are part of the GNU project). Only the individual copyright holders have the authority to sue when a license violation takes place.

Use of licensed software

Software under the GPL may be run for all purposes, including commercial purposes and even as a tool for creating proprietary software, for example when using GPL-licensed compilers. Users or companies who distribute GPL-licensed works (e.g. software), may charge a fee for copies or give them free of charge. This distinguishes the GPL from shareware software licenses that allow copying for personal use but prohibit commercial distribution, or proprietary licenses where copying is prohibited by copyright law. The FSF argues that freedom-respecting free software should also not restrict commercial use and distribution (including redistribution): the GPL explicitly states that GPL works may be sold at any price.

In purely private (or internal) use -with no sales and no distribution- the software code may be modified and parts reused without requiring the source code to be released. For sales or distribution, the entire source code need to be made available to end users, including any code changes and additions- in that case, copyleft is applied to ensure that end users retain the freedoms defined above.

However, software running as an application program under a GPL-licensed operating system such as Linux is not required to be licensed under GPL or to be distributed with source-code availability-the licensing depends only on the used libraries and software components and not on the underlying platform. For example if a program consists only of own original custom software, or is combined with source code from other software components, then the own custom software components need not be licensed under GPL and need not make their code available; even if the underlying operating system used is licensed under the GPL, applications running on it are not considered derivative works. Only if GPLed parts are used in a program (and the program is distributed), then all other source code of the program needs to be made available under the same license terms. The GNU Lesser General Public license (LGPL) was created to have a weaker copyleft than the GPL, in that it does not require own custom-developed source code (distinct from the LGPLed parts) to be made available under the same license terms.

Copyleft

The distribution rights granted by the GPL for modified versions of the work are not unconditional. When someone distributes a GPL'd work plus his/her own modifications, the requirements for distributing the whole work cannot be any greater than the requirements that are in the GPL.

This requirement is known as copyleft. It earns its legal power from the use of copyright on software programs. Because a GPL work is copyrighted, a licensee has no right to redistribute it, not even in modified form (barring fair use), except under the terms of the license. One is only required to adhere to the terms of the GPL if one wishes to exercise rights normally restricted by copyright law, such as redistribution. Conversely, if one distributes copies of the work without abiding by the terms of the GPL (for instance, by keeping the source code secret), he or she can be sued by the original author under copyright law.

Copyleft thus uses copyright law to accomplish the opposite of its usual purpose: instead of imposing restrictions, it grants rights to other people, in a way that ensures the rights cannot subsequently be taken away. It also ensures that unlimited redistribution rights are not granted, should any legal flaw be found in the copyleft statement.

Many distributors of GPL'ed programs bundle the source code with the executables. An alternative method of satisfying the copyleft is to provide a written offer to provide the source code on a physical medium (such as a CD) upon request. In practice, many GPL'ed programs are distributed over the Internet, and the source code is made available over FTP or HTTP. For Internet distribution, this complies with the license.

Copyleft applies only when a person seeks to redistribute the program. One is allowed to make private modified versions, without any obligation to divulge the modifications as long as the modified software is not distributed to anyone else. Note that the copyleft applies only to the software and not to its output (unless that output is itself a derivative work of the program). For example, a public web portal running a modified derivative of a GPL'ed content management system is not required to distribute its changes to the underlying software because its output is not a derivative.

There has been debate on whether it is a violation of the GPL to release the source code in obfuscated form, such as in cases in which the author is less willing to make the source code available. The general consensus was that while unethical, it was not considered a violation. The issue was clarified when the license was altered to require that the "preferred" version of the source code be made available.

License versus contract

The GPL was designed as a license, rather than a contract. In some Common Law jurisdictions, the legal distinction between a license and a contract is an important one: contracts are enforceable by contract law, whereas licenses are enforced under copyright law. However, this distinction is not useful in the many jurisdictions where there are no differences between contracts and licenses, such as Civil Law systems.

Those who do not accept the GPL's terms and conditions do not have permission, under copyright law, to copy or distribute GPL licensed software or derivative works. However, if they do not redistribute the GPL'd program, they may still use the software within their organization however they like, and works (including programs) constructed by the use of the program are not required to be covered by this license. Allison Randal argued that the GPLv3 as a license is unnecessarily confusing for lay readers, and could be simplified while retaining the same conditions and legal force.

Derivations

The text of the GPL is itself copyrighted, and the copyright is held by the Free Software Foundation.

The FSF permits people to create new licenses based on the GPL, as long as the derived licenses do not use the GPL preamble without permission. This is discouraged, however, since such a license might be incompatible with the GPL and causes a perceived license proliferation.

Other licenses created by the GNU project include the GNU Lesser General Public License and the GNU Free Documentation License.

The text of the GPL is not itself under the GPL. The license's copyright disallows modification of the license. Copying and distributing the license is allowed since the GPL requires recipients to get "a copy of this License along with the Program". According to the GPL FAQ, anyone can make a new license using a modified version of the GPL as long as he or she uses a different name for the license, does not mention "GNU", and removes the preamble, though the preamble can be used in a modified license if permission to use it is obtained from the Free Software Foundation (FSF).

Linking and derived works

Libraries

According to the FSF, "The GPL does not require you to release your modified version, or any part of it. You are free to make modifications and use them privately, without ever releasing them." However if one releases a GPL-licensed entity to the public, there is an issue regarding linking: namely, if a proprietary program uses a GPL library, is the proprietary program in violation of the GPL?

This key dispute is whether or not non-GPL software can legally statically link or dynamically link to GPL libraries. Different opinions exist on this issue. The GPL is clear in requiring that all derivative works of code under the GPL must themselves be under the GPL. Ambiguity arises with regards to using GPL libraries, and bundling GPL software into a larger package (perhaps mixed into a binary via static linking). This is ultimately a question not of the GPL per se, but of how copyright law defines derivative works. The following points of view exist:

Point of view: dynamic and static linking violate GPL

The Free Software Foundation (which holds the copyright of several notable GPL-licensed software products and of the license text itself) asserts that an executable which uses a dynamically linked library is indeed a derivative work. This does not however apply to separate programs communicating with one another.

The Free Software Foundation also created the LGPL, which is nearly identical to the GPL, but with additional permissions to allow linking for the purposes of "using the library".

Richard Stallman and the FSF specifically encourage library-writers to license under the GPL so that proprietary programs cannot use the libraries, in an effort to protect the free-software world by giving it more tools than the proprietary world.

Point of view: static linking violates GPL but unclear as of dynamic linking

Some people believe that while static linking produces derivative works, it is not clear whether an executable that dynamically links to a GPL code should be considered a derivative work (see Weak Copyleft). Linux author Linus Torvalds agrees that dynamic linking can create derived works but disagrees over the circumstances.

A Novell lawyer has written that dynamic linking not being derivative "makes sense" but is not "clear-cut", and that evidence for good-intentioned dynamic linking can be seen by the existence of proprietary Linux kernel drivers.

In Galoob v. Nintendo the United States Ninth Circuit Court of Appeals defined a derivative work as having "'form' or permanence" and noted that "the infringing work must incorporate a portion of the copyrighted work in some form", but there have been no clear court decisions to resolve this particular conflict.

Point of view: linking is irrelevant

According to an article in the Linux Journal, Lawrence Rosen (OSI general counsel) argues that the method of linking is mostly irrelevant to the question about whether a piece of software is a derivative work; more important is the question about whether the software was intended to interface with client software and/or libraries. He states, "The primary indication of whether a new program is a derivative work is whether the source code of the original program was used [in a copy-paste sense], modified, translated or otherwise changed in any way to create the new program. If not, then I would argue that it is not a derivative work," and lists numerous other points regarding intent, bundling, and linkage mechanism. He further argues on his firm's website that such "market-based" factors are more important than the linking technique.

There is also the specific issue of whether a plugin or module (such as the NVidia or ATI graphics card kernel modules) must also be GPL, if it could reasonably be considered its own work. This point of view suggests that reasonably separate plugins, or plugins for software designed to use plugins, could be licensed under an arbitrary license if the work is GPLv2. Of particular interest is the GPLv2 paragraph:

You may modify your copy or copies of the Program or any portion of it, thus forming a work based on the Program, and copy and distribute such modifications or work under the terms of Section 1 above, provided that you also meet all of these conditions:

(b) You must cause any work that you distribute or publish, that in whole or in part contains or is derived from the Program or any part thereof, to be licensed as a whole at no charge to all third parties under the terms of this License.

These requirements apply to the modified work as a whole. If identifiable sections of that work are not derived from the Program, and can be reasonably considered independent and separate works in themselves, then this License, and its terms, do not apply to those sections when you distribute them as separate works. But when you distribute the same sections as part of a whole which is a work based on the Program, the distribution of the whole must be on the terms of this License, whose permissions for other licensees extend to the entire whole, and thus to each and every part regardless of who wrote it.

It should be noted that the GPLv3 has a different clause:

You may convey a work based on the Program, or the modifications to produce it from the Program, in the form of source code under the terms of Section 4, provided that you also meet all of these conditions: c)

You must license the entire work, as a whole, under this License to anyone who comes into possession of a copy. This License will therefore apply, along with any applicable Section 7 additional terms, to the whole of the work, and all its parts, regardless of how they are packaged. This License gives no permission to license the work in any other way, but it does not invalidate such permission if you have separately received it.

A compilation of a covered work with other separate and independent works, which are not by their nature extensions of the covered work, and which are not combined with it such as to form a larger program, in or on a volume of a storage or distribution medium, is called an "aggregate" if the compilation and its resulting copyright are not used to limit the access or legal rights of the compilation's users beyond what the individual works permit. Inclusion of a covered work in an aggregate does not cause this License to apply to the other parts of the aggregate.

As a case study, some supposedly proprietary plugins and themes/ skins for GPLv2 CMS software such as Drupal and WordPress have come under fire, with both sides of the argument taken.

The FSF differentiates on how the plug-in is being invoked. If the Plug-in is invoked through dynamic linkage and it performs function calls to the GPL program then it's most likely a derivative work.

Communicating and bundling with non-GPL programs

The mere act of communicating with other programs does not, by itself, require all software to be GPL; nor does distributing GPL software with non-GPL software. However, minor conditions must be followed that ensures the rights of GPL software is not restricted. The following is a quote from the gnu.org GPL FAQ, which describes to what extent software is allowed to communicate with and be-bundled-with GPL programs: 'What is the difference between an "aggregate" and other kinds of "modified versions"?

An "aggregate" consists of a number of separate programs, distributed together on the same CD-ROM or other media. The GPL permits you to create and distribute an aggregate, even when the licenses of the other software are non-free or GPL-incompatible. The only condition is that you cannot release the aggregate under a license that prohibits users from exercising rights that each program's individual license would grant them.

Where's the line between two separate programs, and one program with two parts? This is a legal question, which ultimately judges will decide. We believe that a proper criterion depends both on the mechanism of communication (exec, pipes, rpc, function calls within a shared address space, etc.) and the semantics of the communication (what kinds of information are interchanged).

If the modules are included in the same executable file, they are definitely combined in one program. If modules are designed to run linked together in a shared address space, that almost surely means combining them into one program.

By contrast, pipes, sockets and command-line arguments are communication mechanisms normally used between two separate programs. So when they are used for communication, the modules normally are separate programs. But if the semantics of the communication are intimate enough, exchanging complex internal data structures, that too could be a basis to consider the two parts as combined into a larger program.

The FSF thus draws the line between "library" and "other program" via 1) "complexity" and "intimacy" of information exchange, and 2) mechanism (rather than semantics), but resigns that the question is not clear-cut and that in complex situations, case law will need to decide.

Legal status

The first known violation of the GPL was in 1989 when NeXT extended the GCC compiler to support Objective-C, but did not publicly release the changes. After an inquiry they created a public patch. There was no lawsuit filed for this violation.

In 2002, MySQL AB sued Progress NuSphere for copyright and trademark infringement in United States district court. NuSphere had allegedly violated MySQL's copyright by linking MySQL's GPL'ed code with NuSphere Gemini table without being in compliance with the license. After a preliminary hearing before Judge Patti Saris on 27 February 2002, the parties entered settlement talks and eventually settled. After the hearing, FSF commented that "Judge Saris made clear that she sees the GNU GPL to be an enforceable and binding license."

In August 2003, the SCO Group stated that they believed the GPL to have no legal validity, and that they intended to pursue lawsuits over sections of code supposedly copied from SCO Unix into the Linux kernel. This was a problematic stand for them, as they had distributed Linux and other GPL'ed code in their Caldera OpenLinux distribution, and there is little evidence that they had any legal right to do so except under the terms of the GPL. For more information, see SCO-Linux controversies and SCO v. IBM.

In April 2004, the netfilter/iptables project was granted a preliminary injunction against Sitecom Germany by Munich District Court after Sitecom refused to desist from distributing Netfilter's GPL'ed software in violation of the terms of the GPL. Harald Welte, of Netfilter, was represented by ifrOSS co-founder Till Jaeger. On July 2004, the German court confirmed this injunction as a final ruling against Sitecom. The court's justification was that:

Defendant has infringed on the copyright of plaintiff by offering the software 'netfilter/iptables' for download and by advertising its distribution, without adhering to the license conditions of the GPL. Said actions would only be permissible if defendant had a license grant... This is independent of the questions whether the licensing conditions of the GPL have been effectively agreed upon between plaintiff and defendant or not. If the GPL were not agreed upon by the parties, defendant would notwithstanding lack the necessary rights to copy, distribute, and make the software 'netfilter/iptables' publicly available.

This exactly mirrored the predictions given previously by the FSF's Eben Moglen. This ruling was important because it was the first time that a court had confirmed that violating terms of the GPL could be copyright violation and established case law over the enforceability of the GPL version 2 under German law.

In May 2005, Daniel Wallace filed suit against the Free Software Foundation in the Southern District of Indiana, contending that the GPL is an illegal attempt to fix prices (at zero). The suit was dismissed in March 2006, on the grounds that Wallace had failed to state a valid anti-trust claim; the court noted that "the GPL encourages, rather than discourages, free competition and the distribution of computer operating systems, the benefits of which directly pass to consumers". Wallace was denied the possibility of further amending his complaint, and was ordered to pay the FSF's legal expenses.

On 8 September 2005, the Seoul Central District Court ruled that the GPL was not material to a case dealing with trade secrets derived from GPL-licensed work. Defendants argued that since it is impossible to maintain trade secrets while being compliant with GPL and distributing the work, they are not in breach of trade secrets. This argument was considered without ground.

On 6 September 2006, the gpl-violations.org project prevailed in court litigation against D-Link Germany GmbH regarding D-Link's copyright-infringing use of parts of the Linux Kernel in storage devices they distributed. The judgment provided legal precedent that the GPL is valid, legally binding, and stands in German court.

In late 2007, the BusyBox developers and the Software Freedom Law Center embarked upon a program to gain GPL compliance from distributors of BusyBox in embedded systems, suing those who would not comply. These were claimed to be the first US uses of courts for enforcement of GPL obligations. See BusyBox GPL lawsuits.

On 11 December 2008, the Free Software Foundation sued Cisco Systems, Inc. for copyright violations by its Linksys division, of the FSF's GPL-licensed coreutils, readline, Parted, Wget, GNU Compiler Collection, binutils, and GNU Debugger software packages, which Linksys distributes in the Linux firmware of its WRT54G wireless routers, as well as numerous other devices including DSL and Cable modems, Network Attached Storage devices, Voice-Over-IP gateways, Virtual Private Network devices and a home theater/media player device.

After six years of repeated complaints to Cisco by the FSF, claims by Cisco that they would correct, or were correcting, their compliance problems (not providing complete copies of all source code and their modifications), of repeated new violations being discovered and reported with more products, and lack of action by Linksys (a process described on the FSF blog as a "five-years-running game of Whack-a-Mole") the FSF took them to court.

Cisco settled the case six months later by agreeing "to appoint a Free Software Director for Linksys" to ensure compliance, "to notify previous recipients of Linksys products containing FSF programs of their rights under the GPL," to make source code of FSF programs freely available on its website, and to make a monetary contribution to the FSF.

Compatibility and multi-licensing

Code licensed under several other licenses can be combined with a program under the GPL without conflict, as long as the combination of restrictions on the work as a whole does not put any additional restrictions beyond what GPL allows. In addition to the regular terms of the GPL, there are additional restrictions and permissions one can apply:

1. If a user wants to combine code licensed under different versions of GPL, then this is only allowed if the code with the older GPL version includes an "any later version" statement. For instance, the GPLv3 licensed GNU LibreDWG library can't be used anymore by LibreCAD and FreeCAD who have GPLv2 only dependencies.

2. Code licensed under LGPL is permitted to be linked with any other code no matter what license that code has, through the LGPL does add additional requirements for the combined work. LGPLv3 and GPLv2-

only can thus commonly not be linked, as the combined Code work would add additional LGPLv3 requirements on top of the GPLv2-only licensed software. Code licensed under LGPLv2.x without the "any later version" statement can be relicensed if the whole combined work is licensed to GPLv2 or GPLv3.

FSF maintains a list of GPL-compatible free software licenses with many of the most common free software licenses, such as the original MIT/X license, the BSD license (in its current 3-clause form) and the Artistic License 2.0.

David A. Wheeler has advocated that free/open source software developers use only GPL-compatible licenses, because doing otherwise makes it difficult for others to participate and contribute code. As a specific example of license incompatibility, Sun Microsystems' ZFS cannot be included in the GPL-licensed Linux kernel, because it is licensed under the GPL-incompatible CDDL. Furthermore, ZFS is protected by patents, so distributing an independently developed GPL-ed implementation would still require Oracle's permission.

A number of businesses use multi-licensing to distribute a GPL version and sell a proprietary license to companies wishing to combine the package with proprietary code, using dynamic linking or not. Examples of such companies include MySQL AB, Digia PLC (Qt framework, before 2011 from Nokia), Red Hat (Cygwin) and Riverbank Computing (PyQt). Other companies, like the Mozilla Foundation (products include Mozilla Application Suite, Mozilla Thunderbird and Mozilla Firefox), used multi-licensing to distribute versions under the GPL and some other open-source licenses.

Use for text and other media

It is possible to use the GPL for text documents instead of computer programs, or more generally for all kinds of media, if it is clear what constitutes the source code (defined as "the preferred form of the work for making changes in it"). For manuals and textbooks, though, the FSF recommends the GNU Free Documentation License (GFDL) instead, which it created for this purpose. Nevertheless, the Debian developers recommended (in a resolution adopted in 2006) to license documentation for their project under the GPL, because of the incompatibility of the GFDL with the GPL (text licensed under the GFDL cannot be incorporated into GPL software). Also, the FLOSS Manuals foundation, an organization devoted to creating manuals for free software, decided to eschew the GFDL in favor of the GPL for its texts in 2007.

If the GPL is used for fonts, any documents or images made with such fonts might also have to be distributed under the terms of the GPL. This is not the case in countries like the US and Canada where copyright law is inapplicable to the appearance of fonts, though program code inside a font file may still be covered which can complicate font embedding (since the document could be considered 'linked' to the font). FSF provides an exception for cases where this is not desired.

Reception

Legal Barrier to App Stores

The GPL License is incompatible with many application-distribution-systems, like the Mac App Store, and certain other software distribution platforms (on smartphones as well as PCs). The problem lies in the right "To make a copy for your neighbour", as this right is violated by the integrated DRM-Systems made to prevent copying of paid software. Even if the application is free-as-in-beer in the App Store in question, it might result in a violation of that app store's terms.

Note that there is a distinction between an app store which sells DRM-restricted software under proprietary licenses, and the more general concept of an digital distribution via some form of online software repository: various UNIX-like distros provide app repos, including Fedora, RHEL, CentOS, Ubuntu, Debian, FreeBSD, OpenBSD and so on. These specific app repos all contain GPL-licensed software apps, in some cases even when the core project does not permit GPL-licensed code in the base system (for instance OpenBSD). In other cases, such as the Ubuntu App Store, proprietary commercial software applications *and* GPL-licensed applications are both available via the same system; the reason that the Mac App Store (and similar projects) is incompatible with GPL-licensed apps is not inherent in the concept of an app store, but is rather specifically due to Apple's terms-of-use requirement that all apps in the store utilize Apple DRM-restrictions. Ubuntu's app store does not demand any such requirement: "These terms do not limit or restrict your rights under any applicable open source software licenses."

Microsoft

In 2001, Microsoft CEO Steve Ballmer referred to Linux as "a cancer that attaches itself in an intellectual property sense to everything it touches". In response to Microsoft's attacks on the GPL, several prominent Free Software developers and advocates released a joint statement supporting the license. Microsoft has released Microsoft Windows Services for UNIX which contains GPL-licensed code. In July 2009, Microsoft itself released a body of around 20,000 lines of Linux driver code under the GPL. The Hyper-V code that is part of the submitted code used open-source components licensed under the GPL and was originally statically linked to proprietary binary parts, the latter being inadmissible in GPL-licensed software.

"Viral" nature

Craig Mundie, Microsoft Senior Vice President has described the GPL as being "viral" in 2001. Mundie argues that the GPL has a "viral" effect in that it only allows the conveyance of whole programs, which means programs that link to GPL libraries must themselves be under a GPL-compatible license, else they cannot be combined and distributed.

In the views of Richard Stallman, Mundie's metaphor of a "virus" is wrong as software under the GPL does not "attack" or "infect" other software. Stallman believes that comparing the GPL to a virus is an extremely unfriendly thing to say, and that a better metaphor for software under the GPL would be a spider plant: If one takes a piece of it and puts it somewhere else, it grows there too.

Barrier to commercialization

The FreeBSD project has stated that "a less publicized and unintended use of the GPL is that it is very favorable to large companies that want to undercut software companies. In other words, the GPL is well suited for use as a marketing weapon, potentially reducing overall economic benefit and contributing to monopolistic behavior" and that the GPL can "present a real problem for those wishing to commercialize and profit from software".

Richard Stallman wrote about the practice of selling license exceptions to free software licenses as an example of ethically acceptable commercialization practice. Selling exceptions here means that the copyright holder of a given software releases it (along with the corresponding source code) to the public under a free software license, "then lets customers pay for permission to use the same code under different terms, for instance allowing its inclusion in proprietary applications". Stallman considered selling exceptions "acceptable since the 1990s, and on occasion I've suggested it to companies. Sometimes this approach has made it possible for important programs to become free software". Despite that the FSF doesn't practice selling exceptions, a comparison with the X11 license (which is a noncopyleft free software license) is proposed for suggesting that this commercialization technique should be regarded as ethically acceptable. Releasing a given program under a noncopyleft free software license would permit embedding the code in proprietary software. Stallman comments that "either we have to conclude that it's wrong to release anything under the X11 license-a conclusion I find unacceptably extreme-or reject this implication. Using a noncopyleft license is weak, and usually an inferior choice, but it's not wrong. In other words, selling exceptions permits some embedding in proprietary software, and the X11 license permits even more embedding. If this doesn't make the X11 license unacceptable, it doesn't make selling exceptions unacceptable".

GPLv3 separates community further

Some journalists and toybox developer Rob Landley criticized that with the introduction of the GPLv3 the split between the open source and free software community is wider than ever. As the significantly extended GPLv3 is essential incompatible with the GPLv2, compatibility between both is only given under the optional "or later" clause of the GPL, which was not taken for instance by the Linux kernel. Bruce Byfield noted that before the release of the GPLv3, the GPLv2 was a unifying element between the open-source and the free software community.

Lawrence Rosen, attorney and computer specialist, praised how the community using the Apache license were now able to work together with the GPL community in a compatible manner, as the problems of GPLv2 compatibility with Apache licensed software were resolved with the GPLv3. He said, "I predict that one of the biggest success stories of GPLv3 will be the realization that the entire universe of free and open source software can thus be combined into comprehensive open source solutions for customers worldwide."

MIT LICENSE

The MIT License is a free software license originating at the Massachusetts Institute of Technology (MIT). It is a permissive free software license, meaning that it permits reuse within proprietary software provided all copies of the licensed software include a copy of the MIT License terms. Such proprietary software retains its proprietary nature even though it incorporates software under the MIT License. The license is also GPL-compatible, meaning that the GPL permits combination and redistribution with software that uses the MIT License.

Notable software packages that use one of the versions of the MIT License include Expat, PuTTY, the Mono development platform class libraries, Ruby on Rails, Lua (from version 5.0 onwards), Wayland and the X Window System, for which the license was written.

Various versions

Because MIT has used many licenses for software, "MIT License" is considered ambiguous by the Free Software Foundation. "MIT License" may refer to the "Expat License" (used for Expat) or to the "X11 License" (also called "MIT/X Consortium License"; used for the X Window System by the MIT X Consortium). The "MIT License" published on the official site of Open Source Initiative is the same as the "Expat License".

Differing from the Expat License, the X11 License and the "MIT License" chosen for ncurses by the Free Software Foundation include the clause:

Except as contained in this notice, the name(s) of the above copyright holders shall not be used in advertising or otherwise to promote the sale, use or other dealings in this Software without prior written authorization.

The XFree86 Project uses a modified MIT License for XFree86 version 4.4 onward.

The license includes a clause that requires attribution in software documentation, like the original 4-clause BSD license. The Free Software Foundation contends that this addition is incompatible with the version 2 of the GPL, but compatible with version 3:

The end-user documentation included with the redistribution, if any, must include the following acknowledgment: "This product includes software developed by The XFree86 Project, Inc (http://www.xfree86.org/) and its contributors", in the same place and form as other third-party acknowledgments. Alternatively, this acknowledgment may appear in the software itself, in the same form and location as other such third-party acknowledgments.

License terms

A common form of the MIT License (from OSI's official site, which is the same version as the "Expat License", and which is not identical to the X source code) is defined as follows: Copyright (C) <year> <copyright holders>

Permission is hereby granted, free of charge, to any person obtaining a copy of this software and associated documentation files (the "Software"), to deal in the Software without restriction, including without limitation the rights to use, copy, modify, merge, publish, distribute, sublicense, and/or sell copies of the Software, and to permit persons to whom the Software is furnished to do so, subject to the following conditions:

The above copyright notice and this permission notice shall be included in all copies or substantial portions of the Software.

The software is provided "as is", without warranty of any kind, express or implied, including but not limited to the warranties of merchantability, fitness for a particular purpose and noninfringement. In no event shall the authors or copyright holders be liable for any claim, damages or other liability, whether in an action of contract, tort or otherwise, arising from, out of or in connection with the software or the use or other dealings in the software.

Comparison to other licenses

The MIT License is similar to the 3-clause "modified" BSD license, except that the BSD license contains a notice prohibiting the use of the name of the copyright holder in promotion. This is sometimes present in versions of the MIT License, as noted above.

The original BSD license also includes a clause requiring all advertising of the software to display a notice crediting its authors. This "advertising clause" (since disavowed by UC Berkeley) is present in the modified MIT License used by XFree86.

The MIT License states more explicitly the rights given to the end-user, including the right to use, copy, modify, merge, publish, distribute, sublicense, and/or sell the software.

The Simplified BSD license used by FreeBSD is essentially identical to the MIT License, as it contains neither an advertising clause, nor a prohibition on promotional use of the copyright holder's name.

Also similar in terms is the ISC license, which has a simpler language.

The University of Illinois/NCSA Open Source License combines text from both the MIT and BSD licenses; the license grant and disclaimer are taken from the MIT License.

THE MOZILLA PUBLIC LICENSE VERSION 2.0

The release of the Mozilla Public License Version 2.0 probably flew under the radar when it happened in January 2012.

In fairness, the initial Mozilla Public License (MPL) was admittedly not much used outside of the Mozilla world. Mozilla-branded software source code have traditionally been released under a tri-license comprising the GNU GPL, the GNU LGPL and the MPL itself. Some Mozilla extensions and derivatives decided to follow the same path, but the reality is that the MPL never really spread outside of its originating community (Adobe publishing significant parts of Flex under the MPL is a rare counter-example). This is in sharp contrast to, say, the Apache License or the Eclipse Public License.

Spirit of the MPL

In essence, the MPL was designed as a "middle-ground" license sitting between the extremes of restrictive licenses like the GNU (A)GPL and liberal licenses such as the Apache / BSD / MIT. While the MPL license itself allows derivative works to be released under any license, including a proprietary one, it still requires a form of copyleft at the file level. This consequently puts the MPL in the same bucket as the Eclipse Public License and the GNU LGPL.

In practice, you may take some MPL code and use it as part of your proprietary software. However, you must give access in source form to the MPL-covered parts, and any modification of a piece of MPL-covered code from your side must also be published as MPL-covered code. This is just simple copyleft, really.

The fact that most Mozilla-branded software have been historically released under a tri MPL/GPL/LGPL license is for increased compatibility with third-party libraries, especially those published under the terms of a GNU license. The versions 1.x of the MPL were not (L)GPL-compliant.

A simpler, reusable and pragmatic software license?

A weak copyleft license certainly has some merits, especially when the said license applies at the file level, was written in the open by both opensource advocates and lawyers, and... is free of any political message which you may not necessarily adhere to (yes, I am looking at you Richard).

That being said, the MPL in its original form was not necessarily easy to apply to non-Mozilla projects, so much that derivatives of the MPL were written such as the CDDL by (late) Sun Microsystems.

The latest installment of the MPL looks much more appealing outside of the Mozilla world. Quoting the announcement blog post:

The result of a two year revision process that included feedback and suggestions from the Mozilla community, users of the MPL (both community and corporate), and the broader open source legal community, MPL 2.0 contains several important changes from MPL 1.1. In particular, MPL 2.0:

- is simpler and shorter, using the past 10 years of in-practice application of the license to help better understand what is and isn't necessary in an open source license.
- is modernized for recent changes in copyright law, and incorporates feedback from lawyers outside the United States on issues of applicability in non-US jurisdictions.

- provides patent protections for contributors more in line with those of other open source licenses, and allows an entire community of contributors to protect any contributor if they are sued.
- provides compatibility with the Apache and GPL licenses, making code reuse and redistribution easier.

The explicit compatibility with the GNU and Apache licenses is also an added benefit, especially as it does not involve a complex multi-licenses scheme like it was the case with the old MPL. I recommend reading what Simon Phipps had to say in his "Can Mozilla Unify Open Source?" column for Computer World:

Other coverage of the new license has focussed on the modified patent-peace and other adjusted terms (goodbye, Netscape!) but the most important development in the creation of version 2 of the Mozilla license in my opinion is the inclusion of specific compatibility with the GNU General Public License (GPL). Previously, the Mozilla project used a complex and messy triple license arrangement to allow it to straddle the worlds of copyleft and non-copyleft licensing. Other users of the MPL (and its many vanity-named clones) tended not to bother, with the result that some code-bases were isolated from collaboration with the great universe of GPL-licensed software.

Creative Commons license

A Creative Commons (CC) license is one of several public copyright licenses that enable the free distribution of an otherwise copyrighted work. A CC license is used when an author wants to give people the right to share, use and build upon a work that they have created. CC provides an author flexibility (for example, they might choose to allow only non-commercial uses of their own work) and protects the people who use or redistribute an author's work, so they don't have to worry about copyright infringement, as long as they abide by the conditions that are specified in the license by which the author distributes the work.

There are several types of CC licenses. The licenses differ by several combinations that condition the terms of distribution. They were initially released on December 16, 2002 by Creative Commons, a U.S. non-profit corporation founded in 2001.

Applicable works

Work licensed under a Creative Commons license is governed by applicable copyright law. This allows Creative Commons licenses to be applied to all work falling under copyright, including: books, plays, movies, music, articles, photographs, blogs, and websites. Creative Commons does not recommend the use of Creative Commons licenses for software.

However, application of a Creative Commons license may not modify the rights allowed by fair use or fair dealing or exert restrictions which violate copyright exceptions. Furthermore, Creative Commons licenses are non-exclusive and non-revocable. Any work or copies of the work obtained under a Creative Commons license may continue to be used under that license.

In the case of works protected by multiple Creative Common licenses, the user may choose either.

Types of licenses

The CC licenses all grant the "baseline rights", such as the right to distribute the copyrighted work worldwide, without changes, at no charge. The details of each of these licenses depends on the version, and comprises a selection of four conditions:

The last two clauses are not free content licenses, according to definitions such as DFSG or the Free Software Foundation, and cannot be used in contexts that require these freedoms, such as Wikipedia.

Mixing and matching these conditions produces sixteen possible combinations, of which eleven are valid Creative Commons licenses and five are not. Of the five invalid combinations, four include both the "nd" and "sa" clauses, which are mutually exclusive; and one includes none of the clauses.

Of the eleven valid combinations, the five that lack the "by" clause have been retired because 98% of licensors requested attribution, though they do remain available for reference on the website. This leaves six regularly used licenses:

For example, the Creative Commons Attribution (BY) license allows one to share and remix (create derivative works), even for commercial use, so long as attribution is given.

Versions

As of July 2011, Creative Commons licenses have been "ported" to over 50 different jurisdictions worldwide. No new ports have been implemented in version 4.0 of the license, which was released on 25 November 2013. Version 4.0 discourages using ported versions and instead acts as a single global license which can be used without porting.

Rights

Attribution

Since 2004, all current licenses require attribution of the original author. The attribution must be given to "the best of [one's] ability using the information available". Generally this implies the following:

- Include any copyright notices (if applicable). If the work itself contains any copyright notices placed there by the copyright holder, those notices must be left intact, or reproduced in a way that is reasonable to the medium in which the work is being re-published.
- Cite the author's name, screen name, or user ID, etc. If the work is being published on the Internet, it is nice to link that name to the person's profile page, if such a page exists.
- Cite the work's title or name (if applicable), if such a thing exists. If the work is being published on the Internet, it is nice to link the name or title directly to the original work.
- Cite the specific CC license the work is under. If the work is being published on the Internet, it is nice if the license citation links to the license on the CC website.
- Mention if the work is a derivative work or adaptation, in addition to the above, one needs to identify that their work is a derivative work, e.g., "This is a Finnish translation of [original work] by or "Screenplay based on [original work] by [author]."

Non-commercial licenses

The "non-commercial" option included in some Creative Commons licenses is controversial in definition, as it's sometimes unclear what can be considered a noncommercial setting, and application, since its restrictions differ from the principles of open content promoted by other permissive licenses.

Zero / Public domain

Besides licenses, Creative Commons also offers a way to release material into the public domain through CC0, a legal tool for waiving as many rights as legally possible, worldwide. Development of CC0 began in 2007 and the tool was released in 2009.

In 2010, Creative Commons announced its Public Domain Mark, a tool for labeling works already in the public domain. Together, CC0 and the Public Domain Mark replace the Public Domain Dedication and Certification, which took a U.S.-centric approach and co-mingled distinct operations. In 2011, the Free Software Foundation added CC0 to its free software licenses, making CC0 a recommended way of dedicating software to the public domain.

In February 2012 CC0 was submitted for OSI approval process but due to problems, it was rejected. The OSI FAQ concludes "At this time, we do not recommend releasing software using the CC0 public domain dedication" because of the reservations of being able to waiver copyright (aka "public domain") from a legal standpoint in all jurisdictions. The OSI FAQ further explains that "CC0 was not explicitly rejected, but the License Review Committee was unable to reach consensus that it should be approved, and Creative Commons eventually withdrew the application". In the withdrawal message the Creative Commons representative explained that CC0 was initially developed for the needs of the scientific data community in order to help sharing data freely.

Retired licenses

Due to either disuse or criticism, a number of previously offered Creative Commons licenses have since been retired, and are no longer recommended for new works. The retired licenses include all licenses lacking the Attribution element other than CC0, as well as the following four licenses:

- Developing Nations License: a license which only applies to developing countries deemed to be "non-high-income economies" by the World Bank. Full copyright restrictions apply to people in other countries.
- Sampling: parts of the work can be used for any purpose other than advertising, but the whole work cannot be copied or modified
- Sampling Plus: parts of the work can be copied and modified for any purpose other than advertising, and the entire work can be copied for noncommercial purposes
- NonCommercial Sampling Plus: the whole work or parts of the work can be copied and modified for noncommercial purposes

Legal review

The legal implications of large numbers of works having Creative Commons licensing is difficult to predict, and there is speculation that media creators often lack insight to be able to choose the license which best meets their intent in applying it.

X.net

X.net is a non-profit platform that develops and promotes alternative models for cultural dissemination and royalty management. Its activities revolve around five core themes: free culture, Internet neutrality, technopolitics, network democracy, and new models of sustainability for the digital era. X.net also engages in political lobbying at the national and international levels, by preparing and submitting legislative proposals and viral campaigns.

Initiatives

oXcars

The oXcars' are a non-competitive awards ceremony held at Sala Apolo in Barcelona, Spain, in October each year. They are a public showcase that puts the spotlight on cultural creation and distribution carried out under the paradigms of shared culture. Through presentations and symbolic mentions of works in a series of categories, the oXcars uses parody as a strategy for showing real legal solutions. The award categories include: Music, Animation, Theatre, Human Tools, Future Markets and Great Leftovers of Spanish Culture, among others.

FCForum

The FCForum is an international conference organised by X.net and a network of other groups and activists. It brings together organisations and experts in the field of free/libre culture and knowledge, with the aim of creating a strategic global framework for action and international coordination. It takes place annually in Barcelona.

The first FCForum was held in Barcelona from October 30 to November 1, 2009, to coincide with the 2nd oXcars awards ceremony. The principal organisations and active voices in the world of Free Culture and knowledge participated in the event.

A series of working groups at the Forum produced a unique document known as the "Charter for Innovation, Creativity and Access to Knowledge," which proposes a series of reforms to the Spanish Intellectual Property legislation, Telecoms Package and other issues related to the circulation of information and net neutrality. The Charter was sent to a thousand governments and political and social institutions around the world.

International bodies such as the European Union Committee on Culture and Education and the Government of Brazil (through the Department of Digital Culture) sent official observers to the Forum.

The second FCForum was held in Barcelona from October 28 to 31, 2010, and focused on the new models of sustainability in the digital era. Two documents were drafted as a result of this event: the "Sustainable Models for Creativity and the How-To Manual for Sustainable Creativity'.

D'Evolution Summit

The D'Evolution Summit was created as a civil society response to the European Forum for Cultural Industries, organised by the Spanish Ministry of Culture in collaboration with the Chamber of Commerce of Barcelona, which was held in Barcelona on March 29 and 30, 2010. Authorities, experts and lobby groups participated in the Forum, which focused on five core themes: financing and the cultural industries, intellectual property and royalties management, strategies for the internationalisation of culture, culture and territorial development, and the profiles and skills for culture industry professionals.

The Forum for Cultural Industries lent continuity to the International Conference on Economy and Culture held in May 2009, and took place just before the informal meeting of the 27 Ministers of Culture of the European Union on March 31 within the framework of the Spanish Presidency of the EU.

The D'Evolution Summit was a counter-summit organised at the same time, to demand amendments to Spain's Law of Sustainable Economy (known as the anti-downloads law) and an end to the monopoly of copyright collecting societies.

During three days, the D'Evolution summit organised Internet broadcasts of the proceedings of the Forum for Cultural Industries and the Informal Meeting of Ministers, staged concerts by groups who use free licences, and carried out actions such as the handing out music with free licences to hairdressing salons and the action "We won't carry the bucket for an industry that refuses to adapt to reality" in which the comedian Leo Bassi dressed up as a clown and tried to give a giant inflatable duck to the ministers of culture. D'Evolution also organised viral campaigns and provided information on the topics being discussed at the Forum through social networks.

Parents are the Pirates

Parents are the Pirates is a self-published collective book consisting of contributions by fifty authors who were invited to write or illustrate, in 400 words or less, one of the following topics:

- Culture in the digital era: new "profitabilities"
- The creative ecosystem of the digital age: now or never
- Digital information is what today's memory is made of
- Copying and its benefits
- Lies, bits, the inquisition and P2P
- 13,000,000 pirate homes: piracy does not exist, parents are the pirates
- P2P: Do we really want to follow in the footsteps of Pakistan, China, France and Sudan?

- Lets talk about the middlemen: restructuring in times of crisis. Culture existed before the cultural industry
- Lost profits is counting your chickens before they hatch (and the chickens are culture)
- Public Domain vs benefits for parasites
- The right to quote: the key to the link economy

The book was launched at the first oXcars, in October 2008. It was published under a 2008 season Poetic Licence and is distributed by independent publishing house Traficantes de Sueños.

Legal advice

X.net provides legal advice on copyright, licences, the Spanish levy on private copying, private copies, P2P, copyright collecting societies, broadcast rights and other issues relating to the digital society. They provide artists with information about the licences they can use to cover their work without becoming dependent on a collecting society. They also advise businesses that are being sued by Spanish collective society SGAE and want to know their rights and obligations.

Change of name

On August 2, 2010, lawyers from Spain's largest copyright collecting society, the SGAE, sent a certified fax to the eXgae demanding they shut down the domain name exgae.net and suspend their activities, alleging infringement of the SGAE brand and unfair competition. In the interests of avoiding a long and expensive legal battle, the collective changed its name to X.net, although it continues working in the same sphere of activity.

OSL FOR DOCUMENTATION

GNU Free Documentation License

The GNU Free Documentation License (GNU FDL or simply GFDL) is a copyleft license for free documentation, designed by the Free Software Foundation (FSF) for the GNU Project. It is similar to the GNU General Public License, giving readers the rights to copy, redistribute, and modify a work and requires all copies and derivatives to be available under the same license. Copies may also be sold commercially, but, if produced in larger quantities (greater than 100), the original document or source code must be made available to the work's recipient.

The GFDL was designed for manuals, textbooks, other reference and instructional materials, and documentation which often accompanies

GNU software. However, it can be used for any text-based work, regardless of subject matter. For example, the free online encyclopedia Wikipedia uses the GFDL (coupled with the Creative Commons Attribution Share-Alike License) for all of its text.

History

The GFDL was released in draft form for feedback in September 1999. After revisions, version 1.1 was issued in March 2000, version 1.2 in November 2002, and version 1.3 in November 2008. The current state of the license is version 1.3.

The first discussion draft of the GNU Free Documentation License version 2 was released on September 26, 2006, along with a draft of the new GNU Simpler Free Documentation License.

On December 1, 2007, Jimmy Wales announced that a long period of discussion and negotiation between and amongst the Free Software Foundation, Creative Commons, the Wikimedia Foundation and others had produced a proposal supported by both the FSF and Creative Commons to modify the Free Documentation License in such a fashion as to allow the possibility for the Wikimedia Foundation to migrate the projects to the similar Creative Commons Attribution Share-Alike (CC-BY-SA) license. These changes were implemented on version 1.3 of the license, which includes a new provision allowing certain materials released under the license to be used under a Creative Commons Attribution Share-Alike license also.

Conditions

Material licensed under the current version of the license can be used for any purpose, as long as the use meets certain conditions.

- All previous authors of the work must be attributed.
- All changes to the work must be logged.
- All derivative works must be licensed under the same license.
- The full text of the license, unmodified invariant sections as defined by the author if any, and any other added warranty disclaimers (such as a general disclaimer alerting readers that the document may not be accurate for example) and copyright notices from previous versions must be maintained.
- Technical measures such as DRM may not be used to control or obstruct distribution or editing of the document.

Secondary sections

The license explicitly separates any kind of "Document" from "Secondary Sections", which may not be integrated with the Document, but exist as front-matter materials or appendices. Secondary sections can contain information regarding the author's or publisher's relationship to the subject matter, but not any subject matter itself. While the Document itself is wholly editable, and is essentially covered by a license equivalent to (but mutually incompatible with) the GNU General Public License, some of the secondary sections have various restrictions designed primarily to deal with proper attribution to previous authors.

Specifically, the authors of prior versions have to be acknowledged and certain "invariant sections" specified by the original author and dealing with his or her relationship to the subject matter may not be changed. If the material is modified, its title has to be changed (unless the prior authors give permission to retain the title).

The license also has provisions for the handling of front-cover and back-cover texts of books, as well as for "History", "Acknowledgements", "Dedications" and "Endorsements" sections. These features were added in part to make the license more financially attractive to commercial publishers of software documentation, some of whom were consulted during the drafting of the GFDL. "Endorsements" sections are intended to be used in official standard documents, where distribution of modified versions should only be permitted if they are not labeled as that standard any more.

Commercial redistribution

The GFDL requires the ability to "copy and distribute the Document in any medium, either commercially or noncommercially" and therefore is incompatible with material that excludes commercial re-use. As mentioned above, the GFDL was designed with commercial publishers in mind, as Stallman explained:

The GFDL is meant as a way to enlist commercial publishers in funding free documentation without surrendering any vital liberty. The 'cover text' feature, and certain other aspects of the license that deal with covers, title page, history, and endorsements, are included to make the license appealing to commercial publishers for books whose authors are paid.

Material that restricts commercial re-use is incompatible with the license and cannot be incorporated into the work. However, incorporating such restricted material may be fair use under United States copyright law (or fair dealing in some other countries) and does not need to be licensed to fall within the GFDL if such fair use is covered by all potential subsequent uses. One example of such liberal and commercial fair use is parody.

Compatibility with Creative Commons licensing terms

Although the two licenses work on similar copyleft principles, the GFDL is not compatible with the Creative Commons Attribution-ShareAlike license.

However, at the request of the Wikimedia Foundation, version 1.3 added a time-limited section allowing specific types of websites using the GFDL to additionally offer their work under the CC-BY-SA license. These exemptions allow a GFDL-based collaborative project with multiple authors to transition to the CC-BY-SA 3.0 license, without first obtaining the permission of every author, if the work satisfies several conditions:

- The work must have been produced on a "Massive Multiauthor Collaboration Site" (MMC), such as a public wiki for example.
- If external content originally published on a MMC is present on the site, the work must have been licensed under Version 1.3 of the GNU FDL, or an earlier version but with the "or any later version" declaration, with no cover texts or invariant sections. If it was not originally published on an MMC, it can only be relicensed if it were added to an MMC before November 1, 2008.

To prevent the clause from being used as a general compatibility measure, the license itself only allowed the change to occur before August 1, 2009. At the release of version 1.3, the FSF stated that all content added before November 1, 2008 to Wikipedia as an example satisfied the conditions. The Wikimedia Foundation itself after a public referendum, invoked this process to dual-license content released under the GFDL under the CC-BY-SA license in June 2009, and adopted a foundation-wide attribution policy for the use of content from Wikimedia Foundation projects.

Enforcement

There have currently been no cases involving the GFDL in a court of law, although its sister license for software, the GNU General Public License, has been successfully enforced in such a setting. Although the content of Wikipedia has been plagiarized and used in violation of the GFDL by other sites, such as Baidu Baike, no contributors have ever tried to bring an organization to court due to violation of the GFDL. In the case of Baidu, Wikipedia representatives asked the site and its contributors to respect the terms of the licenses and to make proper attributions.

Criticism

Some critics consider the GFDL a non-free license. Some reasons for this are that the GFDL allows "invariant" text which cannot be modified or removed, and that its prohibition against digital rights management (DRM) systems applies to valid usages, like for "private copies made and not distributed".

Notably, the Debian project and Nathanael Nerode have raised objections. In 2006, Debian developers voted to consider works licensed under the GFDL to comply with their Debian Free Software Guidelines provided the invariant section clauses are not used. The results was GFDL without invariant sections is DFSG compliant. However, their resolution stated that even without invariant sections, GFDL-licensed software documentation "is still not free of trouble", namely because of its incompatibility with the major free software licenses.

Those opposed to the GFDL have recommended the use of alternative licenses such as the BSD Documentation License or the GNU GPL.

The FLOSS Manuals foundation, an organization devoted to creating manuals for free software, decided to eschew the GFDL in favor of the GPL for its texts in 2007, citing the incompatibility between the two, difficulties in implementing the GFDL, and the fact that the GFDL "does not allow for easy duplication and modification", especially for digital documentation.

DRM clause

The GNU FDL contains the statement:

You may not use technical measures to obstruct or control the reading or further copying of the copies you make or distribute.

A criticism of this language is that it is too broad, because it applies to private copies made but not distributed. This means that a licensee is not allowed to save document copies "made" in a proprietary file format or using encryption.

In 2003, Richard Stallman said about the above sentence on the debian-legal mailing list:

This means that you cannot publish them under DRM systems to restrict the possessors of the copies. It isn't supposed to refer to use of encryption or file access control on your own copy. I will talk with our lawyer and see if that sentence needs to be clarified.

Invariant sections

A GNU FDL work can quickly be encumbered because a new, different title must be given and a list of previous titles must be kept. This could lead to the situation where there are a whole series of title pages, and dedications, in each and every copy of the book if it has a long lineage. These pages cannot be removed until the work enters the public domain after copyright expires.

Richard Stallman said about invariant sections on the debian-legal mailing list:

The goal of invariant sections, ever since the 80s when we first made the GNU Manifesto an invariant section in the Emacs Manual, was to make sure they could not be removed. Specifically, to make sure that distributors of Emacs that also distribute non-free software could not remove the statements of our philosophy, which they might think of doing because those statements criticize their actions.

GPL incompatible in both directions

The GNU FDL is incompatible in both directions with the GPL-material under the GNU FDL cannot be put into GPL code and GPL code cannot be put into a GNU FDL manual. At the June 22nd and 23rd 2006 international GPLv3 conference in Barcelona, Eben Moglen hinted that a future version of the GPL could be made suitable for documentation:

By expressing LGPL as just an additional permission on top of GPL we simplify our licensing landscape drastically. It's like for physics getting rid of a force, right? We just unified electro-weak, ok? The grand unified field theory still escapes us until the document licences too are just additional permissions on top of GPL. I don't know how we'll ever get there, that's gravity, it's really hard.

Burdens when printing

The GNU FDL requires that licensees, when printing a document covered by the license, must also include "this License, the copyright notices, and the license notice saying this License applies to the Document". This means that if a licensee prints out a copy of an article whose text is covered under the GNU FDL, he or she must also include a copyright notice and a physical printout of the GNU FDL, which is a significantly large document in itself. Worse, the same is required for the standalone use of just one (for example, Wikipedia) image. Wikivoyage, a web site dedicated to free content travel guides, chose not to use the GFDL because it considers it unsuitable for short printed texts.

Other free content licenses

Some of these were developed independently of the GNU FDL, while others were developed in response to perceived flaws in the GNU FDL.

- Creative Commons licenses
- Design Science License
- Free Art license
- FreeBSD Documentation License
- Open Gaming License
- Open Publication License
- WTFPL

List of projects that use the GFDL

- Most projects of the Wikimedia Foundation, including Wikipedia (excluding Wikinews) - On June 15, 2009, the Section 11 clauses were used to dual-license the content of these wikis under the Creative Commons Attribution Share-Alike license and GFDL.
- An Anarchist FAQ
- Citizendium - the project uses GFDL for articles originally from Wikipedia.
- Free On-line Dictionary of Computing
- Last.fm - artists descriptions are under GFDL
- PlanetMath
- Rosetta Code
- SourceWatch
- The specification documents that define TRAK, an enterprise architecture framework, are released under the GFDL.
- The Virginia Commonwealth University Mathematics Department has begun commercially publishing mathematics texts licensed under the GDFL, including Abstract Algebra by Thomas W. Judson.
- the Baseball-Reference's BR Bullpen, a free user-contributed baseball wiki

FreeBSD Documentation License

The FreeBSD Documentation License is the license that covers most of the documentation for the FreeBSD operating system.

The license is very similar to the 2-clause Simplified BSD License used by the rest of FreeBSD, however, it makes the meanings of "source code" and "compile" less ambiguous in the context of documentation. It also includes a mandatory disclaimer about IEEE and Open Group text in some manual pages.

The Free Software Foundation classes this as a free documentation license, stating that "This is a permissive non-copyleft free documentation license that is compatible with the GNU FDL."

Based on the FreeBSD Documentation License, the BSD Documentation License was created to contain terms more generic to most projects as well as reintroducing the 3rd clause that restricts the use of documentation for endorsement purposes (as shown in the New BSD License).

Public-domain software

Public-domain software is software that has been placed in the public domain: in other words, software for which there is absolutely no ownership such as copyright, trademark, or patent. Software in the public domain can be modified, distributed, or sold even without any attribution by anyone; this is unlike the common case of software under exclusive copyright, where software licenses grant limited usage rights.

Under the Berne Convention, which most countries have signed, an author automatically obtains the exclusive copyright to anything they have written, and local law may similarly grant copyright, patent, or trademark rights by default. The Berne Convention also covers programs. Therefore, a program is automatically subject to copyright, and if it is to be placed in the public domain, the author must explicitly disclaim the copyright and other rights on it in some way, e.g. by a waiver statement. In some jurisdictions, some rights (in particular moral rights) cannot be disclaimed: for instance, civil law tradition-based German law's "Urheberrecht" differs here from the Anglo-Saxon common law tradition's "copyright" concept.

Early academic public-domain software ecosystem

From the 1950s to the 1990s software culture, as original academic phenomena, "public-domain" (usually abbreviated to "PD") software was popular. This kind of freely distributed and shared "free software" combined the nowadays differentiated software classes of freeware, shareware, and free and open-source software and was created in academia, and by hobbyists and hackers. As software was often written in an interpreted language such as BASIC, the source code was needed and therefore distributed to run the software. PD software was also shared and distributed as printed source code (type-in program) in computer magazines (like Creative Computing, SoftSide, Compute!, Byte etc.) and books, like the bestseller BASIC Computer Games. Early on, closed-source software was uncommon until the mid-1970s to the 1980s.

Before 1974, when the US Commission on New Technological Uses of Copyrighted Works (CONTU) decided that "computer programs, to the extent that they embody an author's original creation, are proper subject matter of copyright" software was not copyrightable and therefore always in the public domain. This legislation, plus court decisions such as Apple v. Franklin in 1983 for object code, clarified that the Copyright Act gave computer programs the copyright status of literary works.

In the 1980s, a common way to share public-domain software was by receiving them through a local user group or a company like PC-SIG, of Sunnyvale, California, which maintained a mail-order catalog of more than 300 disks with an average price of US$6. Public-domain software with source code was also shared on BBS networks. Public-domain software was commercialized sometimes by a donationware model, asking the users for a money donation to be sent by mail.

The public-domain "free sharing" and "donationware" commercialization models evolved in following years to the (non-voluntary) shareware model, and software free of charge, called freeware. Additionally, due to other changes in the computer industry, the sharing of source code became less usual.

With the Berne Convention Implementation Act of 1988 (and the earlier Copyright Act of 1976), the legal base for public-domain software changed drastically. Before the act, releasing software without copyright notice was enough for dedicating it to the public domain. With the new copyright act, software was by default copyright-protected and needed an explicit waiver statement or license of the author.

Reference implementations of algorithms, often cryptographic algorithms, meant or applied for standardization are still often given into the public domain, examples are CERN httpd in 1993 and Serpent cipher in 1999. The Openwall Project maintains a list of several algorithms and their source code in the public domain.

Free and open-source software as successor

As a response in the end 1980s of the academic software ecosystem to the change in the copyright system, permissive license texts were developed, like the BSD license and derivatives. Permissive-licensed software, which is a kind of free and open-source software, shares most characteristics of the earlier public-domain software but stands on the legal base of copyright law.

In the 1980s Richard Stallman, who worked long in an academic environment of "public-domain"-like software sharing, noticed the emergence of proprietary software and the decline of the public-domain software ecosystem. In an effort to preserve this ecosystem he created a software license, the GPL, which encodes the "public-domain" rights and enforces them irrevocably on software. Paradoxically, his copyleft approach relies on the enforceability of the copyright to be effective. Copyleft free software shares therefore many properties with public-domain software, but doesn't allow relicensing or sublicensing. Unlike real public-domain software or permissive-licensed software, Stallman's copyleft license tries to enforce the free shareability of software also for the future by not allowing license changes.

To refer to free software (which is under a free software license) or to software distributed and usable free of charge (freeware) as "public-domain" is therefore incorrect. While public domain gives up the author's exclusive rights (e.g. copyright), in free software the author's copyright is still retained and used, for instance, to enforce copyleft or to hand out permissive-licensed software. Licensed software is in general not in the public domain. Another distinct difference is that an executable program may be in the public domain even if its source code is not made available (making the program not feasibly modifiable), while free software has the source code always available.

Post-copyright public domain

With the 2000s and the emergence of peer-to-peer sharing networks and sharing in web development, a new copyright-critical developer generation made the "license-free" public-domain software model visible again, also criticizing the FOSS license ecosystem ("Post Open Source") as stabilizing part of the copyright system. New non-FOSS licenses and waiver texts were developed, notably the Creative Commons "CC0" (2009) and the "Unlicense" (2010), and the growing popularity of permissive software licenses was noticed. Also, the growing problem of orphaned software and digital obsolescence of software raised the awareness of the relevance of passing software into the public domain again for better digital preservation of the digital heritage, unrestricted by copyright and DRM.

Around 2004 there was a debate whether public-domain software can be considered part of the FOSS ecosystem, as lawyer Lawrence Rosen argued in the essay "Why the public domain isn't a license" that software could not truly be given into the public domain, a position that faced opposition by Daniel J. Bernstein and others. In 2012, the status was finally resolved when Rosen changed his mind and accepted the CC0 as an open-source license, while admitting that contrary to previous claims copyright can be waived away, backed by a Ninth circuit's decision.

Passing of software into the public domain

Release without copyright notice

Before the Berne Convention Implementation Act of 1988 (and the earlier Copyright Act of 1976, which went into effect in 1978) works could be easily given into the public domain by just releasing it without an explicit copyright notice and no copyright registration. After the 1988 implementation act, all works were by default copyright protected and needed to be actively given into the public domain by a waiver statement.

Leaving the copyright term

Copyrighted works, like software, are meant to pass into the public domain after the copyright term, losing their copyright privilege. Due to the decades-long copyright protection granted by the Berne Convention, no software has ever passed into the public domain by leaving copyright terms. The question of how fast works should pass into the public domain has been a matter of scientific and public debates, as well as for software like video games.

Public-domain-like licenses and waivers

While real public domain makes software licenses unnecessary, as no owner/author is required to grant permission ("Permission culture"), there are licenses that grant public-domain-like rights. There is no universally agreed-upon license, but multiple licenses that aim to release source code into the public domain.

In 2000 the WTFPL was released as public-domain-like license/ waiver/anti-copyright notice. In 2009 the Creative commons released the CC0, which was created for compatibility with also law domains (e.g. Civil law of continental Europe) where dedicating into public domain is problematic. This is achieved by a public domain waiver statement and a fallback all-permissive license, for the case the waiver is not possible. The Unlicense, published around 2010, has a focus on an anti-copyright message. The Unlicense offers a public domain waiver text with a fallback public-domain-like license inspired by permissive licenses but without attribution clause. In 2015 GitHub reported that of their approx. 5.1 million licensed projects hosted almost 2% use the unlicense, approx. 102,000 projects. Another option is the Zero Clause BSD license, released in 2006 and aimed at software.

As result, such licensed public-domain software has all four freedoms but is not hampered by the complexities of attribution (restriction of permissive licensed software) or license compatibility (issue with copyleft licensed software).

Public-domain software

See also Category:Public-domain software with source code, Category:Public-domain software

Classical PD software (pre-1988)

Public domain software in the early computer age was for instance shared as type-in program in computer magazines and books like BASIC Computer Games. Explicit PD waiver statements or license files were at that time unusual. Publicly available software without a copyright notice was assumed to be, and shared as, public-domain software.

Notable general PD software from that time include:

- ELIZA (1966)
- SPICE (1973)
- BLAS (1979)
- FFTPACK (1985)
- Video games are among the earliest examples of shared PD software, which are still notable today:
- Spacewar! (1962)
- Hamurabi (1969)
- Star Trek (text game) (1971)
- Hunt the Wumpus (1972)
- Maze War (1974)
- Colossal Cave Adventure (1976)
- Android Nim (1978)
- Rogue (video game) (1980)
- Ballerburg (1987)

Many PD software authors kept the practices of public-domain release without having a waiver text, not knowing or caring for the changed copyright law and creating therefore a legal problem. On the other hand, magazines started in the mid-1980s to claim copyright even for type-in programs that were seen as PD before. Only slowly PD software authors started to include explicit relinquishment or license statement texts.

Examples of modern PD software (post 1988)

These examples of modern PD software (after the Berne Convention Implementation Act of 1988) are either under proper public domain (e.g. created by a US governmental organization), under a proper public-domain-like license (for instance CC0), or accompanied by a clear waiver statement from the author. While not as widespread as in the pre-2000s, PD software still exists nowadays. For example, SourceForge listed 334 hosted PD projects in 2016, GitHub 102,000 PD projects under the unlicense alone in 2015. In 2016, an analysis of the Fedora Project's packages revealed public domain was the seventh most popular "license".

The award-winning video game developer Jason Rohrer releases his works into the PD, as do several cryptographers, such as Daniel J.

Bernstein, Bruce Schneier and Douglas Crockford, with reference implementations of cryptographic algorithms.

- BLAST (1990)
- CERN's httpd (1993)
- ImageJ (1997)
- Serpent (cipher) (1999)
- SQLite (2000)
- reStructuredText (2002)
- I2P (2003)
- youtube-dl (2006)
- 7-Zip's LZMA SDK (2008)
- Diamond Trust of London (2012)
- Glitch (2013)
- The Castle Doctrine (2014)
- SHA-3 (2015)
- One Hour One Life (2018)

Public-domain-equivalent license

Public-domain-equivalent license are licenses that grant public-domain-like rights and/or act as waivers. They are used to make copyrighted works usable by anyone without conditions, while avoiding the complexities of attribution or license compatibility that occur with other licenses.

No permission or license is required for a work truly in the public domain, such as one with an expired copyright; such a work may be copied at will. Public domain equivalent licenses exist because some legal jurisdictions[which?] do not provide for authors to voluntarily place their work in the public domain, but do allow them to grant arbitrarily broad rights in the work to the public.

The licensing process also allows authors, particularly software authors, the opportunity to explicitly deny any implied warranty that might give someone a basis for legal action against them. While there is no universally agreed-upon license, several licenses aim to grant the same rights that would apply to a work in the public domain.

Licenses

In 2000, the "Do What the Fuck You Want To Public License" (WTFPL) was released as a public-domain-equivalent license for software. It is distinguished among software licenses by its informal style and lack of a warranty disclaimer. In 2016, according to Black Duck Software, the WTFPL was used by less than 1% of FOSS projects.

In 2009, Creative Commons released CC0, which was created for compatibility with jurisdictions where dedicating to public domain is problematic, such as continental Europe. This is achieved by a public-domain waiver statement and a fall-back all-permissive license, for cases where the waiver is not valid. The Free Software Foundation and the Open Knowledge Foundation approved CC0 as a recommended license to dedicate content to the public domain. The FSF and the Open Source Initiative, however, do not recommend the usage of this license for software due to inclusion of a clause expressly stating it does not grant patent licenses. In June 2016 an analysis of the Fedora Project's software packages placed CC0 as the 17th most popular license.

The Unlicense software license, published around 2010, offers a public-domain waiver text with a fall-back public-domain-like license, inspired by permissive licenses but without an attribution clause. sIn 2015 GitHub reported that approximately 102,000 of their 5.1 million licensed projects, or 2%, use the Unlicense.

The Zero Clause BSD license removes half a sentence from the OpenBSD template license, leaving only an unconditional grant of rights and a warranty disclaimer. It is listed by the Software Package Data Exchange as the Zero Clause BSD license, with the SPDX identifier "0BSD." It was first used by Rob Landley in Toybox and is OSI-approved.

Reception

In the free-software community, there has been some controversy over whether a public domain dedication constitutes a valid open-source license. In 2004, lawyer Lawrence Rosen argued in the essay "Why the public domain isn't a license" that software could not truly be given into public domain, a position that faced opposition by Daniel J. Bernstein and others. In 2012, Rosen changed his mind, accepted CC0 as an open-source license, and admitted that, contrary to his previous claims, copyright can be waived away.

In 2011, the Free Software Foundation added CC0 to its free software licenses and called it "the preferred method of releasing software in the public domain," while in general recommending the GNU General Public License.

In February 2012, when the CC0 license was submitted to the Open Source Initiative for approval, controversy arose over a clause which excluded any relevant patents held by the copyright holder from the scope of the license. This clause was added with scientific data in mind rather than software, but some members of the OSI believed it could weaken users' defenses against software patents. As a result, Creative Commons withdrew their submission, and the license is not currently approved by the OSI.

In June 2020, following a request for legacy approval, OSI formally recognized the Unlicense as an approved license meeting the OSD.

Google does not allow its employees to contribute to projects under public domain equivalent licenses like the Unlicense and CC0, while allowing contributions to 0BSD licensed and US government PD projects.

Free-software license

A free-software license is a notice that grants the recipient of a piece of software extensive rights to modify and redistribute that software. These actions are usually prohibited by copyright law, but the rights-holder (usually the author) of a piece of software can remove these restrictions by accompanying the software with a software license which grants the recipient these rights. Software using such a license is free software (or free and open-source software) as conferred by the copyright holder. Free-software licenses are applied to software in source code and also binary object-code form, as the copyright law recognizes both forms.

Pre-1980s

In the early times of software, sharing of software and source code was common in certain communities, for instance academic institutions. Before the US Commission on New Technological Uses of Copyrighted Works (CONTU) decided in 1974 that "computer programs, to the extent that they embody an author's original creation, are proper subject matter of copyright", software was not considered copyrightable. Therefore, software had no licenses attached and was shared as public-domain software. The CONTU decision plus court decisions such as Apple v. Franklin in 1983 for object code, clarified that the Copyright Act gave computer programs the copyright status of literary works and started the licensing of software.

Free-software licenses before the late 1980s were generally informal notices written by the developers themselves. These early licenses were of the "permissive" kind.

1980s

In the mid-1980s, the GNU project produced copyleft free-software licenses for each of its software packages. An early such license (the "GNU Emacs Copying Permission Notice") was used for GNU Emacs in 1985, which was revised into the "GNU Emacs General Public License" in late 1985, and clarified in March 1987 and February 1988. Likewise, the similar GCC General Public License was applied to the GNU Compiler Collection, which was initially published in 1987. The original BSD license is also one of the first free-software licenses, dating to 1988. In 1989, version 1 of the GNU General Public License (GPL) was published. Version 2 of the GPL, released in 1991, went on to become the most widely used free-software license.

1990s to 2000s

Starting in the mid-1990s and until the mid-2000s, the open-source movement pushed and focused the free-software idea forward in the wider public and business perception. In the Dot-com bubble time, Netscape Communications' step to release its webbrowser under a FOSS license in 1998, inspired many other companies to adapt to the FOSS ecosystem. In this trend companies and new projects (Mozilla, Apache foundation, and Sun, see also this list) wrote their own FOSS licenses, or adapted existing licenses.

This License proliferation was later recognized as problem for the Free and open-source ecosystem due to the increased complexity of license compatibility considerations. While the creation of new licenses slowed down later, license proliferation and its impact are considered an ongoing serious challenge for the free and open-source ecosystem.

From the free-software licenses, the GNU GPL version 2 has been tested in to court, first in Germany in 2004 and later in the USA. In the German case the judge did not explicitly discuss the validity of the GPL's clauses but accepted that the GPL had to be adhered to: "If the GPL were not agreed upon by the parties, defendant would notwithstanding lack the necessary rights to copy, distribute, and make the software 'netfilter/ iptables' publicly available." Because the defendant did not comply with the GPL, it had to cease use of the software. The US case (MySQL vs Progress) was settled before a verdict was arrived at, but at an initial hearing, Judge Saris "saw no reason" that the GPL would not be enforceable.

Around 2004 lawyer Lawrence Rosen argued in the essay Why the public domain isn't a license software could not truly be waived into public domain and can't be interpreted as very permissive FOSS license, a position which faced opposition by Daniel J. Bernstein and others. In 2012 the dispute was finally resolved when Rosen accepted the CC0 as open source license, while admitting that contrary to his previous claims copyright can be waived away, backed by Ninth circuit decisions.

In 2007, after years of draft discussion, the GPLv3 as major update of the GPLv2 was released. The release was controversial due to the significant extended scope of the license, which made it incompatible with the GPLv2. Several major FOSS projects (Linux kernel, MySQL, BusyBox, Blender, VLC media player) decided against adopting the GPLv3. On the other hand, in 2009, two years after the release of the GPLv3, Google open-source programs office manager Chris DiBona reported that the number of open-source projects licensed software that had moved to GPLv3 from GPLv2 was 50%, counting the projects hosted at Google Code.

2010s

In 2011, four years after the release of the GPLv3, 6.5% of all open-source licensed projects were GPLv3 while 42.5% were still GPLv2 according to Black Duck Software data. Following in 2011 451 Group analyst Matthew Aslett argued in a blog post that copyleft licenses went into decline and permissive licenses increased, based on statistics from Black Duck Software.In 2015 according to Black Duck Software and GitHub statistics, the permissive MIT license dethroned the GPLv2 as most popular free-software license to the second place while the permissive Apache license follows already at third place. In June 2016 an analysis of Fedora Project's packages revealed as most used licenses the GPL, MIT, BSD, and the LGPL.

Definitions

OSI-approved open-source licenses

The group Open Source Initiative (OSI) defines and maintains a list of approved open-source licenses. OSI agrees with FSF on all widely used free-software licenses, but differ from FSF's list, as it approves against the Open Source Definition rather than the Free Software Definition. It considers Free Software Permissive license group to be a reference implementation of a Free Software license. [clarification needed] Thus its requirements for approving licenses are different.

FSF-approved free-software licenses

The Free Software Foundation, the group that maintains the Free Software Definition, maintains a non-exhaustive list of free-software licences.

The Free Software Foundation prefers copyleft (share-alike) free-software licensing rather than permissive free-software licensing for most purposes. Its list distinguishes between free-software licenses that are compatible or incompatible with the FSF's copyleft GNU General Public License.

Conditions in free-software licenses

There exists an ongoing debate within the free-software community regarding the fine line between what restrictions can be applied and still be called "free".

Only "public-domain software" and software under a public-domain-like license is restriction-free. Examples of public-domain-like licenses are, for instance, the WTFPL and the CC0 license. Permissive licenses might carry small obligations like attribution of the author but allow practically all code use cases. Certain licenses, namely the copyleft licenses, include intentionally stronger restrictions (especially on the distribution/ distributor) in order to force derived projects to guarantee specific rights which can't be taken away.

Copyleft

The free-software share-alike licenses written by Richard Stallman in the mid-1980s pioneered a concept known as "copyleft". Ensuing copyleft provisions stated that when modified versions of free software are distributed, they must be distributed under the same terms as the original software. Hence they are referred to as "share and share alike" or "quid pro quo". This results in the new software being open source as well. Since copyleft ensures that later generations of the software grant the freedom to modify the code, this is "free software". Non-copyleft licenses do not ensure that later generations of the software will remain free.

Developers who use GPL code in their product must make the source code available to anyone when they share or sell the object code. In this case, the source code must also contain any changes the developers may have made. If GPL code is used but not shared or sold, the code is not required to be made available and any changes may remain private. This permits developers and organizations to use and modify GPL code for private purposes (that is, when the code or the project is not sold or otherwise shared) without being required to make their changes available to the public.

Supporters of GPL claim that by mandating that derivative works remain under the GPL, it fosters the growth of free software and requires equal participation by all users. Opponents of GPL claim that "no license can guarantee future software availability" and that the disadvantages of GPL outweigh its advantages. Some also argue that restricting distribution makes the license less free. Whereas proponents would argue that not preserving freedom during distribution would make it less free. For example, a non-copyleft license does not grant the author the freedom to see modified versions of his or her work if it gets publicly published, whereas a copyleft license does grant that freedom.

PATENT RETALIATION

Further information: Patent retaliation

During the 1990s, free-software licenses began including clauses, such as patent retaliation, in order to protect against software patent litigation cases – a problem which had not previously existed. This new threat was one of the reasons for writing version 3 of the GNU GPL in 2006. In recent years, a term coined tivoization describes a process where hardware restrictions are used to prevent users from running modified versions of the software on that hardware, in which the TiVo device is an example. It is viewed by the FSF as a way to turn free software to effectively non-free, and is why they have chosen to prohibit it in GPLv3. Most newly written free-software licenses since the late 1990s include some form of patent retaliation clauses. These measures stipulate that one's rights under the license (such as to redistribution), may be terminated if one attempts to enforce patents relating to the licensed software, under certain circumstances. As an example, the Apple Public Source License may terminate a user's rights if said user embarks on litigation proceedings against them due to patent litigation. Patent retaliation emerged in response to proliferation and abuse of software patents.

Hardware restrictions

Version 3 of the GNU GPL includes specific language prohibiting additional restrictions being enforced by hardware restrictions and digital rights management (DRM), a practice FSF calls tivoization after Tivo used GPL'd software on devices that disallowed user modification of that software.

Attribution, disclaimers and notices

The majority of free-software licenses require that modified software not claim to be unmodified. Some licenses also require that copyright holders be credited. One such example is version 2 of the GNU GPL, which requires that interactive programs that print warranty or license information, may not have these notices removed from modified versions intended for distribution.

Practical problems with licenses

License compatibility

Licenses of software packages containing contradictory requirements render it impossible to combine source code from such packages in order to create new software packages. License compatibility between a copyleft license and another license is often only a one-way compatibility. This "one-way compatibility" characteristic is, for instanced, criticized by the Apache Foundation, who provides the more permissive Apache license which doesn't have this characteristic.

Non-copyleft licenses, such as the FOSS permissive licenses, have a less complicated license interaction and normally exhibit better license compatibility. For example, if one license says "modified versions must mention the developers in any advertising materials", and another license says "modified versions cannot contain additional attribution requirements", then, if someone combined a software package which uses one license with a software package which uses the other, it would be impossible to distribute the combination because these contradictory requirements cannot be fulfilled simultaneously.

Thus, these two packages would be license-incompatible. When it comes to copyleft software licenses, they are not inherently compatible with other copyleft licenses, even the GPLv2 is, by itself, not compatible with the GPLv3.

Purpose of use

Restrictions on use of a software ("use restrictions") are generally unacceptable according to the FSF, OSI, Debian, or the BSD-based distributions. Examples include prohibiting that the software be used for non-private applications, for military purposes, for comparison or benchmarking, for good use, for ethically questionable means, or in commercial organizations.

While some restrictions on user freedom, e.g. concerning nuclear war, seem to enjoy moral support among most free software developers, it is generally believed that such agendas should not be served through software licenses; among other things because of practical aspects such as resulting legal uncertainties and problems with enforceability of vague, broad and/or subjective criteria or because tool makers are generally not held responsible for other people's use of their tools. Nevertheless some projects include legally non-binding pleas to the user, prominently SQLite. Among the repeated attempts by developers to regulate user behavior through the license that sparked wider debate are Douglas Crockford's (joking) "no evil" clause, which affected the release process of the Debian distribution in 2012 and got the JSMin-PHP project expelled from Google Code, the addition of a pacifist condition based on Asimov's First Law of Robotics to the GPL for the distributed computing software GPU in 2005, as well as several software projects trying to exclude use by big cloud providers.

Definition conflicts

As there are several defining organizations and groups who publish definitions and guidelines about FOSS licenses, notably the FSF, the OSI, the Debian project, and the BSDs, there are sometimes conflicting opinions and interpretations.

Permissive versus copyleft opinions

Many users and developers of BSD-based operating systems have a different position on licensing. The main difference is the belief that the copyleft licenses, particularly the GNU General Public License (GPL), are undesirably complicated and/or restrictive. The GPL requires any derivative work to also be released according to the GPL while the BSD license does not. Essentially, the BSD license's only requirement is to acknowledge the original authors, and poses no restrictions on how the source code may be used.

As a result, BSD code can be used in proprietary software that only acknowledges the authors. For instance, Microsoft Windows NT 3.1 and macOS have proprietary IP stacks which are derived from BSD-licensed software. In extreme cases, the sub- or re-licensing possibilities with BSD or other permissive licenses might prevent further use in the open-source ecosystem. For instance, MathWorks' FileExchange repository offers the BSD license for user contributions but prevents with additional terms of use any usage beside their own proprietary MATLAB software, for instance with the FOSS GNU Octave software.

Supporters of the BSD license argue that it is more free than the GPL because it grants the right to do anything with the source code, provided that the attribution is preserved. The approach has led to BSD code being used in widely used proprietary software. Proponents of the GPL point out that once code becomes proprietary, users are denied the freedoms that define free software. As a result, they consider the BSD license less free than the GPL, and that freedom is more than a lack of restriction. Since the BSD license restricts the right of developers to have changes recontributed to the community,[dubious – discuss] neither it nor the GPL is "free" in the sense of "lacking any restrictions."

Debian

The Debian project uses the criteria laid out in its Debian Free Software Guidelines (DFSG). The only notable cases where Debian and Free Software Foundation disagree are over the Artistic License and the GNU Free Documentation License (GFDL). Debian accepts the original Artistic

License as being a free software license, but FSF disagrees. This has very little impact however since the Artistic License is almost always used in a dual-license setup, along with the GNU General Public License.

Controversial borderline cases

The vast majority of free software uses undisputed free-software licenses; however, there have been many debates over whether or not certain other licenses qualify for the definition.

Examples of licenses that provoked debate were the 1.x series of the Apple Public Source License, which were accepted by the Open Source Initiative but not by the Free Software Foundation or Debian and the RealNetworks Public Source License, which was accepted by Open Source Initiative and Free Software Foundation but not by Debian.

Also, the FSF recommended GNU Free Documentation License, which is incompatible with the GPL, was considered "non-free" by the Debian project around 2006, Nathanael Nerode, and Bruce Perens. The FSF argues that documentation is qualitatively different from software and is subject to different requirements. Debian accepted, in a later resolution, that the GNU FDL complied with the Debian Free Software Guidelines when the controversial "invariant section" is removed, but considers it "still not free of trouble". Notwithstanding, most GNU documentation includes "invariant sections". Similarly, the FLOSS Manuals foundation, an organization devoted to creating manuals for free software, decided to eschew the GFDL in favor of the GPL for its texts in 2007, citing the incompatibility between the two, difficulties in implementing the GFDL, and the fact that the GFDL "does not allow for easy duplication and modification", especially for digital documentation.

SLUC is a software license published in Spain in December 2006 to allow all but military use. The writers of the license maintain it is free software, but the Free Software Foundation says it is not free because it infringes the so-called "zero freedom" of the GPL, that is, the freedom to use the software for any purpose.

Market share

While historically the most widely used FOSS license has been the GPLv2, in 2015, according to Black Duck Software the permissive MIT license dethroned the GPLv2 to the second place while the permissive Apache license follows at third place. A study from 2012, which used publicly available data, criticized Black Duck Software for not publishing their methodology used in collecting statistics. Daniel German, professor in the Department of Computer Science at the University of Victoria in Canada, presented a talk in 2013 about the methodological challenges in determining which are the most widely used free-software licenses, and showed how he could not replicate the result from Black Duck Software.

A GitHub study in 2015 on their statistical data found that the MIT license was the most prominent FOSS license on that platform.

In June 2016 an analysis of the Fedora Project's packages showed as most used licenses the GPL family, followed by MIT, BSD, the LGP family, Artistic (for Perl packages), LPPL (for texlive packages), and ASL. The GNU GPLv2+ was the single most popular license

BIBLIOGRAPHY

- "Brief Definition of Open Source Licenses". Open Source Initiative. Retrieved April 25, 2013.
- Popp, Dr. Karl Michael (2015). Best Practices for commercial use of open source software. Norderstedt, Germany: Books on Demand. ISBN 978-3738619096.
- Haumba, Eric Nelson (2018). Open Licensing Models for Strengthening Access to Information: Opportunities for Authors. YMCA Library: Uganda Textbook-Academic and Non-Fiction Authors Association- UTANA. ISBN 9789970428052.
- Hillman, Robert; O'Rourke, Maureen (January 2009). "Rethinking Consideration in the Electronic Age". Hastings Law Journal. 61 (2009): 313–14, 328–35.
- Stallman, Richard (18 November 2016). "Why Open Source misses the point of Free Software". The GNU Project. Retrieved 1 October 2018.
- "Relationship between the Free Software movement and Open Source movement", Free Software Foundation, Inc
- Wheeler, David A. (2015). "The fight for freedom". Archived from the original on 4 July 2017. Retrieved 17 February 2016.
- Hancock, Terry (29 August 2008). "What if copyright didn't apply to binary executables?". Free Software Magazine. Archived from the original on 25 January 2016. Retrieved 25 January 2016.
- Apple Computer, Inc. v. Franklin Computer Corporation Puts the Byte Back into Copyright Protection for Computer Programs in Golden Gate University Law Review Volume 14, Issue 2, Article 3 by Jan L. Nussbaum (January 1984)
- "Downloads". Creative Commons. 16 December 2015. Retrieved 2015-12-24.
- "Version 1.0 license". anonscm.debian.org. Archived from the original on 2013-06-02. Retrieved 2016-06-19.
- "Top 20 licenses". Black Duck Software. 31 May 2016. Archived from the original on 2016-07-19. Retrieved 2016-05-31.

- "11/17: Lulan Artisans Textile Competition". 18 June 2009.
- Till Kreutzer. "Validity of the Creative Commons Zero 1.0 Universal Public Domain Dedication and its usability for bibliographic metadata from the perspective of German Copyright Law" (PDF).
- "Using CC0 for public domain software". Creative Commons. 15 April 2011. Retrieved 2011-05-10.
- "Various Licenses and Comments about Them". GNU Project. Retrieved 2015-04-04.
- Timothy Vollmer (27 December 2013). "Creative Commons 4.0 BY and BY-SA licenses approved conformant with the Open Definition". creativecommons.org.
- The Open Source Initiative FAQ. "What about the Creative Commons "CC0" ("CC Zero") public domain dedication? Is that Open Source?". opensource.org. Retrieved May 25, 2013.
- Anwesha Das (22 June 2016). "Software Licenses in Fedora Ecosystem". anweshadas.in. Retrieved 2016-06-27.
- Joe Brockmeier (2010). "The Unlicense: A License for No License". ostatic.com. Archived from the original on 2016-03-24.
- "The Unlicense". unlicense.org. Archived from the original on 2018-07-08. Retrieved 2020-05-12.
- Ben Balter (9 March 2015). "Open source license usage on GitHub.com". github.com. Retrieved 2015-11-21.
- "Zero-Clause BSD | Open Source Initiative". opensource.org. Retrieved 2018-12-18.
- Schwartz, Leo (March 7, 2022). "Amateur open-source researchers went viral unpacking the war in Ukraine". Rest of World. Retrieved 8 March 2022.
- Richelson, Jeffrey (2016). The US Intelligence Community. ISBN 978-0813349183.